Reaction to *O, Mountaineers!*

Danny Kuhn unveils a salient account history of West Virginia many fail to consider given West Virginia's current demographics. However, the brutal unknown may provide insight regarding many of the factors that prevent minorities, specifically Black Americans, from considering the state today. Kuhn's pioneering work goes through the painstaking research to uncover a brutal past of West Virginia, and lovers of history will experience a treacherous but necessary journey to bring West Virginia's full history to light. Moreover, Kuhn also captures Black American contributions to the rich history of West Virginia. These hopeful accounts display a degree of Black resilience to oppressive conditions and how Blacks succeeded in the face of seemingly insurmountable odds. When given the freedom and equitable access to resources, they were just as capable as any American. If you value West Virginia's history and want to continue unlocking its past glory and faults, I highly recommend adding O, Mountaineers! to your library. - **Dr. Adam Starks, author of Broken Child Mended Man**

History is outstanding. What you have compiled and shared on African-American West Virginians is an incredible download, eye opening view of history that, though a native West Virginian, I would never have gotten any other place. Thank you, Danny Kuhn, for adding to the education of this senior citizen. Blessings! – **Charles Shaw, Senior pastor, Real Life Christian Center, Huntington, West Virginia**

WITH HARD-TO-FIND GENEALOGICAL INFORMATION

O, *Mountaineers!*
Volume II: Noted (or Notorious) African-American West Virginians

BORN - LIVED - DIED

With genealogical information

Danny R. Kuhn

DEDICATION

One of the determining factors in a successful life is having an outstanding mentor. I have been blessed with two. One of them is **Davis N. Lewis** of Lewisburg, the first Deputy Chief United States Probation Officer for the Southern District of West Virginia, as well my advisor, proponent, cheerleader, encourager, and friend. "You should write a book someday," he once said. This one is dedicated to him, with gratitude.

CONTENTS

INTRODUCTION

First, what this book is not: it's not an encyclopedic listing of famous and/or influential Black West Virginians, with "just the facts" biographies. Such a work would be very useful, especially if regularly updated, but this isn't it. Instead, think of this as a conversation between us, on your porch. We're telling each other stories about people we've known, or heard or read things about. Some of them have been dead for two centuries or more. Some of them live down the road today, and might stop in if they drive by and see us sitting here.

Yes, of course you will find great accomplished Americans like Bill Withers and Katherine Johnson and Steve Harvey. You will also find many, either born or lived here at one time, who may not be well known but left no less important a legacy. In some cases, their pieces are more involved than those for the more famous, since their stories are harder to find but no less intriguing. For example:

- The world's longest career as a jewel thief, an honor held by a coal miner's daughter from Slab Fork.
- A thoracic surgeon who was an "artificial heart" pioneer.
- A pastor born a "Free Black" in Greenbrier County, who founded the Mother Emmanuel Church in Charleston, South Carolina, the site of a horrific hate crime in 2015.
- A watchman who saw his town being invaded by an armed mob and raised the alarm. The great irony is that the watchman was Black, and the armed mob John Brown's abolitionists.
- The last people born into bondage still living in West Virginia at over a hundred years of age.
- Many "First" African-Americans elected to state offices, most disappointedly late, and, to date, disappointedly "Only."
- A young man whose story could have inspired the plot of *To Kill a Mockingbird*, except he wasn't even in the vicinity when the "victim" cried wolf.
- John Henry. John Hardy!
- The real Johnny B. Goode, and Sweet Georgia Brown.

Not all the stories are positive, of course. We have also produced our share of thieves and killers, hence the (or Notorious) part of the title. But, all in all, there are more inspirational stories than those otherwise, and West Virginia's influence has been greater than could be expected from a small, rural state.

One more thing about the format. Remember the "sitting on your porch" analogy. I use the first person (just like that!) throughout, and my emphasis is on the stories, not the chronology. If a subject's grandmother did something of note, we'll explore that as well. Or, the subject's brother-in-law's barber's wife, even. We allow the stories to lead us where they will.

Strictly technical or academic works should be objective and devoid of a point of view, I hear. I can write that way, and did so for years producing reports and training materials and other documents for the federal court. But now I write for myself. No, slavery and the myth of the Noble Lost Cause and Jim Crow and lynching and racism and continued inequalities in opportunity are not "political opinions that should be respected even though they are different from yours." They are not treated as such here, just as they would not be if we were sitting on your porch. I purposely try to give some family history behind most of our subjects, because, in the words of native West Virginian and historian/genealogist Dr. Henry Louis Gates Jr., we Appalachians are always interested in the question, "Who are your people?" As you may already know, genealogy is harder for African-Americans, for obvious reasons. Using census records and other resources, I do my best to give the subjects' family context. I have included contemporary accounts, such as newspaper stories and obituaries, when they can be found, and, if I happen to have a personal connection to any of the subjects (as, perhaps surprisingly, I do with someone on the "notorious" side of things) you will hear about it. Sitting on your porch, would you expect anything different? If you once roomed with someone later convicted of two murders, wouldn't you mention it?

I try to insert a bit of humor with the whole endeavor where possible, and present pieces short enough to hold your interest, yet long enough to learn something and give the big picture of the times and circumstances. I fully expect some copies of this work will live in the bathroom, and I'm certainly okay with that.

A note on the length: I know you will think of many, many other African-Americans born, who lived, or who died in West Virginia whose stories should be told here. Some might even bring a "I can't BELIEVE he left out so-and-so!" response. I agree. This book is almost 90,000 words in length, though, and publishing books longer than that presents problems with production cost per copy vs. what people are generally willing to spend on a paperback. I had to make decisions based on the interesting aspects of the story, with preference going to those whose tales are not as well-known. For that reason, Maceo Pinkard (you may not recognize his name, but you definitely know his work) from Bluefield made it into the final manuscript, but Randy Moss got cut. How often has that happened in his career?

And, finally, a note on terms: as inspirational as many of these stories are, some of them were hard to write, and some things are just as unsettling to read. It is difficult using the terms of the day, such as Mulatto, and recounting slaves in documents as property, and citing how many of our subjects or their parents were the results of slaves being raped by their owners, or vivid descriptions of lynchings or other murders, or reprinting the way Blacks were often portrayed in the newspapers of the day. There is no joy in it, trust me. But, it is the way it was, and recording it differently would be dishonest. You will find I use the term Black and White capitalized when referring to one's race. Those are simply style choices for ease of reading.

This is Volume II of the *O, Mountaineers!* series (Volume I is available on Amazon and at TAMARACK in Beckley) and I hope to do more someday, perhaps on sports figures or entertainers or politicians or criminals. Come to think of it, maybe the last two could be combined, due to the substantial overlap. Stay tuned.

I have learned so much writing this book. Most of it is heartwarming and funny and makes me proud to be a Mountaineer. Some of it is sad, or even disturbing. But, all of it is part of our legacy as West Virginians. I hope you enjoy our visit. -Danny R. Kuhn, 2021

1 BORN

Dr. Jared Maurice Arter (1850 – 1930), educator and missionary
Born a slave, he saw the Civil War play out on his doorstep, and became an influential man of faith as well as a chronicler of the times.

The tip of West Virginia's eastern panhandle was quite a busy place in the leadup to and during the Civil War. It's just over forty miles to a flying crow from Harpers Ferry to Manassas, but, aside from Ft. Sumter nearer my current residence, nowhere was more important early in the conflict.

Jared Arter was born on a plantation owned by William Schaeffer, halfway between Harpers Ferry and Charles Town. His mother, Hannah, was enslaved there, while his father, Jeremiah, was owned by William Grove of Duffield. Jeremiah was almost forty years older than Hannah, and died seven years after Jared's birth.

William Schaeffer, in addition to being a planter, was an inspector at the United States Arsenal in Harpers Ferry. He left home at 5:00 AM on horseback each morning to go to work, and the morning of October 16, 1859 was no different. Except, of course, that John Brown and his men would set into motion the events that led to the third bloodiest, but perhaps inevitable, war in the history of the western hemisphere. (To complete that thought, historians believe the Mexican Revolution of 1910-1920 claimed a million casualties, and the War of the Triple Alliance in Paraguay, 1864-1870, around 800,000. The American Civil War was estimated to have killed approximately 650,000.) Young Jared remembered it as a time of great excitement and anxiety, with soldiers marching through the area and rumors flying.

We know how the siege ended, and the aftermath. Jared and his mother witnessed the hanging of four of Brown's men. Over the next several years, the Schaeffer plantation found itself between Union and Confederate lines, its "big house" taken over and used by one army or the other, and all the residents, both slave and free, hunkering in their homes with gunfire rampant outside.

Just after emancipation but before the War's end, Hannah, with a new husband and a combined family of nine children in tow, moved to Washington DC. Jared, a young teenager, found a position as a house servant with a successful miller in Georgetown. After being threatened by the owner, he became a bellboy at a hotel, where his industriousness was noticed by a patron, who offered to take barely-15-year-old Jared in and educate him, provided he remained "bound" to him as a servant until age 21, in upstate New York. He was treated well by the family of W. W. Ayers, a merchant and farmer, though sometimes not as well by the White schoolmistress and his classmates.

Jared sought, and was granted, early release from his contract with Mr. Ayers, and returned to Washington. He worked at manual labor between the city and Harpers Ferry for the next several years, buying a small house in Bolivar with his brother William. Eventually, the whole family came back from Washington and occupied the house, while Jared and William went to Pittsburgh for better wages. It took a few years to save enough to do so, but, in 1873, Jared had enough in pocket to come back to Harpers Ferry to fulfill his true ambition: enter Storer College. That same year, he experienced a religious conversion, and would eventually become an ordained minister.

His higher education career stretched over the next two decades, interspersed by periods teaching in various schools in West Virginia, Virginia, and Maryland. After Storer, he received a Ph.D. at Pennsylvania State College, and degrees at Hillsdale College in Michigan, and Chicago Theological Seminary. He returned to teach at Storer for a time, and even served as the superintendent of a school in Hilltop, near Oak Hill, in Fayette County for a year, all of which was usually done while also pastoring churches. He helped found a Bible college in Cairo, Illinois, the town where one can stand at the point in the city park and see the Ohio and Mississippi join right in front of you.

Jared married Emily "Emma" Carter in Jefferson County during 1890. (In today's nomenclature, she would have been known as Emily Carter-Arter, I suppose) After her death, he married Maggie Wall, a Mississippi native, in Kanawha County during 1910. Sadly, but as was common in the day, most of their children died young.

We know about Jared's life in great detail, because he wrote an autobiographical piece titled *Echoes From a Pioneer Life,* published by A. B. Caldwell Publishing of Atlanta, in 1922. It is available to read free online, on the *Documenting the American South* website maintained by the University of North Carolina. It doesn't take long to read, and it's worth the time. From the little enslaved boy holding onto his mother's apron while watching John Brown's men at the end of a rope, to one of the most educated men of his day, Jared's story is an extraordinary one.

Leon Brown "Chu" Berry (1908 – 1941), saxophonist *Charlie Parker and Cab Calloway both gave this innovative entertainer credit for his influence.*

To this day, saxophone collectors look upon the Conn New Wonder Series II instruments produced in the 1920s with awe, the Holy Grail of the hobby. Though never officially dubbed that by the company, they are known as "Chu Berry" models.

Okay, forget that Chu actually played a slightly different model, the Conn Transitional, but that doesn't really matter. It's all in the name!

Chu was the son of Brown (1856 – 1928) and Margaret Glasgow (1881 – 1945) Berry, who were living at 1002 Chapline Street in Wheeling when Chu was born. Brown worked in a shoe store and they owned their home. Brown was the son of Nathaniel Berry, and had been born in Harrisonburg, Virginia (according to his death certificate) well before the end of the Civil War, and, since there is no trace of him as a youngster in the 1860 census, he was probably born into slavery. He died of a stroke in 1928. *The Wheeling Intelligencer* reported:

LIFE-LONG RESIDENT OF WHEELING; FUNERAL SERVICE ON FRIDAY

Brown N. Berry, aged 72, died Tuesday afternoon at 1:10 o'clock at his home, 1002 Chapline Street, following a lengthy illness. He was a life-long resident of Wheeling. He had been employed for many years by the late J. N. Vance, where he worked until his retirement in 1918. Mr. Berry was the oldest member of the Simpson M. E. Church and was affiliated with Eureka Lodge, 1307, Grand United Order of Odd Fellows. He is survived by his widow, Mrs. Margaret Berry, sons, Leon and Nelson Berry, and one daughter, Anna Berry. Two brothers, Crawford Berry and Ernest Berry, and three sisters, Mrs. Emanuel Williams, Mrs. Robert Hill, and Mrs. Lucy Field also survive.

Margaret was the daughter of Abraham and Margaret Robinson Glasgow, of Rixeyville, Virginia. She also died at the family home, of heart disease, in 1945. She and Brown had married in Wheeling in 1907.

Chu attended Lincoln High School in Wheeling, and then West Virginia State College in Institute. His career began locally but his talent put him on an upward trajectory with increasingly famous bands, and as a studio musician backing such greats as Bessie Smith and Billie Holiday. In 1937, he landed with the incomparable Cab Calloway, helping turn the group into a true Jazz orchestra.

The jazz journalism of the day was something to behold. For example, *The Harrisburg (PA) Evening News* had this to say about Chu's plying, in the March 18, 1941 issue:

So then there's Chu Berry. Even hanging by his toes from the chandelier, he could play sax that would make a jitterbug out of a hibernating bear. But this is commercial, strictly on the up and up, and Chu Berry wraps his licks in a blanket and of blues and the next number is "Night and Day." Charade music. Very pretty."

"…make a jitterbug out of a hibernating bear." That's the kind of reviews we need today!

But, unfortunately, his career was cut short. On October 28, 1941, the band was traveling to an engagement in Toronto, Ohio. Near the town of Conneaut, the car in which Chu was a passenger swerved out of control and crashed. Chu died of his injuries three days later.

In his honor, the Pabst Blue Ribbon Beer Company (who would have thought that brew so familiar to old coal miners in times past would breath a new life with Millennials, as PBR?) established an annual award for the country's most promising young saxophonist. From the *Pittsburgh Courier*, December 13, 1941:

In an effort to keep alive the memory of Leon "Chu" Berry, Cab Calloway's late but great saxophonist, the Pabst Blue Ribbon Beer Company, who through its national colored representative William Graham, will create a special trophy for the saxophonist winner in The Courier's Third Annual Band and Musicians Contest. The award will be known as the "Chu" Berry Memorial… (O)ne of the greatest tenor saxophonists that ever lived, "Chu" Berry was killed several weeks ago in an auto accident while en-route to a dance engagement with Cab Calloway in Ohio.

Just after Chu's death, the same publication had described him as "a great musician, instrumentally tops in his chosen field. Fat and jovial, he was the kind of fellow that you would trust your sister with and tell your troubles to."

Quite a tribute, indeed.

Chu was initially laid to rest in Wheeling's Peninsula Cemetery. But, in 1964, part of that hallowed ground was excavated to make room for the I-70 Wheeling Tunnel. He, as well as his parents, were relocated to the Greenwood Cemetery.

Ethel Caffie-Austin (1949 -   ), West Virginia's First Lady of Gospel The subject of the 1999 documentary His Eye is on the Sparrow, Ethel inspires the meek and the mighty with her music.

Without doubt, the person who benefits most from my research and writing is me, and I definitely don't mean in the form of royalty checks. I learn so much, and am exposed to so many stories new to me. One of the many things I have learned more about is West Virginia's gospel music, and its First Lady.

Being Catholic, I am certainly no stranger to religious music, but, what a difference! In my church, if a song is less than four hundred years old and the slightest bit upbeat, it will almost certainly draw the ire of some older (or even "neo-traditionalist") congregants as "that *new* music." Ethel, we need you!

Ethel was born in Bluefield, but grew up near Mt. Hope, where her father was a coal miner and Pentecostal minister. Like so many Black families included in this book, the Caffie family came to the coalfields from the deep south. Her father was born in Alabama in 1896, a sharecropper. When he confronted the overseer after being cheated, he was told to leave town or be killed. The McDowell County coalfields were in need of workers, and that's where he ended up.

Ethel was a musical child prodigy, becoming adept at the piano at age six, accompanying church services at nine, and directing the choir at eleven. She was fortunate to have an excellent teacher, Eunice B. Fleming, the first African-American to give a Master's Recital at Marshall University and to sing at a Marshall commencement (1973). As she grew, she developed a full, rich voice that, to my ear, reaches down into your soul and does not let you ignore it.

Her story is an inspiring one. She was adopted by her parents, and thought she was an only child all her life until she found out, in her 50s, that she has multiple siblings who grew up nearby and were even her childhood playmates. After attending Mt. Hope High School (where she was active in the Future Business Leaders of America), Ethel attended West Virginia Tech in Montgomery, majoring in English. She later moved to Charleston.

Why an English major, instead of music? It's an oft-repeated story: while supportive, her parents felt English would offer a more secure future. (My father really wanted me to major in accounting. I would have been a horrible, and horribly unhappy, accountant.)

Like most roads worth traveling, hers has not been smooth. Ethel is a cancer survivor, and her doctors had prepared her for the possibility she may never be able to sing again, or, perhaps, even to talk. But, skilled medical treatment (and Divine intervention) saved her vocal cords, and she is now able to continue her life's work.

Ethel sees her music not as a worship service add-on, but as a full ministry. She takes it into prisons, schools, and housing projects, and to music festivals across America and Europe. One of her special gifts is teaching, conducting workshops to help spread not only joy, but skill. She has produced instructional videos, and founded the Black Sacred Music Festival. She was inducted into the West Virginia Music Hall of Fame in 2020.

The Kentucky Educational Television documentary about Ethel, *His Eye is on the Sparrow: Ethel Caffie-Austin, Minister of Black Sacred Music* (1999) is available to view online, and I highly recommend it. In addition to the music, Ethel delivers an outstanding lecture on the history of Black gospel music, which, as we know, is also the history of jazz and rock-and-roll.

Dr. Ancella Radford Bickley (1930 –   ), educator and historian
She not only recorded history, she made it, as the first full-time Black student at Marshall University.

Just as everyone interested in American history should know the name Carter G. Woodson, everyone interested in West Virginia history should know the name Ancella Radford Bickley. She has done more to promote the recording of Black history in the Mountain State than anyone I know, and her personal connection to my undergraduate alma mater, Marshall University, is historic in itself.

Ancella is a true Huntingtonian, with roots that stretch back far in the river city, but also to Cuba. Her paternal grandparents, Anderson and Julia Ann Peters Radford, are found in the census living on Patch Street in Huntington in 1900, with 15-year-old Willard, Ancella's father, one of five children still at home. Anderson died in 1917, of "Paralysis of the throat," and his death record lists him as a janitor. While the 1900 census lists him as Black, the 1910 uses the term "Mulatto," and gives his occupation as a laborer at the car works, or railroad shop. His house, on 27th Street, is owned, without mortgage. Willard is still living at home that year. In fact, he is still living with his mother Julia, by then a widow, during the following census in 1920, but in a mortgaged house. And, the extended family was still together in the year of Ancella's birth, 1930, but by then Willard, a watchman in the railroad shop, had been joined by his wife Lillian, a native alien from Cuba, who had immigrated in 1927. Willard's mother Julia died of complications from a fractured hip in 1950, at the age of 84.

The same year her grandmother died, Ancella earned her BA in English from West Virginia State, and then came home to Huntington for graduate school at Marshall, becoming the institution's first full-time Black student. She received her MA in 1954, and eventually also earned an Ed.D in English from West Virginia University in 1974. She had a distinguished career as an educator, retiring as Vice President of Academic Affairs at West Virginia State.

Throughout her career, and accelerating after her retirement, Ancella collected and promoted West Virginia's Black history. She has written numerous stories and articles, and conducted and published interviews for Marshall's Oral History of Appalachia Program. Her publications include:

The Remarkable Story of a Black Appalachian Woman. Ancella R. Bickley and Lynda Ann Ewen, editors; historical afterword by Joe Trotter. Athens: Ohio University Press, 2001.

In Spite of Obstacles: A History of the West Virginia Schools for the Colored Deaf and Blind, 1926-1955. Institute, WV Dept. of Education and the Arts, 2001.

Our Mount Vernons: Historic Register Listings of Sites Significant to the Black History of West Virginia. Ancella Bickley

Honoring Our Past: Proceedings of the First Two Conferences on West Virginia's Black History. Edited by Joe William Trotter, Jr. and Ancella Radford Bickley. Charleston, WV: Alliance for the Collection, Preservation and Dissemination of West Virginia's Black History, 1991.

History of the West Virginia State Schools Association. Washington: National Education Association. 1979.

Ancella is married to Nelson R. Bickley, who had a long legal career in the Mountain State, and they are now retired in Florida. In my personal experience with him during my career with the federal court, I know Nelson has the authoritative bearing and voice that are, I am sure, the envy of any other lawyers sharing the courtroom.

Dennis Michael Blevins (1948- 1970), wide receiver *His and other promising young lives were cut short in one of our greatest tragedies.*

There are moments you remember, news flashes across the television or radio. November 14, 1970 holds one of those memories for me. If my now-early-60s mind recalls it correctly, we were watching *The Newlywed Game* on the black-and-white Philco when the news bulletin came across. At only eleven years old, a coal miner's son living on a small farm at the end of a three-mile dirt road, I certainly had no assurance I would be able to attend college, and knew little about Marshall. But, seven years later, that was my choice, and the events of that cold, foggy, rainy, ill-fated evening still loomed large, as it continues to do in our state's collective memory today.

And, not just our state's. For years (and still), I traveled around the country conducting training programs for the federal court. I never made much of my resume and avoided lengthy introductions, preferring to get right to the presentation, but there was almost always a bio printed in the program, listing my "BA, Marshall University; MA, West Virginia University." I estimate about a quarter of the time, someone in the audience actually read it, and, during a break or after the presentation, approached me and mentioned it. That frequency increased after the 2006 film *We Are Marshall*, starring Matthew McConaughey.

Most of us know the basics. The Thundering Herd football team was returning from a 17 – 14 defeat by the East Carolina University Pirates, when the McDonnell Douglas DC-9 chartered by the University came into the Tri-State Airport too low, and clipped trees about a mile short of the runway, bursting into flames and crashing. Head Coach Rick Tilley, five members of his coaching staff, and thirty-seven players were killed, as well as several prominent team supporters, including a city councilman, state legislator, and four doctors. There were no survivors. The intensity of the fire and force of the crash were so severe that some of the remains were unidentifiable, and buried together at Spring Hill Cemetery. To this day, it remains the deadliest sports-related air tragedy in American history.

Dennis "the Menace" Blevins, a 6 foot, 181 pound wide receiver wearing number 80, was one of those players.

Dennis was the son of Solomon and Helen Holley Blevins of Hale Street in Bluefield, and had several siblings. When Dennis was four years old, his baby brother Larry, aged just a year and a half, died of accidental burns. Dennis graduated from Park Central High School in Bluefield, which, along with the Genoa High School with which it merged, was home to the town's African-American students for many years. The school district did not achieve partial integration until 1957, and Park Central's final class graduated in 1969, its students integrating and merging with Bluefield High School. The old Park Central building later became the Mt. Zion Pentecostal Church facility. Dennis earned Class AA All-State honors in football, basketball, and track, and a scholarship to play for the then-struggling Thundering Herd.

A natural three-sport athlete who was both fast and hard-working, he had the advantage of playing in what is, still today, considered one of the finest high school football stadiums in the country: Bluefield's Mitchell Stadium, built as a New Deal project in 1936, and seating 10,000. To go from Mitchell to Marshall's Fairfield, which had already been crumbling for decades even then, was probably a bit of a letdown when it came to physical plant. A junior at the time of the crash, Dennis (who was commonly called by his middle name, Michael) was known as friendly and outgoing, and making an extra effort to take care of other students from "back home."

As with most tragic events, news was spotty at first. Dennis's brothers Edward and Ronnie drove to Huntington early on November 14 hoping to find that their brother had survived. Of course, no one had done so.

For Marshall grads and fans, Huntingtonians, and many other West Virginians, the November 1970 crash holds a place similar, in some ways, to November 22, 1963. There was "before," and "after." But, as time goes on and those lives continue to be honored, there are some signs of renewal. I noted above that, when reading that I am a Marshall grad, I often receive comments about the tragedy. In recent years, though, those comments are accompanied by the mentions of Randy Moss, Byron Leftwich, and Chad Pennington.

While I was only eleven, my future federal court boss (in his capacity as Chief United States Probation Officer for the Southern District of West Virginia) and friend Ted Philyaw, originally from Oceana and also, like me, a coal miner's son, was a student at Marshall in 1970. Like so many others, he went to the crash site in Wayne County in the aftermath of the event. Debris was scattered everywhere, even days later. He picked up a couple pieces of it, probably honeycombed fuselage insulation. One of those pieces now lies in my "important stuff" box, with other mementos that would mean little to anyone else.

You aren't forgotten, Dennis. None of you are.

Robert L. Burnette (1918 - 1957), musician and band leader *His All Star run ended in tragedy, but rose to make more music.*

There were so many talented local and regional bands in the Mountain State's past, and The Burnette All Stars (sometimes called Burnette and his All Stars or Burnette's All Star Band, and often without the final "e") was one of them. Band members came and went, as is common in the business, but founder Robert L. Burnette of Bluefield recruited Lee Shadrack "Chad Lee" Manns, William Morrison, Harold T. Herndon, and Donald Smalls from Bluefield, vocalist Juanita Ritz from Princeton, and Charles Lash from Pulaski, Virginia. As early as November 1952, an announcement in the *Hinton Daily News* read: *DANCE NOV. 27. A dance will be held at the Paradise Club Thursday night Nov. 27. Music will be furnished by Burnette and his All Stars of Bluefield, from 10:00 till 2:00. Admission $1.25.* If you wanted to go out for Halloween in the year I was born (1959), an ad in the *Raleigh Register* (Beckley WV) offered this enticing invitation: *DANCE at the TWIN OAKS Country Club 10 to 2 Saturday, Oct. 31ˢᵗ Music by BURNETTE ALL STARS - Public invited-*

But, by then, the Burnette All Stars was a "reconstituted" band, having barely survived a great tragedy two years before. Returning from a gig in Kingsport all packed into a 7-passenger limousine owned by Manns and being driven by Herndon, the car crashed into a utility pole in front of Lebanon High School, around 7:00 AM. Burnette and Lash died shortly thereafter, with Manns soon following. This from the *Lebanon* (Va.) *News*, July 25, 1957:

Three Are Killed In Main Street Auto Crash Here Sunday

MUSICIANS' AUTO CRASHES INTO UTILITY POLE ON MAIN STREET EARLY SUNDAY MORNING; FIVE OTHER BAND MEMBERS HOSPITALIZED

The worst automobile wreck to take place within the city limits of Lebanon occurred Sunday morning about 7 o'clock in front of the Lebanon High School building when a limousine loaded with Negro musicians plowed into a utility pole killing two of the musicians and hospitalizing six others; the two men dying a few hours after being taken to the local hospital. The rock 'n roll band was from Bluefield and had filled an engagement at Kingsport Saturday night. Robert L. Burnette of Bluefield, leader of Burnette's All-Star Bluefield Band, died in the Lebanon General Hospital five hours after the 7 o'clock crash. Four hours later Charles Lash of Pulaski, Va., expired in the same hospital. He was a passenger in the right front of the car, while Burnette rode a jump-seat in the rear of the auto. Injured Listed: Injured in the crash were Juanita Ritz of Princeton, band vocalist; Chad

Lee Manns, owner of the car, of Bluefield; William J. Manns, also of Bluefield; Harold T. Herndon of Lincolntown, N. C.; Donald Harris and Donald Small, both of Bluefield. Trooper L. W. Collins said the band had played a Saturday night engagement at an auditorium in Kingsport, Tenn., and was returning home at the time of the accident. The car, driven by Herndon according to state police, swerved onto the sidewalk and into a utility pole in front of Lebanon High School on U. S. 19. Herndon said he dropped off to sleep and recalled nothing prior to the crash, Trooper Collins related. The officer said apparently all occupants of the car were sleeping when Herndon dozed. Crash Impact: Burnette was thrown over the back of the driver's seat and onto the hood of the car as it was forced into the driver's seat. The impact drove the pole, imbedded in concrete, into the front seat, between Miss Ritz and Lash. Chad Lee Manns was listed in "critical" condition, while all other bandsmen were considered "satisfactory" with cuts and bruises. Death of the two pushed to five the number of highway deaths in Russell County to date this year, and the Virginia road toll soared to 444, three more than had met death in the same period last year.

Unfortunately, Lee Shadrack "Chad Lee" Manns also died later in the day, as reported in the *Bluefield Daily Telegraph*, later on July 25, 1957:

THIRD MUSICIAN DIES OF INJURIES

Lee Shadrack Manns, 47-year-old Bluefield rock 'n roll musician, died yesterday In Lebanon General Hospital from injuries suffered in a Sunday highway accident that already claimed two members of the Burnette's All-Star Band.
Manns was owner of the nine-passenger limousine that crashed into a utility pole in front of Lebanon high School, claiming the lives of Robert L. Burnette of Bluefield, leader of the musical group, and 17-year-old Pulaski, Va., musician Charles Lash. Manns lived at 318 Park Street in Bluefield, where his widow, Irene, survives. The body is at Sinkford and Richardson Funeral Home where arrangements will be made.

Seven bandsmen in all were involved in the crash. Juanita Ritz of Princeton, band vocalist, and Harold T. Herndon of Lincolntown, N. C., and Bluefield, who was driving the car, both were in good condition there yesterday.

William Morrison and Donald Smalls, both young Bluefield musicians, have been released from the hospital. State police said apparently all members of the troupe, including the driver, were sleeping at the time of the crash.

The death of Manns pushed the Virginia road toll to 449, two less than had met death on the highway by the same date last year. His also was the sixth Russell County fatality for the year.

By the way, 449 highway deaths mid-year for the Commonwealth of Virginia was on track to be slightly more than the 2020 toll, 838 for the entire year. Today, there are many more people and cars, but, thankfully, those cars are much safer.

LEBANON CRASH CLAIMS 3d VICTIM

A third man died yesterday of injuries received Sunday when a limousine carrying members of a band crashed in Lebanon, Russell county.

Lee Shadrack Manns, 47, Negro, of Bluefield, W. Va., died in a Lebanon hospital. Also fatally injured in the single vehicle accident were Robert L. Burnette, 39, of Bluefield, leader of the Burnette All Stars band, and Charles Lash, 17, of Pulaski. Five other band members were injured.

While I have not been able to find a complete obituary, Robert L. Burnette appears to have been the son of Isaac and Lucy Verline Gee Burnette, of Rock. While both Isaac and Lucy Verline are listed as Black in the 1920 census, they are actually listed as White in their 1917 Mercer County marriage record, while Robert and his sister Alzie are listed as "Mulatto." An Isaac Burnett from Princeton later died of an acute coronary occlusion in Spencer State Hospital, and this could well have been our musician Robert's father. Like all families, Robert's was complicated in its own way, that old records do not always clear up for us.

After the tragic loss, the band continued with new members. One was "Ike" Harris, quite an athlete and an Army veteran as well as a piano player. His parents Jacob and Mary "Minnie" Medley Harris were married in Summers County on January 28, 1925, and Ike died in Louisville, Kentucky in 2008:

Bluefield Telegraph, July 2, 2008:

LOUISVILLE, Ky. — Donald (Ike) Elmore Harris, the fifth youngest of six, was born November 17, 1939 in Lovern, West Virginia to the late Jacob Winston Harris and Minnie Medley Harris. He died Wednesday, June 25, 2008 at St. Mary Elizabeth Hospital in Louisville following a brief illness. Reared and educated in Bluefield, West Virginia, Donald attended Genoa Junior High and Park Central High Schools and was on the Basketball Teams that won West Virginia State Basketball Championship. As a young boy he was baptized at Scott Street Baptist Church. He was also in the Boy Scout Troop at that Church. He played piano for the Burnett All Stars Band for several years. He served in the Army Special Force s during the Vietnam War, and was stationed in Hawaii as part of his tour of duty. Donald was married for a number of years, and with his wife Jackie, two children were born, Eloise and Derrick Harris.

He attended numerous trade schools and earned certificates in electricity, electronics, refrigeration, and computer robotic technology. He used this training to become a journeyman in the Maintenance Department at General Electric. He retired from this position in November, 2000.Donald was an entertainer. He loved playing keyboard for the BB Taylor Blues Band and for his own Band, the Donald Harris Blues Band. Donald was preceded in death by his parents, Jacob and Minnie Harris; and a sister, Mildred Deborah Davis, (Charles, also deceased).He leaves to Cherish his memory, daughters Donna, Christina, and Eloise and son, Derrick; sisters, Brinnie Marcella, (Patsy) Whitehurst, Sarah Jean Heath, Tassie Esther Hare, and one brother, Jacob Jerome Harris, (Amrizene); and a host of nieces, nephews, and other relatives and friends. Funeral Services will be conducted on Thursday, July 3, 2008, 1:00 p.m. at Chapel Funeral Home, 1335 Bland Street Bluefield, W.Va. with the Rev. Robert Johnson officiating the service. The family will be receiving friends one hour prior to the service. Burial will follow at the family Cemetery in Lovern, W.Va. Chapel Funeral Home and Cremations served the Harris family.

Another veteran of the reconstituted Burnett All Stars was Albert "Bucky" Clemons, who even played with *The Drifters* and *The Coasters* at one point.

Warco-Falvo Funeral Home, Washington, PA:

Albert L. "Bucky" Clemons, 77 of Washington passed away on Saturday-May 9, 2020. He was born May 14, 1942 in Bluefield, West Virginia the son of the late Colbert Hunt and Elizabeth Clemons. Mr. Clemons was employed as a crane operator at Washington Steel for over 20 years from where he retired. He was a member of the Nazareth Baptist Church, Washington where he played the piano and organ in the church choir. Mr. Clemons enjoyed playing the piano in traveling bands, most notably with the Burnett All Stars. He also played with the Coasters and the Drifters. Mr. Clemons also enjoyed the precious times that he spent with his family. He will be dearly missed by all that knew and loved him.

Surviving is his wife, Linda L. Clemons of Washington; eight children, Denny, Odessa, Regina (Amos), Ron, Dana (Keith), Kenn (Kendra), Todd (Calli) and Colbert; three brothers, Larry, Charles and Gregory; three sisters, Barbara, Carolyn and Sharon. Many grandchildren and a host of nieces and nephews also survive.

In addition to his parents, Mr. Clemons was preceded in death by a sister, Bridget.

We hope there will always be a place for local bands, even in a world of streaming everything else remotely. Go out and hear one this weekend, if you can, in memory of the Burnette All Stars.

Richard H. Cain (1825 – 1887), minister and Congressman *The roots of Mother Emmanuel AME church reach to Greenbrier County.*

We sometimes forget that, prior to the Civil War, there were many Black Americans were who not enslaved. The Greenbrier County census records from 1830 – 1860 have more than three hundred listings for "Free Blacks." One who was born there was Richard Harvey Cain, whose father was a Free Black, and whose mother was of Native American ancestry. When Richard was about seven years old, his family "moved west" to Gallipolis, Ohio.

Crossing the Ohio River from Point Pleasant meant more than it does today. Ohio was free soil. That meant the very curious and bright young Richard could go to school, a privilege denied even "Free Blacks" in much of the south. Coming from a devout family, Richard's first education came in Sunday school classes. He worked on steamboats plying the Ohio River for a while, but entered the ministry of the Methodist Church. His first assignment, in 1844, was in Hannibal, Missouri. One has to wonder if he ever encountered a precocious waif named Clemens, whose family moved to Hannibal in 1839, while there. He also made a living as a barber at one time.

The Methodist Church, at the time, was still segregated. Unable to accept that hypocrisy, Richard transferred to the AME Church in 1848. Feeling a need to continue his education to become a more effective pastor, he returned to Ohio to attend Wilberforce University, the very first college to be owned and operated by African-Americans. It was founded in 1856 as a collaboration by the Methodist Episcopal Church and the African Methodist Episcopal (AME) church. When the Civil War broke out, he and the other students attempted to join the Union Army, but it did not begin accepting Black soldiers until later in the War, and even then, in strictly segregated units commanded by White officers. The U. S. Armed Services did not become fully integrated until July 26, 1948, by President Truman's executive order.

Unable to serve in uniform, Richard spent the War as pastor at the Bridge Street Church in Brooklyn, New York. When the War ended, he was reassigned to the AME Church in Charleston, South Carolina, which had not been allowed to operate openly for years. The original church, called the Hempstead Church, had been burned after one of its founders, Denmark Vesey, was executed after a "secret trial" found him guilty of being involved in a slave revolt plot. After the War, the new pastor consolidated various branches of the small congregation and soon the membership swelled to more than two thousand souls. We know that congregation today as Mother Emmanuel.

If you have visited Charleston, you have probably seen the stately, glowing-white stucco building on Calhoun Street. That edifice dates from 1891, after the wooden structure in which Richard Cain served was destroyed by the 1886 earthquake.

When taking one of the popular narrated carriage rides around the historic city, tourists used to hear mainly about the architecture of the beautiful building. Sadly, after June 17, 2015, that changed.

The first decade of Reconstruction held hope for a more equitable society in the defeated south. Reverend Cain founded a pro-civil rights newspaper that brought him name recognition throughout the state.

He was elected to the state senate in 1868, and the Greenbrier County native was elected to the United States House of Representatives four years later.

Fueled by both conviction and years of practice behind the pulpit, Richard was a most eloquent speaker. During the debate over the Civil Rights Bill in 1874, he made a speech that still resonates today:

"Sir, social equality is a right which every man, every woman, and every class of persons have within their own control. They have a right to form their own acquaintances, to establish their own social relationships. Its establishment and regulation are not within the province of legislation. No laws enacted by legislators can compel social equality. Now, what is it we desire? What we desire is this: inasmuch as we have been raised to the dignity, to the honor, to the position of our manhood, we ask that the laws of this country should guarantee all the rights and immunities belonging to that proud position, to be enforced all over this broad land....

(T)he gentleman who so eloquently spoke on this subject the other day, {a colleague from North Carolina} a few months ago entered a restaurant at Wilmington and sat down to be served, and while there a gentleman stepped up to him and said, "You cannot eat here." All the other gentlemen upon the railroad as passengers were eating there; he had only twenty minutes, and was compelled to leave the restaurant or have a fight for it. He showed fight, however, and got his dinner; but he has never been back there since. Coming here last week I felt we did not desire to draw revolvers and present the bold front of warriors, and therefore we ordered our dinners to be brought into the cars, but even there we found the existence of this feeling; for, although we had paid a dollar a piece for our meals, to be brought by the servants into the cars, still there was objection on the part of the railroad people to our eating our meals in the cars, because they said we were putting on airs. They refused us in the restaurant, and then did not desire that we should eat our meals in the cars, although we paid for them. Yet this was in the noble State of North Carolina. Mr. Speaker, the colored men of the south do not want the adoption of any force measure. No; they do not want anything by force. All they ask is that you will give them the right to enjoy precisely the same privileges accorded to every other class of citizens.

We believe in the Declaration of Independence, that all men are born free and equal, and are endowed by their Creator with certain inalienable rights, among which are life, liberty, and the pursuit of happiness. And we further believe that to secure those rights governments are instituted. And we further believe that when governments cease to subserve those ends the people should change them. Inasmuch as we have toiled with you in building up this nation; inasmuch as we have suffered side by side with you in the war; inasmuch as we have together passed through affliction and pestilence, let there be now a fulfillment of the sublime thought of our father—let all men enjoy equal liberty and equal rights. Our wives and our children have high hopes and aspirations; their longings for manhood and womanhood are equal to those of any other race. The same sentiment of patriotism and of gratitude, the same spirit of national pride that animates the hearts of other citizens, animates theirs. In the name of the dead soldiers of our race, whose bodies lie at Petersburg and on other battle-fields of the South; in the name of the widows and orphans they have left behind; in the name of the widows of the confederate soldiers who fell upon the same fields, I conjure you let this righteous act be done. I appeal to you in the name of God and humanity to give us our rights, for we ask nothing more."

A fierce advocate for government intervention to ensure civil rights, he was caught in the tide of regression as the country lost it appetite for Reconstruction. The Republican Party became more focused on economic issues than on continuing the legacy of Lincoln, and southern Democrats succeeded in rewriting the War's history in one of the greatest long-term public relations coups ever. Richard was not re-nominated in 1878.

Returning to the ministry, he was elected as bishop of the Texas-Louisiana AME Conference in 1880, and cofounded Paul Quinn College (which still exists) in Waco. He was reassigned to the Mid-Atlantic/New England Conference in 1884, and served as its bishop until his death in Washington on January 18, 1887.

There is little mentioned in most biographies about Richard Cain's family. Onc source says his wife was named Lara, and his daughter Anna Jane Cain Cook.

After retiring from the federal court in West Virginia in in 2010, I moved to Myrtle Beach. Charleston, South Carolina, is one of my favorite cities and close enough for frequent day trips. I had visited it on Saturday, June 13, 2015, and walked past the landmark church on Calhoun Street. Four days later, 21-year-old Dylann Roof entered Mother Emmanuel at 8:16 p.m., and sat next to the pastor, Reverend Pinckney, during Bible study. Almost an hour later, he began to disagree with their discussion of scripture and, when the participants began to pray, he pulled a Glock from his pack. Reloading five times, he killed six women and three men, ages 41 to 87. Before he opened fire, he said, "I have to do it. You rape our women and you're taking over our country. And you have to go."

Roof was a fan of the multitude of White Supremacist and Neo-Nazi propaganda sites so easily found on the Internet. He posed for photos with the Confederate battle flag, holding guns.

After receiving a tip from a passerby, authorities arrested Roof almost 250 miles away. He was brought to Charleston, where he made his first court appearance. Survivors and victims' family members also appeared, and spoke directly to Roof, with words of forgiveness.

I could not have done that. Could you?

The Magistrate who presided over that hearing, James Gosnell, Jr., said, on the record, that, along with the dead victims and their families, "there are (also) victims on this young man's side of the family." Magistrate Gosnell, by the way, had been reprimanded in 2003 for using a racial slur from the bench.

Roof has been sentenced to both life without parole, and to death, in separate proceedings. From prison, he wrote, "I would like to make it crystal clear, I do not regret what I did. I am not sorry. I have not shed a tear for the innocent people I killed."

Reading that, after the passage from Greenbrier County native Richard Cain's speech above, tells us that we won the War, but we have far to go to win the Peace, even after more than 150 years.

Cornelius H. Charlton (1929 – 1951), Medal of Honor recipient A West Virginia hero's journey to his final resting place was longer than it should have been.

The Congressional Medal of Honor is a rare thing. During a public tour of the Pentagon, you can visit a room dedicated to Honorees, and see their individual names. The medal was commissioned in 1861, to recognize personal acts of valor committed "conspicuously by gallantry and intrepidity." Of the 3,469 medals awarded to soldiers, sailors, airmen, Marines, and Coast Guardsmen since its inception, almost half were awarded to Civil War participants. So, modern recipients are rare, indeed.

The splendor of that Pentagon memorial would seem to have little in common with East Gulf, West Virginia. Like so many once-bustling coal camps across the southern part of the state, there really isn't a town there anymore. A sign and a few houses between Rhodell and the next semi-abandoned settlement of Killarney is all that's left. But, there is a connection. His name was Cornelius H. Charlton. He was born in East Gulf on July 26, 1929, one of seventeen children born to coal miner Van Charlton and his wife, Clara. After moving among various coal camps, Van and Clara took advantage of the domestic labor shortage during World War II and moved their family to the Bronx, New York City. I'm sure that was quite an adjustment. Van became the superintendent of an apartment building.

With the war raging, young Cornelius wanted to enlist, but his parents would not allow it until he graduated from high school. Soon after the war ended, they signed permission for the youth to enter the United States Army at age seventeen. He served his first term with occupation troops in Germany, and his reenlistment in occupied Japan.

When the cold war became hot, Cornelius, who by that time had a comfortable job in Okinawa, volunteered to go to Korea. A natural soldier, Cornelius was soon made platoon leader.

The young Raleigh Countian's platoon, among others, was tasked with taking a hill with Chinese entrenchments near Chipo-ri in June 1951. When a neighboring platoon's leader was shot, Cornelius took it over as well. His actions that day sound like those of a Hollywood war movie hero, but were all too real. He single-handedly destroyed two Chinese positions, but received a chest wound in the process. Despite the injury, Charlton led his men forward to a Chinese mortar bunker, which was responsible for many American casualties. Even after receiving additional wounds from a grenade, he continued firing until the bunker was immobilized, before dying on the battlefield.

That seems like exactly the kind of valor that should be recognized by the Congressional Medal of Honor. How many American soldiers lived to fight another day because of his actions at that mortar installment, we do not know.

What we do know, though, is that, had Cornelius Charlton somehow survived those acts of bravery, valor, and heroism and returned to East Gulf, West Virginia to visit childhood friends, he would have been riding in the back of the bus. Cornelius Charlton was an African-American. The number of American lives he saved and his self-sacrifice would not have changed much for him on the 1950s home front.

The brave soldier's remains' story should have ended in 1951, with being returned to America for burial among other heroes at Arlington National Cemetery, but it did not. The United States Army did not offer the Charlton family a plot in Arlington as a final resting place. So, instead, Cornelius was returned to West Virginia and buried in a segregated coal camp cemetery in Bramwell. There he rested until 1989, when he was reburied with full honors in the American Legion cemetery in Beckley. He was the only African-American buried there.

A Congressional Medal of Honor recipient being denied burial at Arlington is a bit of a story, and the *Los Angeles Times* picked it up. Living Medal honorees were incensed, and mounted a campaign to have Cornelius moved to the National Cemetery. In the light of publicity, the Pentagon discovered it had made an 'administrative error' and the remains of the brave young man from East Gulf were finally moved to Arlington on November 12, 2008. May he rest in peace.

Fannie Cobb Carter (1872 – 1973), educator and school integration activist *In a "long life, well lived," she saw results of the change she helped bring about.*

More and more people are living to be a hundred years old, and its sobering to think about the change one can see in a single lifetime. My grandmother, for example, could remember the first automobile she ever saw, yet also lived in the age of cellphones and laptops.

When it comes to civil rights activism, few lifetimes could rival that of Fannie Cobb Carter. She was born on Dickinson Street in Charleston. Her mother, Margaret (at least, according to the census) was still living in during the 1900 census, in a rented house on upper Lewis Street, listed as a 44-year-old widow, with her 25-year-old school teacher daughter Fannie. Margaret died of heart disease in 1941 and is again listed as widowed, but, unfortunately, none of the records I found give her late husband's name.

The difficulty of family history research is present with Margaret, however. The 1900 census, as noted above, lists her as Fannie's mother. But, other sources say Fannie's mother died while Fannie was young, and Fannie then lived with her grandmother. The story goes that, as a child, Fannie went to the Colored School on Quarrier Street until that time, when she was allowed to be taught alongside the children of Charles Lewis, by whom her grandmother was employed as a servant. So, I can't tell you for sure much more about Fannie's parents, other than that, in a 1972 interview in the *Charleston Daily Mail,* Fannie said both her parents were paid servants, and her grandparents all born into slavery..

Fannie went on to Storer College in Harpers Ferry, where she earned a teaching degree in 1891. Just before the turn of the century, she attended Hampton Institute, and even toured Europe with the Hampton Institute Singers, surely a heady experience for a young lady from Charleston. During her career, she also did professional development work at Oberlin College, Columbia, the University of Chicago, and The Ohio State University. (I know I would hear about it from my Buckeye friends if I hadn't added "The" to OSU!)

She taught in Kanawha County public schools (for the grand salary of $40.00 per month) at a time when Black teachers were uncommon anywhere in the state. Determined to change that, Fannie left the public system to help organize the Education Department at the West Virginia Colored Institute, now West Virginia State University, in 1908, staying for 12 years. After that, she was appointed as superintendent of the West Virginia Industrial Home for Colored Girls in Huntington, and held that position until 1935, when she returned to Kanawha County as Director of Adult Education for the Board of Education there.

Her work in education not unnoticed outside of the state, she moved to Washington DC to become Dean of the National Trade and Professional School for Women and Girls in 1945, and remained well past the age most folks retire. She re-retired and came home to Charleston in 1962. She was active in civic organizations throughout her life.

Fannie married Emory Rankin Carter, a lawyer originally from Lancaster County, Virginia in 1911. Daniel Stratton performed the ceremony. Fannie and Emory did not have children. Emory's father had been a Justice of the Peace there, and Emory became interested in the law at an early age. After earning a law degree from Howard University in 1900, he relocated to Charleston a couple of years later, reportedly with less than five dollars in his pocket. Over the years, his practice thrived and he took a particular interest in real estate, buying land on the south side of the river that most businessmen at the time felt had no future, being steep wilderness unfit for development.

We now call that area South Hills. Look through the real estate prices there today, and you see that, apparently, Emory was right.

The short *Charleston Daily Mail* death notice for Emory, January 15, 1925, simply states:

Funeral services for Emory R. Carter, colored, who died Tuesday afternoon, will be held at the First Baptist church, Washington street, Friday afternoon at 2:30.

But, fortunately, we have an excellent picture of Emory's life from *History of the American Negro, West Virginia Edition*, Volume VII, original edition, edited by A.B. Caldwell, 1923, A.B. Caldwell Publishing Co., Atlanta, Georgia:

EMORY RANKIN CARTER

Among the capable and successful men of the colored Bar of West Virginia must be mentioned Emory Rankin Carter, of Charleston, who has been identified with the Capital City for more than twenty years. Mr. Carter is a native of the Old Dominion, having been born in Lancaster County, in the eastern part of the State, on September 24, 1874. His father, Emanuel Carter, who was engaged in farming and oystering, was a man of intelligence and of standing in the community, and was for a number of years the Justice of the Peace in his township. The mother of our subject was, before her marriage, Caroline Wiggins, dtr. of Jesse and Roxie Wiggins.

Growing up in Lancaster County, young Carter laid the foundation of his education in the local public schools. For his higher literary work, he went to the Petersburg Normal and Collegiate Institute and completed his course there in 1896. For his law course, he matriculated at Howard University, where he won his L.L.B. degree.

As a boy young Carter had become interested in the procedure of his father's court and early determined to be a lawyer. Of course, the way was not easy. Hard work and close application told on his health, and while he was admitted to the bar at Richmond in 1901, it was two years after his graduation, before he settled down to devote his full time to the practice of law. He was at Newport News, Va. for a few months and spent a short time in Ohio and in Pittsburgh. He worked in Florida for a part of two tourist seasons. This brought him up to 1902. In that year he came to Charleston, where he has since resided. When he reached the city he had $3.16, and was a stranger, but he had his education and a will to work. Also there was something about him which inspired confidence, so that from the beginning he had the co-operation of some of the best people of the city. His practice has been almost entirely civil, and grew apace as the man and the character of his work became known. He was not slow to visualize the future of Charleston and invested his earnings in real estate which has had steady enhancement.

In politics Mr. Carter is a Republican, but has not sought office. He is a prominent and active member of the Baptist church in which he is a trustee. He has been Superintendent of his local Sunday School and is now teacher of a Bible Class.

On October 2, 1911, Mr. Carter was married to Miss Fannie C. Cobb, one of the State's most accomplished teachers. Mr. Carter has been an intelligent observer of conditions both in the country and in the city and believes that the three outstanding needs of the race today may be summed up in as many words "Education-property-business."

Fannie became a revered fixture in the Charleston education community. Think about the change she witnessed: After surely hearing her grandparents' stories about slavery and emancipation, she watched Representative Shirley Chisholm's name be placed into nomination at the 1972 Democratic primary in Miami, Florida, after Chisholm won the New Jersey primary.

But, without doubt, one of the highlights of her later professional life was the 1954 *Brown v. Board of Education of Topeka* case, ruling "Separate but Equal" unconstitutional, and effectively integrating public schools. She had been a tireless advocate of integration, at a time when many of the most influential Black educators were of mixed opinion, setting up a rivalry between raised-in-West Virginia-Booker T. Washington and W. E. B. Du Bois.

She told the *Daily Mail:* "To say why I have lived for 100 years is not easy. But, I guess I really didn't have any choice. When you have lived in an atmosphere where everybody has been so friendly and helpful, it seems you ought to take life seriously and live to be at least 100."

From the *Charleston Daily Mail*, March 30, 1973:

A Charleston woman who celebrated her 100th birthday last Sept. 30, and was widely known in educational circles, died Thursday flight at St. Francis Hospital following a long illness.

Mrs. Fannie Cobb Carter graduated from Storer College in Harpers Ferry in 1891, and later attended Oberlin College, Ohio State University, Columbia University and several other institutions.

Mrs. Carter traveled in the United States and abroad for education purposes.

Mrs. Carter, who was born in 1872, the year before the first train came through Charleston, kept abreast of current news.

She was against strip mining and last year, during an interview, explained:

"I would rather see little children playing on the hillsides. And I like to see cows and horses there."

An early riser, she always voted before breakfast and confided that she "used to be a staunch Republican but found out all the devils aren't on the Democratic side. Sometimes I vote the other way now."

She didn't like the idea of calling Negroes "blacks." She preferred to talk about "just people" instead of blacks and whites.

Mrs. Carter never met Gov. Moore but she remembers when George Wesley Atkinson was governor in 1899.

"He invited Booker T. Washington back to West Virginia and had him go all over the state," she said.

She danced at a reception honoring the prominent Negro educator.

She was born in a house on Dickinson Street, between Quarrier and Lee streets.

She was superintendent of the first West Virginia industrial School for Colored Girls in Huntington, dean of women for 17 years in the National Trade and Processional School for Women and Girls in Washington, D.C., and Teague Elementary school in Charleston.

Mrs. Carter in 1909 instituted the teacher training department at West Virginia State College, then known as West Virginia Collegiate Institute where she worked several years.

She later returned to private business in Charleston where she became a charter member of the Women's Improvement League.

There are no immediate survivors.

The body is at Preston Funeral Home.

A few years after Fannie died, Charleston began to recognize the legacy she left behind, when the mayor at the time proclaimed "Fannie Cobb

Carter Day." From the *Charleston Sunday Gazette-Mail State Magazine*, June 5, 1977:

Next Saturday has been proclaimed "Fannie Cobb Carter Day" by Mayor Hutchinson, who notes that the late Charleston resident will be honored by the Association for the Study of Afro-American Life and History. A plaque will be placed in the Science and Culture Center in recognition, sponsors say, of "her distinguished service to mankind."

Mrs. Carter, affectionately known to many as "Miss Fannie," is recognized as an educator, humanitarian, and centenarian. She will be memorialized at 6 p.m. Saturday in the theater of the Science and Culture Center.

In addition to the presentation of the plaque by the association, the Charleston-Institute Chapter of the Links will present to the Archives a commemorative book of letters and other memorabilia about Mrs. Carter, says Delia Brown Taylor, president of the Links. The Links and members of the center's staff are cosponsors of the memorial.

The program, Mrs. Taylor says, includes music by First Baptist Church Sanctuary Choir and a performance by the St. James Episcopal Church Dancers.

This is a fitting part of the tribute. Those of us who knew Miss Fannie and shared her confidence realize that Negro American music and dance held special appeal to her as art forms and as means of being what she termed "ambassadors of goodwill."

That belief went back to her European travels with the Hampton (Va.) Institute Singers in the late 1890's, although she herself wasn't a singer. Hampton was one of several schools that she attended and where she later taught during her career as an educator. Significantly, it was the Fisk Jubilee Singers of Fisk University who first took Negro spirituals and folk songs to the concert halls of Europe and drew waves of applause in the 1880's. On top of that, "they made money for Fisk and for themselves as individual students. From it all flowed the goodwill that Miss Fannie felt inherent in the touching music that grew out of the black experience.

"We used to know how to dance and sing, but now it seems that all we know how to do is raise hell," Miss Fannie once complained to me.

She wondered whether we American blacks during the latter part of the sizzling 1960's weren't in danger of creating our own poisonous stereotype. It was during the height of inner-city riots marked by the angry self-destructive cry of "Burn, baby, burn."

Mrs. Carter didn't believe in the double-standard, one for whites and another for blacks.

"Right is right if nobody does it, and wrong is wrong if everybody does it," she would say.

She was candid, although she often spoke to her friends in confidence about personal and public matters on her mind. An obvious intent of confidence was to avert a chain of mindless and malicious gossip, but at the same time to help her clear up some question or maybe to put a rumor to rest about this or that. She had a .peculiar way of swearing one to secrecy.

"If I hear this again," Miss Fannie would caution, "I shall say, 'Mr. Peeks is my friend, but he makes mistakes.'"

Yet she spoke on the record about topical and controversial matters. One notable occasion was the week before her 100th birthday when she was interviewed by John Morgan in a Gazette story Sept. 23,1972.

She told Morgan she was against strip mining.

"I would rather see little children playing on the hillsides. And I like to see cows and horses there."

She was all for then-Secretary of State John D. Rockefeller IV becoming governor.

"I think Rockefeller will make West Virginia a garden spot if he is given a chance," she said, adding, "He can't be blamed if he was born rich and white. He would make a fine official for West Virginia."

By comparison, she said she didn't know Gov. Moore. This question, however, made her sound a bit devious if not politic, in the judgment of those in whom she confided.

She once said she didn't know Sen. Robert C. Byrd, D-W.Va. but added softly, "I don't think his heart is right." Miss Fannie had reason to doubt the junior senator from the Mountain State, now Senate Majority Leader, because as one wag put it, "Byrd made a reputation for himself by minding the morals of the poor in Washington."

The reference was to his crackdown on so-called "welfare cheats" when he was chairman of the Senate appropriations subcommittee for the District of Columbia in the early 1960's. "Taxpayers are subsidizing illegitimacy," Byrd maintained.

He raised the old question of welfare reform for the District of Columbia and for the nation as a whole, but the question was overtaken and politically drowned out by the war on poverty. Now the welfare reform question is back again.

"It's a question that Miss Fannie understood all too well for those on welfare and those off, and for those honestly interested in welfare reform as opposed to those who would make political hay out of it.

Miss Fannie was quite aware of welfare problems in the nation's capital, where she spent many years. In 1945, she became associated with Miss Nannie H. Burroughs, president of the National Trade and Professional School for Women and Girls in Washington. Mrs. Carter was dean of this institution and later acting president for a combined period of about 17 years.

The school was supported mainly by the women's auxiliary of the National Baptist Convention, the largest black denomination in the country. One of its major aims was to give wayward girls and unwed mothers a second chance for a high school education and to learn a marketable skill. It was something of a forerunner of the jobs corps.

Miss Fannie had an abiding faith in young people, as witnessed by the many friends she made among them throughout her lifetime. She differed with them on questions of separating generations, but without marring friendship and the high esteem in which she was held.

She, for example, preferred to be called a "Negro" rather than a "Black" even with a capital "B." Since Orientals weren't referred to as "yellows," she pointed out, it made no sense to her for Negroes to be called "blacks." She believed that "Black English" was something for the birds.

She had been part of the fight through the years for the spelling of Negro with a capital "N," as was the case with capitalizing Indian, Jew or the name of any other ethnic or racial group. It wasn't until the early 1930's that the fight for the recognition of a name was won. The New York Times and the New York Board of Education capitulated and agreed to write Negro in the "upper case," printer's parlance for capital letters.

Mrs. Carter believed in the ideals of racial integration, but not at the expense of the Negro American past and ethnic recognition.

"Disbanding our schools in West Virginia is leaving my people no connection with the history of education in West Virginia," she said. "We've made large contributions."

She was appalled that the trophies won by black Garnet High School athletes over the years were shunted aside in a cabinet at the Mattie V. Lee Home. She was even more appalled that the name of Garnet was changed to John Adams when the school was integrated as a junior high school.

"This is our fault for not calling attention to what is surely an oversight," she remarked. "Our people need a voice, not to create trouble but to call attention to things like this. Integration is no good unless it is in goodwill.

"There's no doubt we gained and yet we lost. I'm not sure yet whether the gain is equal to the loss."

Those remarks were made on her 90th birthday in 1962. She lived to see the name of Garnet restored to the old school building as the Garnet Adult Education School. She saw other changes during the next 10 years that pleased her and indicated that integration was a positive gain.

In sports, she regarded the black stars and superstars with their six-figure salaries as an opportunity come true, for more individual blacks to get into the main stream of American business. She used to count ways how she thought this could be done through franchises, partnerships and the like.

Her husband was lawyer-businessman Emory R. Carter who had an eye for real estate. Mrs. Carter delighted in recalling how people referred to her husband as crazy when he bought land south of the Kanawha River. In those days, practically all of present South Hills was nothing but a wilderness. Her husband died in 1925 and the couple had no children.

But Mrs. Carter experienced motherhood as the mother of other people's children, some of whom were motherless and fatherless, too. She was prepared. She was graduated from Storer College at Harpers Ferry in 1891. She did postgraduate work at Ohio State University, Oberlin College, the University of Chicago, and Columbia University.

She took postgraduate studies mostly during the summer after she started teaching in Charleston before the turn of the century. She taught in the city for nine years. She also set up the teacher training department at West Virginia Collegiate Institute, now West Virginia State College. She also taught at Bluefield State College.

In 1926, she was named superintendent of the first Industrial Home for Colored Girls in Huntington, where she remained for 10 years. After that, she returned to Charleston and became director of adult education for Negroes in Kanawha County.

As a result of all this, Miss Fannie took a wealth of teacher and administrative experience to Washington when she joined Miss Nannie H. Burroughs at the National Trade and Professional School for Women and Girls.

For words and deeds, Miss Fannie is being honored by the Association for the Study of Afro-American Life and History. The association was founded in 1915 by a former West Virginia coal miner, Carter Godwin Woodson, who earned a doctor's degree in history at Harvard University.

In 1975, the association started the two-year National Historic Marker Project for honoring prominent and pioneering black Americans. Each year, 100 bronze markers, like the one for Mrs. Fannie Cobb Carter, are placed at birthplaces and other sites of commemoration.

The first marker was dedicated to Dr. Woodson and placed in New Canton, Va., Dec. 19, 1975, on the 100th anniversary of his birth. The project was started with a $75,000 grant from the Amoco Foundation, under the present executive director of the association, Dr. J. Rupert Picott.

The historic marker and commemorative musical tribute Saturday to Mrs. Carter is open to the public.

Nice. The piece captures how outspoken the small, but fiery, lady was, even at 100. But, if one proclaims a "Day" to recognize the historic legacy of a person who lived a century, shouldn't one have done it while the subject was still around to see it? I mean, Fannie gave us plenty of time to arrange things. "Just sayin,'" as we see in social media.

In that same *Daily Mail* interview (September 29, 1972), Fannie said, "I'm interested in people, both Black and White. Life is like a piano. It has two kinds of keys, both black and white. If you don't play on both of them, you will never get harmony."

You still teach us today, Fannie.

John Robert Clifford (1848 – 1933), attorney, teacher, soldier, and journalist *He set the stage for Brown v. Board of Education more than a half century sooner.*

Having worked in the federal legal system much of my life, I know it's easy to make fun of lawyers, until you need one. J. R. Clifford, as he preferred to be called, was West Virginia's first Black attorney.

J. R. was born in Williamsport, which was in Hardy County then, but Grant County now after a boundary change. His parents, Isaac and Mary Clifford, and grandparents were Free Blacks, and had lived in the area for generations. Today, the tiny town of Williamsport is not exactly a center of diversity, with statistics showing 99.2% of the total 2,655 population self-identifying as White, and the remaining 0.8 % Black. The Cliffords must have been people of some means, because they sent J. R. to school in Chicago to be educated, because of limited opportunities in the area. When he was in his early teens, the Civil War broke out, and, at age 15, he joined what was officially titled the United States Colored Troops, serving in Company F, 13th Regiment, Heavy Artillery. He was a Corporal when the War ended.

Still a teenager, he took up barbering to make a living, and attended writing school in Ohio. He opened his own writing school in Wheeling, and then in Martin's Ferry, Ohio before enrolling in Storer College in Harpers Ferry. Becoming a teacher in Martinsburg, he persuaded white attorney J. Nelson Wirner to allow him to study law with him, and had a successful career the rest of his life, but was not officially admitted to the West Virginia State Bar until 1887, its first African-American member. J. R. and his wife Mary had ten children.

From 1882 through 1917, J. R. published *The Pioneer Press*, one of the most important newspapers of the day aimed at a Black audience. This brought him to national attention, and he became friends with W. E. B. Du Bois, helping him found the Niagara Movement, the forerunner of the NAACP. (J. R. objected to the new organization's use of the term "Colored" in its name, by the way) He was elected as a delegate to the Republican National Convention in 1884, but, unfortunately, his race was evidently a problem for some of the other delegates and candidates.

Now, to that court case, with a little background: In 1896, the Supreme Court upheld the "Separate but Equal" principle of legal racial segregation in its landmark *Plessy v. Ferguson*. Homer Plessy deliberately violated Louisiana's "Separate Car Act" that required separate (but, uh, equal...we all know how that worked out) accommodations for train cars. Homer boarded the "Whites only" car, and his defense was that the law was unconstitutional. The Louisiana Supreme Court disagreed, and, eventually, so did the U. S. Supreme Court. Separate but "equal" was safe as a legal avenue for discrimination for more than a half century afterwards.

Homer Plessy, from New Orleans, actually had very little Black ancestry, being legally categorized at the time as an "Octoroon," or a person of seven-eighths White and one-eighth Black ancestry. What terms, back then! He was born to a family that had come to America as free from Haiti, and Whites from France. Because his appearance was White, he could have ridden the railroad car with no problem, but he was willing to be arrested to test the law, buying a first-class ticket and coordinating with the local Citizens' Committee, formed to fight segregation laws.

Just two years later, the Tucker County, West Virginia Board of Education decided it could save a few bucks by shortening the school year from nine months to five…but only for Black students. The white kids still had a full school year, in their segregated schools.

How equal was that?

J. R. represented Mrs. Carrie Williams, the Colored School's principal. He asked her to continue teaching the full term, even without funding, while he litigated the matter, and then filed suit for Mrs. Williams's back pay. The case was styled *Williams v. Board of Education*, and he won. Tucker County appealed to the West Virginia Supreme Court, and J. R. won again, which set precedent for African-American school rights across the state.

There were very few civil rights court victories in southern states in those days, but Carrie Williams's back pay, $121.00, represented one of them. It would not be until *Brown v. Board of Education of Topeka* in 1954 that the "separate but equal" principle was found to be unconstitutional, overruling *Plessy v. Ferguson*. That case, argued by the NAACP's chief counsel Thurgood Marshall with financial support in the amount of $75,000 from the United Auto Workers, began a decade of white supremacist backlash across the south. Arkansas Governor Orval Faubus called out the National Guard to block Black students entry into Little Rock Central High School, and it worked until President Eisenhower called in the 101st Airborne Division from Fort Campbell, Kentucky to enforce integration. In Mississippi, Medgar Evers sued to enforce the law, and was murdered. Alabama Governor George Wallace personally blocked the door of the University of Alabama to prevent two Black students from enrolling.

And then there was our neighbor, Virginia. Their politicians got their pointy little heads together and thought, you know, this new law says we have to integrate our schools, but there's nothing in the Constitution that says we have to HAVE public schools to begin with, so let's let counties just close 'em all down. If we can't have it our way, we'll just take our future and out tax money and marbles and go home, opening private schools, which the law do not affect, for those who can afford them. That lasted in Prince Edward County all the way until 1964.

On October 4, 1933, J. R., 85, fell down the stairs in his Martinsburg home and hit his head, causing a cerebral hemorrhage. He died the next day. Having served our country well, J. R. rests in Arlington National Cemetery, as is fitting.

Martin Robison Delany (1812 – 1885), physician, soldier, writer, and abolitionist *One of the first four Black men admitted to Harvard, he was a true "Renaissance man" of his age.*

The role of "Free Blacks" in the Civil War has been under appreciated. Until the 1989 movie *Glory*, about the 54th Massachusetts Infantry, starring Denzel Washington and Morgan Freeman, and the 1997 TNT television film *Buffalo Soldiers*, about Black members of the U. S. Cavalry during the Apache Wars starring Danny Glover, most Americans thought little about African-American soldiers in wars prior to World War I. But, it is estimated that 179,000 Black soldiers, a full 10% of the force, served in the U. S. Army during the Civil War, and another 19,000 in the Navy, and nearly 30,000 of them gave their lives for the cause. As with White soldiers, of course, more died of infection or disease than being killed on the battlefield. Delany, the highest ranking Black officer during the Civil War, was born a "Free Black" in Charles Town, and went on to be one of the most influential voices for equality for decades.

Martin's status seems a bit complicated by today's standard. His father, Samuel Delany, was enslaved. But, his mother Patty was a free woman. According to the Virginia law of the day, children were born into the status of their mothers, so Martin was a freeman. All four of his grandparents were born in Africa, so he was not as far removed from the continent as many, even of the day, since the United States officially banned the importation of slaves on January 1, 1808. Patty's father was a nobleman from the Niger Valley, kidnapped and brought to Virginia, and supposedly returned to Africa after obtaining his freedom through his status. But, his wife Gracie, who had also been kidnapped and enslaved, was freed and decided to stay in America instead of accompanying her husband.

Now, even for free Blacks, living in the slave south was perilous, with the constant threat of being kidnapped and sold into slavery, or having their status challenged. That's just what happened with Martin when he was a child, but his mother walked twenty miles to Winchester in order defend his status in court, and did so successfully. While in Charles Town, the family obtained a copy of one of the most popular teaching books of the day, The *New York Primer and Spelling Book*, from a traveling peddler, and Martin learned to read and write, which was illegal in Virginia at the time, even for free Blacks. And, remember, Martin's father was still enslaved, which probably made the infraction even worse in the eyes of the law. So, when the transgression was discovered, Patty moved with her children up the valley to Chambersburg, in the free state of Pennsylvania, in 1822. Eventually, Samuel was allowed to buy his own freedom and rejoined his family.

Martin was a voracious reader and learner. Since there were few higher education opportunities for Blacks even in "Free" Pennsylvania, he was largely self-educated. In his late teens, he traveled west to Pittsburgh by foot (more than 150 miles) and worked as, among other things, a barber. He continued his education at the Bethel Church School for Black People and Jefferson College, and the exceptionally bright young man eventually became apprenticed to a White abolitionist doctor. He became active in the local Vigilance Committee that acted not only in community protection but also similarly to the Underground Railroad, and traveled through the Midwest and South, a dangerous undertaking at the time, while still in his twenties. He married Catherine Richards, from a successful Pittsburgh merchant family, in 1843, and they eventually had eleven children. He founded the first African-American newspaper published west of the Alleghenies, *The Mystery*, and his abolitionist articles became read nationwide, coming to the attention of Frederick Douglass, who hired Martin to write for his paper in 1847. Just three years later, Martin, whose interests turned back to medicine, was one of the first four men to be admitted to Harvard, in the Medical School. Sadly, none of them were able to graduate, because White backlash was so strong that they could not remain at the school. The first Black graduate didn't come along until well after the Civil War. Edwin Howard (Medicine), George L. Ruffin (Law), and Robert T. Freeman (Dental) all graduated in 1869, and Richard Greener (1844 – 1922) from Philadelphia earned a BA in 1870. Greener went on to become the dean of Howard University School of Law.

Martin became a prolific writer and activist, and even traveled to Africa to explore the possibility of obtaining land for freed and fugitive slaves there. When the Civil War broke out, he became an avid recruiter for the Black regiments, himself rising to a Major in the 104th Regiment of the United States Colored Troops, the highest ranking African-American ever in the U. S. military up to that point. Relocating to South Carolina after the War, he was appointed as a judge. After Reconstruction, he saw the onset of Jim Crow, and moved to Ohio to again practice medicine, and still expressed sentiments for the possibility of relocating African-Americans to Africa.

He became associated with Wilberforce University in Ohio, but developed tuberculosis and died in 1885. Not long after his death, a fire at the University destroyed many of his papers.

Ann Kathryn Flagg (1924 – 1970), educator, actress, and playwright *It was a "Great Gettin' Up Morning'" for American theater thank to this Charlestonian.*

If you have never heard the great Mahalia Jackson sing the spiritual *Great Gettin' Up Morning*, please seek it out. The song, and even her entire album by that name, is available on streaming services. But, a play taking its name from the song is just as moving, and was even made into a movie debuting on CBS back in 1964. It stars the great groundbreaker Nichelle Nichols (of *Star Trek* fame), and Don Marshall (Dan Erickson in *Land of the Giants*…remember that one?), as well as Paulene Myers (*The Sting, My Cousin Vinny*). The subject was quite topical for the time: An African-American family faces conflicting views of the past and concern about the future as it prepares to send two young children off to the first day of a newly-integrated school in the South.

Ann Kathryn Flagg, the playwright who produced both the original stage and teleplay versions, knew something about segregated schools, because that's what she attended growing up in Charleston, West Virginia.

Ann was the daughter of Francis and Frances Hawkins Flagg, who were married in Kanawha County by C. W. Thompson in 1924, illustrating the sometimes overlooked difference in spelling between the male and female version of the first name. Francis was the son of Henry and Adeline Sweeney (note: her death certificate incorrectly says "Snelling") Flagg. Henry was born in Charleston, and Adeline in Talcott. Adeline died in 1917, and lists her parents as W. R. "Snelling" and Annie Huffman "Snelling." William R. Sweeney and Anna/Annie Huffman had married in Hinton in 1880, he 20 and the son of Lewis and Ann Sweeney, and she 16, the daughter of Adaline Huffman.

In 1930, Ann and her mother were living with Ann's parents, Patterson and Lydia Hawkins, on Sentz Street in Charleston. Patterson was a drug store manager and Lydia a homemaker. Frances was working as a hotel maid. Ann's father Francis is found living with his father Henry and stepmother Ora on Truslow Avenue, and working as a janitor.

After finishing at Charleston's segregated Garnet High School, Ann attended West Virginia State in Institute, and was among eight students from the school listed in the 1944-45 edition *of Who's Who in American Colleges and Universities,* along with Frederick Duncan from Florida, Edna Farmer from Beckley, Lloyd Hurst from Virginia, Frederick Jefferson from Bramwell, Thomas Jenkins from Massachusetts, Beatrice King from Virginia, and John Calvin Parker, also a Virginian. Ann served as president of the West Virginia State Players, and graduated Magna cum Laude.

Always interested in theater, Ann taught drama in Northampton County, Virginia after graduating, and toured with the American Negro Repertory Players. She returned to the Mountain State to teach at the Dunbar School in Fairmont (which still stands at 103 High Street), which served grades 1-12 as the only school for Black students in Fairmont, and the only high school for Black students in all of Marion County. After desegregation, it was used as an annex to Fairmont

Junior High School and then as an elementary school, but has been closed since 2007. As with several closed schools dear to the hearts of former students, there is an effort to turn the still-sound building into a museum and community center, and we hope the Dunbar School Foundation continues to find success in that endeavor.

In 1952, Ann was appointed Director of the Children's Theater at Karamu House in Cleveland, Ohio. She moved to Chicago in 1961 to pursue a Master's degree at Northwestern University, and it was there she wrote *Great Getting' Up Mornin,'* for which she won a first place prize in the National Collegiate Playwriting Contest. During much of this time, she also taught drama in the Evanston IL public schools, and then at the Foster School, later renamed the Martin Luther King, Jr. Laboratory School. In 1966, she began to teach playwriting at Southern Illinois University in Carbondale, but only for a year before returning to Evanston.

Ann suffered from emphysema, and died from the disease at the young age of 46. She left her papers to Northwestern University, where they remain archived today. She is memorialized by the American Alliance for Theater and Education by the annual presentation of the Ann Flagg Multicultural Award "to an individual, organization, or theatre company making significant contributions to the field of theatre or drama for youth or arts education dealing with multicultural issues and/or reaching diverse audiences and constituencies."

A fitting legacy for a little girl from Charleston who loved words, don't you think?

Henry Louis "Skip" Gates, Jr. (1950 -   ), historian, author, and film maker *He helps us with that obligatory Mountaineer question, "Who are your people?"*

His father worked in a paper mill and as a janitor, and his mother cleaned houses. He was injured playing football when he was 14 years old, and walks with a cane. This Harvard professor, personal friend of

President Obama, Yale and Cambridge graduate, and prolific filmmaker, was no silver-spoon recipient.

One would think that, of all people, Henry's genealogy would be an open book. It's not often possible with African-Americans, though. He is the son of Henry Louis Sr. (1913 – 2010) and Pauline Augusta Coleman Gates. Both the Gates and Coleman families had been in the Cumberland Maryland-Keyser (West) Virginia area since before the Civil War. He is descended from John Redman, a "free Black" who fought in the American Revolution.

In addition to having written more than twenty books, Dr. Gates has hosted numerous documentaries for PBS, as well as the ongoing series *Finding Your Roots*. He works with famous people from many different backgrounds to help them discover their own family histories, using both traditional and DNA methods. His most recent documentaries, *Reconstruction: America After the Civil War* and *The Black Church* are as good as it gets for those who love American history.

In addition to adding so much to the academic study of American history, he has popularized genealogy for laymen in a way not done before. Many of his guests discover skeletons in their closets, and what they had always been told, what was "known" in the family about "who begat who," isn't always true. I have found that to be the case with my own family history (no, I am not really of German descent, despite the surname), and many of you probably have as well.

It's flattering that the two most successful history documentary producers in America today, Gates and Ken Burns, both have West Virginia roots. Burns was actually a guest on *Finding Your Roots*, and, despite having been born in New York, found he had slave-holder ancestry, traced back from his grandparent's family, and his grandparents were from West Virginia. For that story, stream the *Finding Your Roots* episode featuring Burns, and I cordially invite you to read about it in my last book, *O, Mountaineers! Noted (or Notorious) West Virginians Born-Lived-Died,* Volume I of this series.

I love both historians' work, but, from what I have seen and read Gates would definitely be my preference with which to have beer and nachos and conversation. In fact, having a beer was the way some non-history-loving people may have first heard of him. On July 16, 2009, he returned home from a trip to China. When he tried to open the front door of his historic Cambridge, MA home, it was stuck, and he tried to force it open.

A Black man seen trying to jimmy open the door of a historic home in an affluent Cambridge neighborhood? It's not hard to guess what happened. When Cambridge Police Sergeant James Crowley showed up, Skip had gotten the door open, was on his cell phone with a maintenance company about having it fixed, and had stepped inside. Sergeant Crowley came onto the porch and ordered Dr. Gates out of it.

Dude, this is my house. I've been away, and the door was stuck. I'm a Harvard professor. Can you prove it? Sure can. Here's my identification and driver's license. (I am, of course, paraphrasing the conversation)

Crowley followed Dr. Gates into the house. Search warrant? Ask permission? Um, no. Dr. Gates did, indeed, question the officer's actions in terms we would not, perhaps, use in front of Grandma, but when he asked other officers who had shown up by then for Crowley's name and badge number, Crowley arrested the guy for disorderly conduct, on his own front porch. Gates was handcuffed, marched to a cruiser, booked and held for four hours.

The charges were, of course, later dropped. But Sergeant Crowley refused to apologize for his actions or admit any wrongdoing, and was supported by the Cambridge Police Superior Officers Association. In fact, officer Justin Barrett of the nearby Boston Police Department, emailed *The Boston Globe* referring to Dr. Henry Louis Gates Jr. as a "banana-eating jungle monkey" who he would have pepper-sprayed.

Barrett, at least, was fired. Crowley, on the other hand, never suffered any consequences of which I am aware. In fact, as can be guessed, he became an overnight hero to the *Fox News* crowd. I know that statement is a bit of a stereotype, and, if it offends you, I am...still convinced it's mostly true. So there.

President Obama and Skip Gates are long-time friends. The President felt he saw an opportunity to use the situation as a tool to help bring the country together. He invited both men to the White House to talk, over beers.

I would like to have beers with Skip Gates and Barack Obama someday, but under different circumstances.

Dr. Gates accepted, stating, "My entire academic career has been based on improving race relations, not exacerbating them. I am hopeful that my experience will lead to greater sensitivity to issues of racial profiling in the criminal justice system." Today, Dr. Gates says he has an amicable relationship with the officer who arrested him, proving he is a man with a more forgiving nature than yours truly. As expected, President Obama received vapid right-wing vitriol for his simple action of inviting the two to meet.

That was in 2009, before we knew the names George Floyd, Breonna Taylor, Eric Garner, Michael Brown, Tamir Rice, Walter Scott, Alton Sterling, Philando Castile, Stephon Clark, and so many others who lost their lives over the past dozen years. Invite me to have a beer with you, and I'll be there, but I am afraid we need much, much more.

We see Dr. Gates today as a middle-aged, distinguished and acclaimed Harvard professor, but think back to the 22-year-old "Skip" Gates, just out of college, son of a janitor and house cleaner from West Virginia. That year, 1973, he had just graduated from Yale, and found a temporary job as a summer correspondent for *Time* magazine. He was assigned to a segment in a series on Black expatriates, investigating why they had remained in self-imposed exile even after the civil rights gains of the 1960s.

His piece of it was to travel to Paris, France and interview James Baldwin and Josephine Baker. How's that for a 22-year-old-form-West-Virginia's first gig?

Novelist, essayist, poet, and activist James Baldwin (1924 – 1987), author of *The Fire Next Time* and *If Beale Street Could Talk*, had lived there for several years, and his house guests often included folks we've heard of, including Harry Belafonte, Sidney Poitier, Nina Simone, Miles Davis, Ray Charles…you know, just regular friends stopping by when they were in town. How would you like to have been at the table for those visits?

Baldwin is famous for another meeting, as well. On May 24, 1963, Attorney General Robert F. Kennedy invited Baldwin and others to his New York City apartment overlooking Central Park, in hopes of reaching some sort of agreement to help quell unrest associated with the civil rights movement, then reaching a climatic stage. Also at the meeting were James's brother David, Harry Belafonte, Edwin Berry of the Chicago Urban League, psychologist Kenneth Clark, NAACP official June Shagaloff, playwright Lorraine Hansberry (*A Raisin in the Sun*), singer Lena Horne, MLK advisor Clarence Jones, Freedom Rider Jerome Smith, and White actor Rip Torn.

The meeting didn't go well. "We were a little shocked at the extent of his naivete. We told him that though the Kennedy administration has done some things the Eisenhower Administration never did, its actions have yet to affect the masses of Negro people." Belafonte, in a telephone call with Dr. King that night, called the meeting "a disaster." Shortly thereafter, Baldwin, Torn, and Jones were placed under surveillance, and their telephones tapped by the FBI.

Josephine Baker (1906 – 1975) was a truly unique entertainer, and I do not overuse that word. Born in St. Louis, she was a chorus line dancer in New York City during the Harlem Renaissance. At age 19, she appeared in *"La Revue Negre"* in Paris. It changed her life. "One day I realized I was living in a country where I was afraid to be Black," she said. "I felt liberated in Paris. People didn't stare at me."

They didn't stare, but they definitely *watched*. Her act included partially nude erotic dancing, including one set wearing a costume made of a skirt of artificial bananas. She sometimes appeared with a live cheetah, and recorded many jazz records that were hits in Europe, but not so much in the United States. Ernest Hemingway, Pablo Picasso, and Jean Cocteau all befriended her. She was a superstar in the hedonistic Paris of the 1920s and early 1930s, and her singing became more musically sophisticated, as critics would say, later in her career.

But, the world changed. The invading Nazis were also enamored of her, and invited her to parties at embassies and ministries, charming everyone she met, drinking wine and making small talk.

And soaking up all the information she could about troops, locations, equipment, movements, personnel changes, etc., funneling it all to the French Resistance. After the war, she was awarded high honors by French President Charles de Gaulle for her heroism. In 1951, she was invited back to tour the United States, but insisted on desegregating the audience. When that became a problem for the patrician Stork Club in Manhattan, she canceled the rest of her engagements and was not allowed to re-enter the United States for a decade.

That was James Baldwin and Josephine Baker in Paris. Enter 22-year-old West Virginian Skip Gates. He first met Baker at her favorite restaurant in Monte Carlo, and then they traveled together to Baldwin's house in St. Paul de Vence, where they talked until dawn, through a considerable amount of food and wine.

I am sure the resulting feature article was fascinating, but, unfortunately, we can't read it. You see, after Skip Gates spent the night eating and drinking wine and talking with these two true African-American icons, *Time* decided not to run it, claiming that, even though they had originally commissioned it, the two subjects were really "passé'," a couple of relics no longer of real interest.

We can thank *Time* for that decision, as pathetic as it was from a literary and historical viewpoint. It caused native West Virginian Henry Louis Gates Jr., barely out of adolescence, to rethink his career. It was evidence, to him, that he could accomplish more as a critic than a reporter to help shape America's sense of Black culture, for which we are richer today.

Skip, if you're reading, I really like Guinness and French Broad Oatmeal Porter. Call me. Any time. And if Barack just happens to also be available...

Elizabeth Mason Brown Harden Gilmore (1909 – 1986), businesswoman, activist, and first African-American to serve on the West Virginia Board of Regents, and *Silas Harden (1889 – 1946), mortician.* Meet a mid-century Charleston "power couple."

While working in Charleston all those years, I often passed the stately Classical Revival brick mansion with the columned portico at 514 Leon Sullivan Way (once Broad Street). I didn't know its interesting history, or that it is listed on the National Register of Historic Places. The house, built before 1900, was the home and business of Elizabeth Harden Gilmore, and that business was a funeral home. Elizabeth was the first woman to be licensed as a mortician and funeral director in the state, as an Assistant Director in 1938, and full Director in 1940.

But, the house didn't begin as a funeral home. Instead, it stands as a testament to Dominic Minotti, an immigrant from Favaro, Italy, who came to the Land of Opportunity just out of his teens, shortly after the Civil War. He became a successful building contractor. Beautiful stonework in buildings and bridges constructed by Italian masons, including Minotti, more than a hundred years ago still stand all over West Virginia. He built many of the piers for the bridges connecting Charleston with Kanawha City and South Charleston. He died in 1925, a member of the Knights of Columbus like yours truly.

When Minotti's wife died twelve years later, the mansion became a boarding house for a time, and was then offered for sale. Our subjects Elizabeth and her husband Silas had operated a funeral home on Alderson Street along with George Harvey. The business was first known as Harvey and Harden, and then, after Elizabeth's licensure, Harden and Harden. After her husband's death from cerebral thrombosis in December 1946 at age 57, Elizabeth bought the Minotti mansion and, from 1947 onward, it became her home and business for the rest of her life. The bottom floor served as the funeral home, the second floor the family living quarters, and the third floor an apartment for out-of-town guests.

Silas was the son of James and Caroline "Cali" Brown Harden. James was a laborer who was born in Ohio, and they lived in a rented house on Hansford Street. After his death, Elizabeth married Virgil Melvin Gilmore.

Just within the past year, I read that a burial fund in West Virginia had been found to have been a not-so-good investment, failing to pay what was promised after collecting premiums for years. Apparently, that's nothing new. In 1942, Silas successfully sued the American Eagle Burial Fund and won, being awarded $205 damages and $15 attorney fee. (I wonder how far $15 will get you with a lawyer today?) The fund, many of whose clients were coal miners who had premiums withheld directly from their paycheck, claimed the right to designate a funeral home (probably at a negotiated lower price), but that wasn't "in the contract," making it necessary for Silas to sue after a family chose Harden and Harden's services over the preferred provider, as we would say today. The case, by the way, was decided by Circuit Judge Clarence W. Meadows, who three years later became West Virginia's first governor to have been born in the 20th century, and also the first from my home County of Raleigh.

Elizabeth was a true funeral professional during a time when women were rare in the business. She made the newspaper several times as a voice on such matters. When funeral homes started becoming air conditioned (Harden and Harden was one of the first in town, by the way), she still provided the iconic "funeral fans" for families after most businesses stopped doing so. Are there still a couple of these, perhaps with the image of Jesus Praying in the Garden, tucked in a drawer somewhere in your house?

On November 29, 1959, the *Gazette-Mail* ran an article about the growing popularity of cremation, interviewing several local stakeholders, including Elizabeth. It reads, in part,

...Mrs. Gilmore was one of the most sympathetic persons interviewed on the subject of cremation. She said that "one of the most impressive services we've had involved a young woman whose ashes were shipped here from another state in a beautiful bronze urn. There was a memorial service with the urn before a background stand of red roses. Many people said it was the most beautiful service they ever saw. It was like a reacquaintance with an old friend, one who had been away and returned on a non-physical basis."

On the other hand, the representative of my denomination interviewed, Fr. Roy A. Lombard of Christ the King Catholic Church in Dunbar, was less welcoming. "The Church absolutely forbids cremation voluntarily except in cases of contagion or where the law requires it," he said.

For the record, the Church eventually came around. Today, it allows cremation, but still frowns upon ashes being scattered or kept in an urn on the mantle. Good thing, since I'm prepaid! But definitely not with the American Eagle Burial Fund. We see how that turned out.

If Elizabeth's professional service and business sense were the whole of it, she would still be exceptional and worthy of note here. But, even more than that, she is remembered today as a civil rights activist. She was an adamant opponent of segregation, and fought against it on all fronts, but particularly in public businesses, the Girl Scouts, housing, and in education. She formed a women's club that opened Charleston's first integrated daycare center even before *Brown v. Board of Education*, successfully fought to integrate the state Girl Scout camp, and cofounded the state's first chapter of the Congress of Racial Equality (CORE) in 1958. Yes, the same organization that, a few years later, sent the Freedom Riders into the south, and whose bus was firebombed in Anniston, Alabama.

One of Elizabeth's early targets was much closer to home. For many of us, it's inconceivable that there are grown Charlestonians who don't remember The Diamond Department Store, a Charleston landmark for most of the twentieth century, closing in 1983 and eventually being converted into state government offices. The Diamond had a lunch counter on the first floor, and a full cafeteria on the fifth floor, and a shopping/eating day at The Diamond, especially during the Christmas season with its elaborate window displays, was a quintessential Kanawha Valley experience for a couple of generations.

But, the eating part? White people only. That is, until Elizabeth and CORE came along. They organized a boycott of the store, which lasted for almost two years. Tired of losing the Black community's business, the store desegregated its facilities on May 3, 1960.

Just after that, Elizabeth was interviewed by Don Marsh for the *Sunday Gazette-Mail,* to talk about integration. It's a long article, but here are excerpts:

Sunday Gazette-Mail, May 22, 1960, by Don Marsh

Mrs. Elizabeth Gilmore remembers the first time she decided to actively demonstrate against segregation.

"It must have been 25 years ago," she said. "Lady Baden-Powell, whose husband started the Boy Scouts, was in Charleston and a program was arranged for her at old Garnet High School. My Girl Scouts were invited to take part. We found that they had been placed off state, hidden in a corner, and were supposed to sing spirituals. Now, I have nothing against spirituals. They're a part of American music, but the whole idea upset me so much, the hurt of those passed-over lilt girls, I decided to do something about it. I implied that unless new arrangements were made, I would take my little brown skinned girls and march out, right in the middle of the program. Well, something was done. They sat on the stage and they held up their heads.

I guess I've always been something of a protester. My daughter calls me 'Mrs. Anthony' and Carrie Nation. But my grandmother taught us not to be ashamed because we were negroes. She said to look people in the eye when we talked to them. She told us we were as good as anybody else, no better, but as good."

Two years ago, Mrs. Gilmore's protest against racial segregation resulted in her helping to organize a Charleston chapter of the Congress of Racial Equality, the first, and so far only, CORE chapter in West Virginia. CORE, a national organization, is pledged to direct nonviolent action against segregation. Such action has included sitting in restaurants and refusing to leave until receiving service (sit-ins), standing in restaurants, theater lines and the like (stand-ins), picketing, and boycotting.

Activity of the Charleston group, so far, has been limited to the lunch counters of variety stores. Eventually, each of the targets changed from a segregated to an integrated policy.

There are 14 active members of CORE here and about 400 associate ones. Active members pledge to take part in demonstrations when they are asked.

"I am convinced of the efficiency of direct action," Mrs. Gilmore said. "If our people had used it a generation or two ago, we wouldn't be witnessing things today that shock and sadden people of good will of all races. Many people feel as I do. That's why we're opposed to the idea that if we keep our places and wait patiently these things will come to us. We've been waiting for almost a hundred years and whatever we've got, we've had to fight for. It wasn't given us. That's why we believe in direct action. Segregation, making a person an inferior citizen, is a bad thing, an evil thing. I think the majority of white people would gladly see the end of it if it could be done in a way that would not involve them personally. I think the majority would welcome, if it were put to a popular vote, and ordinance that would say, 'we will have no more of this.' I think people would welcome a way of life where a man could walk with dignity and live his life to the extent of his potentialities, as a Christian, as a human, as a brother, in a free society."

Mrs. Gilmore, as many other observers, thinks that Charleston residents are tolerant toward minority groups. But, she adds, tolerance or sympathy is not enough; specific improvements are the tings needed.

Restaurants and hotels, she thinks, will end their policy of refusing service to Negroes in the near future not because they felt that it was the proper thing to do but because pressure was brought against them.

"There are other things to remember when you talk about how tolerant Charleston is," she said, "employment for one. We desperately need some semblance of fair employment. It is the most important thing of all. The greater portion of our ills can be laid to lack of employment opportunities. If we had good jobs, we could have better educations, decent homes, better medical care, all the things that money can buy to enhance a good life....

(M)rs. Gilmore thinks that critics of CORE, those who do not believe in protest action, do not understand what it is to be a Negro. "They can't realize the slights, the rebuffs, the humiliation," she said. "They don't see the tears in their children's eyes. They don't know the sadness, the frustration...

(M)rs. Gilmore, a graduate of West Virginia State College, is principal owner of Harden and Harden Funeral Home. "My people came over the Appalachians from Virginia before the Civil War because they wanted to find a better way and a better place to live," she said.

Elizabeth served on the Kanawha Valley Council of Human Relations, and was the first African-American appointed to the Board of Regents, overseeing higher education in the state. She served for almost a decade, and was President for one year. She was also, at one time, the only female member of the Charleston Area Chamber of Commerce.

Elizabeth's daughter, also named Elizabeth, became an aerodynamics programmer with General Electric. For the duration of Elizabeth's life, she referred to herself as "Negro," not Black. She cited family history: "I'm old-fashioned. My maternal grandmother was from England and my maternal grandfather was from Spain, so, I figure I'm as much anything as I am Black. My great-grandmother came over the mountains to the Kanawha Valley four generations ago looking for a better life. She had six children and only the supplies her master had given her."

While all that family history may be hard to verify today, Elizabeth's influence in Charleston is not, at all.

Harold Everett "Hal" Greer (1936 – 2018), athlete and Basketball Hall of Famer. *This Huntington native scored 21,586 career points in the NBA, and the street signs changed in front of Marshall's Old Main.*

One of my many deficits is that I am just not a big basketball fan. But, while I was a junior at Marshall University during a time when its football team, still not having recovered from the tragic plane crash, was generally dismal (thank goodness for Moorhead State's football program, giving us at least one victory), the main thoroughfare running alongside the school was renamed from 16th Street to Hal Greer Boulevard, and I learned some proud West Virginia basketball history.

We first encounter Hal in the 1940 census, living with his rather large family in a rented residence on Tenth Avenue in Huntington, with parents William (45) and Jessie (40, along with eight siblings, ages 2 to 20 years old. William and Jessie were both born in Kentucky, completed the eighth grade but not high school, and had an annual income of $1,200.00. Jessie was a "Janitress" in the office of the C&O

building, and died in 1950 of a pulmonary embolism after having a hysterectomy.

Hal attended Frederick Douglass High School in those segregated days. The school was founded in 1891 on the corner of 8th Avenue and 16th Street, which is now, fittingly, Hal Greer Boulevard. Carter G. Woodson was a graduate in 1896, and became principal only four years later. A new building, which I still think is Huntington's most attractive architecturally from that era, was built on 10th Avenue and Bruce Street in 1924-26 and is now a community center. The original school was renamed Barnett Elementary, and was demolished in 1994.

Legendary coach Cam Henderson (1890 – 1956) coached at Marshall 1935 – 1955, and was the supposed inventor of the fast break and the 2-3 zone defense. He recruited Hal to play for the Thundering Herd, even though there were no other Black athletes playing on the major college teams in the state. Hal was the first, and, since Marshall played against several schools even further south, had potential to become a conference issue. Like so many other sports pioneers, though (Jackie Robinson and Jesse Owens come to mind), Hal's performance and character overcame those challenges.

Led by Hal, Marshall won the Mid-American Conference in 1956, but lost to Morehead (there the Eagles are again) in the first round of the NCAA tournament. Hal was chosen by the old Syracuse Nationals in the second round of the 1958 NBA draft and played with them for five seasons before the team moved to Philadelphia and became the Philadelphia 76ers. He and a tallish young Philly native named Wilt Chamberlain led the team to the NBA championship in 1967. He played in ten NBA All-Star games and was the MVP of the 1968 contest. To this day, Hal's records for points scored, field goals, field goal attempts, games played, and minutes played stand for the 76ers.

After retiring from active play in 1973, Hal coached a couple a minor league and private academy teams in Pennsylvania. Marshall retired his jersey (number 16), as did the 76ers (number 15). When he was inducted into the Basketball Hall of Fame in 1982, he became the first Black West Virginia athlete to become a member of a major sport Hall of Fame.

The poor kid from a crowded rented house on 10th Avenue did good, during a time when it was even harder than it would have been today.

Minnie Buckingham Harper (1886 – 1978), legislator. *When she became a member of the House of Delegates, she also became America's very first Black woman legislator.*

There is always a "first," and West Virginia has had its share, many good but some not. This one is good. There were many Black state legislators during Reconstruction, but then came Jim Crow, and the number was cut drastically. All, of course, were men. Women did not even have the national vote until 1920, though a few states had suffrage before that. While Minnie Buckingham Harper came to the West Virginia House of Delegates through appointment rather than election, her place in history is significant and secure.

Because the 1890 census was lost to fire, we first encounter Minnie at age 15, living with her rather large family in the Scott Depot area of Putnam County. Her father, Elisha Buckingham, was a "tinner," according to the census.

A what? Today, we are more familiar with the term tinsmith. After the salt industry began to diminish and before the chemical plants began to line the banks of the Kanawha, steel production in the form of "tin cans" for food preservation was an up-and-coming industry. A typical worker stood in front of a formidable machine all day to feed sheets of steel through it, and, in those days, the cans were soldered with a tin amalgam, which early on contained lead, with sometimes disastrous results when it leached into the preserved food. For example, there is some evidence the 1845 Arctic expedition of Sir John Franklin ended in tragedy because of lead poisoning, or perhaps other factors; historians differ in their opinions on the matter. Some of the ill-fated expedition's members were exhumed from the ice almost 150 years later, and scientists found evidence of high lead levels. Oh, and of cannibalism, after the "tinned food" ran out. Now, that's cold.

The Buckinghams were a mixed-race family. Elisha, 59, was White, and his wife Lora Ann, 45, Black. The children, seven of them in the household at the time, are all listed as Black, instead of the term "Mulatto" found so frequently in previous census records. Minnie was the next-to-youngest, and there must have been a few older, because Her mother is listed as having ten living children. Lora Ann's maiden name was Brooks, and she died a widow in 1924.

At least, that's what it looks like in 1900. Two of Minnie's older siblings found in the household at the time have death records in Putnam County. Anna died in 1942, and Brady died in 1944. Both death certificates list their father's name as Fredrick, and their race as white. Perhaps Elisha was known by his middle name, and these children were of light complexion and chose to identify as Caucasian. Such is the daily plight of a genealogist studying census records.

In any event, Minnie married Ebenezer Howard Harper in Keystone, McDowell County on May 7, 1923. Ebenezer was a lawyer who had been born in Tazewell County, and there was a considerable age difference, his being 21 years her senior. Ebenezer was a graduate of Howard University, and a committeeman-at-large for the West Virginia Republican Party. He was elected to the House of Delegates in 1926, the first Black from McDowell to do so, but he died in the middle of his term. As is prescribed in such events, the county Executive Committee recommended a replacement to the governor, Howard Gore, and unanimously chose Minnie. During her tenure, she served on the Federal Relations, Railroads, and Labor committees.

Active politics evidently didn't appeal to Minnie as a career, though. She chose not to run for a term of her own, and eventually moved back to Putnam County. She lived a long life, dying in Winfield at the age of 91. From Minnie's appointment, it was more than two decades before another Black woman would take her place in the West Virginia legislature, when Elizabeth Drewry was elected from McDowell County in 1950.

Patrice Harris (1960 -   ) physician The precedent-setting President of the American Medical Association is a proud Mountaineer.

The American Medical Association is a big deal. It's the most powerful and prestigious physician's group in the country, and has always had great influence in public health policy. Not many psychiatrists have been elected its president. Not many women have been elected its president. Not many African-Americans have been elected its president, and none combined all those attributes. Add to all that being a West Virginian, and Dr. Patrice Harris, from Bluefield, rolls all those into one.

Growing up in our southern split city, she knew she wanted to be in a helping profession. Her choice of colleges was set when her father took her to a football game in the 1970s, to see Bluefield native Dwayne Woods, a two-time All-State running back, play for the Mountaineers.

After graduation from Bluefield High School (she was a majorette), she attended WVU for a BA in Psychology (Magna Cum Laude) and then a MA, before entering WVU Medical School in 1988, graduating in 1992. She was the only African-American in her class, and sixty family members were in the audience for the commencement.

Originally intending to become a pediatrician, she changed to psychiatry in her third year. She once told the *Atlanta Business Chronical* that she encountered a psychiatric patient during a rotation and was so intrigued by it that she changed academic gears.

The patient thought he was Axel Rose. "I became fascinated with how the human brain works, how this blob of tissue can make somebody believe that he is somebody else. I simply fell in love with psychiatry." She left Morgantown after gradation for a psychiatry residency at Emory, where she also became a senior policy fellow at Emory's law school, adding background in public policy and child advocacy. She became the Director of Health Services for Fulton County, Georgia, and a frequent contributor on public health policy on NBC, NPR, CNN, and other legitimate media outlets.

Her childhood medical role model? Dr. Marcus Welby. "He not only took care of their health needs, he took an interest beyond the examination room," she once told the *Bluefield Daily Telegraph*. "I wanted to be a physician since the eighth grade."

Dr. Harris is the daughter of Titus and the late Barbara Harris. Titus was a railroad worker, and Barbara was a math teacher at Central and Bluefield High School. Their story is a common and romantic one: young lady goes off to college and meets a local boy, or vice versa. Barbara was from Bristol, Virginia and came to Bluefield State to major in Education.

Dr. Harris is an Atlanta Falcons fan, but when it comes to college football, it's all WVU. She still serves on the WVU Foundation Board of Directors, and regularly attends meetings. Her father relocated to Atlanta as well, but they return to southern West Virginia to visit relatives, and have even been known to time their visits in order to attend the cross-town (and cross-state) rivalry Bluefield-Graham football game. She and her cousins purchased the family home in Bluefield and have renovated it as a family meeting place; she credits her father's large and supportive family as being a defining factor in her life. Titus is one of ten children, and Dr. Harris is an only child who received lots of attention and encouragement from the great big family group. Lots of encouragement is an important thing. Just ask Dr. Harris.

Broderick Stephen "Steve" Harvey (1957 –), entertainer. *This coal miner's son from Welch has become one of America's most recognizable and beloved personalities. His is a true American success story, coupling talent with passion and hard work.*

The Great Migration of African-Americans into the southern West Virginia coalfields brought together a rich mix of people seeking economic betterment and, often, safety from the dangerous Jim Crow south. There are numerous references to families that relocated from Alabama to McDowell County in this book. Today, McDowell has the second highest percentage of Black population in the state, at 8.3

percent, between No. 1 Gilmer County at 11 percent, and No. 3 Raleigh County at 8.1 percent. The rest of the top ten is rounded out by Berkeley, Kanawha, Jefferson, Mercer, Cabell, Fayette, and Summers, ranging from 7.8 to 4.5 percent. On the other hand, Calhoun, Clay, Lincoln, Roane, and Tyler, by the way, all share the bottom of the list at only 0.3 percent, and a whopping 21 counties have less than one percent Black population.

Our ubiquitous television personality was born in Welch to Jesse "Slick" Harvey (1914 – 2000) and Eloise Vera Canner/Connor Harvey (1914 – 1997). Jesse was a coal miner, born in Alabama to John and Clara Simons Harvey. Like so many others, he suffered from Black Lung Disease. The elder John's father was also named John, whose wife's maiden name was Haig. Steve's maternal grandparents were Fredrick William (1893 – 1972) and Hattie Prillaman (1892 – 1961) Connor/Canner. They are buried at Restlawn Memorial Gardens on New Hope Road in Princeton. Jesse and Eloise were married at Elbert on September 12, 1936. The 1940 census shows them living in Adkin (near Gary), in a rented house, with daughters Ramona, 2, and Pauline, 8 months. Brother Terry would later join the family before "surprise" baby Steve came on the scene, when his parents were 42 years old. Jesse and Eloise are buried in Cleveland, Ohio's Lakeview Cemetery.

When Steve was only four years old, the family became part of yet another great migration, this time from the coalfields to the northern industrial cities. With almost no money, they relocated to Cleveland, where Jesse began working construction. The family lived on East 112th Street, which is now officially named Steve Harvey Way. Steve graduated from local Glenville High School in 1974. He attended Kent State, where he majored in Advertising. His first two years there were, shall we say, not exactly an academic success. Steve once admitted, in an interview with *Premier Gospel,* "When I went to college, I backslid; I got all off track. I went to college, man, and lost my mind. It was…I couldn't believe it, man. I mean, I could stay out at night…there were girls…You know, I went to college and lost my mind. I lost my mind and at the same time, I found myself." He did pledge to Omega Psi Phi, and met a fellow student from Cleveland who was the son of a Baptist minister. His name is Arsenio Hall. How would you like to have hung out with those two as college kids?

After his less-than-successful Kent State experience, Steve decided to return to his native state and give college another try, at WVU, and the mountains (and, perhaps, some life lessons learned in Ohio) did the trick. But, even with a degree, he struggled to support himself. At various times, he worked as a carpet cleaner, insurance salesman, mechanic, and mailman. He even tried boxing. None of these turned into successful careers, though, and he admitted to himself that his passion was comedy. Steve first performed stand-up at the Hilarities Comedy Club in Cleveland, in October 1985. He pursued comedy gigs and a big break relentlessly, traveling to wherever he could find an audience while continuing to clean carpets.

When his gigs didn't provide a room, Steve slept in his Ford Tempo (remember those?) and bathed at truck stops or swimming pool showers. For three years, Steve Harvey, today one of America's brightest stars, was homeless.

How far a person will go to achieve his or her dream is a true test of character. Steve could have continued living in his car and chasing gigs until he finally gave up, but, instead, he persisted, and his passion and talent eventually prevailed. Johnnie Walker, the Scotch importer, annually sponsored what it called a National Comedy Search. In the contest's second year, Steve reached the finals.

At that time, the Johnnie Walker was a very big deal in the world of comedy, and Steve's career took off. By 1993, he was the host of *Showtime at the Apollo*, a syndicated variety show filmed at New York's legendary Apollo Theater. Here, his very special talent as a host was honed to an art. In 1994, the Welch native was offered the starring role in the ABC sitcom *Me and the Boy*, which he also helped write. The show aired on Tuesday nights, between *Full House* and *Home Improvement*. It rose to number 20 in the ratings, but, for some reason, ABC cancelled it after only one season. Steve went on to star in *The Steve Harvey Show* on the WB Network, from 1996 through 2002. The show portrayed Steve as a teacher at a westside Chicago high school, and teamed him with real-life friend Cedric Kyles, aka Cedric the Entertainer.

Steve's incredible energy and work ethic never ceased, because, while filming the show, he continued doing stand-up, touring with the Kings of Comedy, which also included Cedric, D. L. Hughley, and Bernie Mac. It became the highest-grossing comedy tour in history. *The Original Kings of Comedy*, later renamed *Steve Harvey's Big Time Challenge*, aired on the WB Network 2003 – 2005. Plus, during this time and continuing today, Steve hosts *The Steve Harvey Morning Show*, a nationally-syndicated radio broadcast.

How on earth does he do it all? Throw in motivational speaking, writing books, numerous specials, movie appearances…the man is incredible.

Then came *Family Feud,* which Steve began hosting in 2010. The show had its roots in the mid-1970s, with droll Englishman Richard Dawson as host. It went through several revivals with various hosts over the years, but, when Steve took the helm, the show's ratings soared. Then came a syndicated TV talk show, and his rise to become America's most prolific television emcee, including the Miss Universe pageant (okay, there was that, but he handled it with a sincere apology), New Year's Eve from Times Square, NFL Honors, and many more events. He has won multiple Emmys and other awards.

A couple of years ago, I spent 18 days in Los Angeles, working my side gig as a trainer for the federal court. On my weekend downtime, I took the obligatory tourist bus tour to Hollywood, got off at Hollywood and Vine, and walked to find my fellow West Virginian's (and fellow coal miner's son) star on the Walk of Fame. I was very proud to see it.

Steve has been married three times, and has four children and three stepchildren. He credits his wife Marjorie with making him a better man. Like any public figure, he has not been without controversy when it comes to political views, and occasionally an off-the-cuff remark meant as a joke falls flat. I am a member of that club myself. But, I cannot think of a Hollywood figure more relatable. Somehow, I believe I could sit down with Steve at the Sterling Drive-In on Stewart Street in Welch, have lunch, and not feel the least bit uncomfortable. And, apparently, millions of Americans and other fans worldwide feel the same, even if they couldn't find Welch on the map to save themselves from disaster.

I'll have the steak sandwich. It's excellent. I think Steve is Vegan, though, so something else for him.

Though he is perhaps the hardest working person in the entertainment business, Steve knows where to lay the credit. In words my mother might frown at, but I understand perfectly well, he once said, "If you think you can make it without God, your ass is trippin'."

Message received, Steve.

Hamilton Hatter (1856 – 1942), academic and educator. *Born into slavery, he helped build a higher education legacy that lives on today.*

With many of our subjects born in bondage, it's difficult to trace their family. Hamilton Hatter's is known. His parents, Frank and Rebecca McCord Hatter; his paternal grandparents James and Matilda Hatter, and his maternal grandparents William and Lettie McCord, were all slaves in the eastern panhandle area. As a youngster, he became a skilled carpenter and mechanic, and even received a patent later in life for a corn harvester.

After emancipation, Hamilton attended Storer College in Harpers Ferry, and then Nichols Latin School in Lewiston, Maine, graduating in 1883. He stayed on in Maine for the next five years, managing a sawmill and doing graduate work at Bates College, before returning to Storer to teach in 1888. In 1892, he became the first Black West Virginian to receive a nomination for the West Virginia House of Delegates (as a Republican; he did not win the seat). His reputation must have been impressive, because then-West Virginia Governor Virgil A. Lewis appointed him as Principal of the new Bluefield Colored Institute when it opened with forty students in 1896. He remained head of the school until his retirement in 1906, when his protégé and fellow Storer alum Robert Page Sims took the office.

During World War I, he was a supporter of Woodrow Wilson and was a frequent speaker defending the President's policies.

Hamilton died of heart disease at his home located at 204 Park Street in Bluefield, and is buried in Oak Grove Cemetery, Bluewell.

Antoine Hickman, (1959 –   ), convicted killer. *One of the Mountain State's most notorious murderers was once described as "a nice young man" by his school principal. Also:* **Ronando Holland (1959 – 2005), college professor.** *A brilliant mind and gifted educator, taken too soon. A tale of three very different 1977 Marshall freshmen and what connected them.*

Unless it's restful sleep or you are a caring healthcare professional working night shift (like my wife), it's seldom that anything good happens between 2:00 and 3:00 AM. That was the case in Charleston on Friday, June 26, 1981. Antoine Hickman, 22 at the time, had an argument with a woman at a bar, which turned into a disturbance with other patrons outside on the sidewalk. A witness watched Hickman get into a yellow Cadillac being driven by Allen Mackie, 21, of Charleston. The car was spotted separately by two Charleston police officers, 33-year Charleston PD veteran Lieutenant Delbert. J. Roush, 61, and Patrolman Eddie R. Duncan, 32.

On the policemen's order, Mackie got out of the car, but Hickman refused to do so, and the officers ordered him out a second time. As Hickman did, he opened fire on the officers with a snub nosed .38 Special revolver. Roush was shot once in the chest. Duncan, who had only been on the force three years, was hit under the arm and in the back, with one bullet passing through his heart.

Hickman and Mackie fled. The officers died. They were the first Charleston officers to die in the line of duty in more than thirty years.

As the day dawned, a manhunt began. That evening, Hickman's mother, Ernestine Irving, and his brother Juan made a short appeal on the local evening news for Antoine to turn himself in. Shortly after it aired, the PD received a call that Hickman was ready to do so, and officers were dispatched to an address just a few blocks from the scene of the crime.

Now, if you will indulge me, we will turn the clock back four years, to the summer of 1977. The new crop of freshmen was on Marshall University's campus for orientation. Fresh young faces, excited and confused, were everywhere. In those days before the legal drinking age was raised to 21, signs for free "Smokers" and "Rush parties" were on every lamppost, with Greek and other organizations hoping to attract pledges. The local bars, plentiful by any standard, were standing room only. (Including, for any MU alumni of the era who wish to wax nostalgic, Boney's Confectionary, aka "The Hole.")

I was amongst that gaggle. For a barely 18-year-old kid who had hardly been out of southern West Virginia, lived on a farm at the end of three miles of dirt road, and whose parents had not graduated from high school, that was an exciting time. Huntington could have been New York City for me that day.

For orientation, rooms and roommates for the two nights were randomly assigned. Mine was in Buskirk Hall, one of the older dorms housing women during regular term. When I arrived with my cardboard suitcase and white canvas Nike tennis shoes (because I could not afford the white leather ones popular at the time), my roommate had already checked in, because there were clothes and toiletries in the closet and on the bottom bunk bed. "I'll meet my roommate later. Maybe we'll become friends," I thought.

I did, indeed, meet my orientation roommate later that afternoon, during a break after standing in line after line for classes, and advisor approval to take more than the prescribed number of hours my first semester (that strategy, as well as testing out of many classes via the CLEP program, must have worked, since I was only 20 when I graduated with my BA). Returning to the room, I turned the key and walked in to find him with a young woman, on the bunk bed mattress pulled into the floor. They were both naked.

Had I thought to knock first? Probably not. I was just dropping off my papers, to head back out, and didn't expect for anyone to be in the room. I quickly apologized and left, hesitant to return and meet my roomie (hopefully under different circumstances) later that evening. It was sure to be..ah..awkward.

He was nowhere to be seen when I returned, but, just after I had settled in at the small desk to look over my big stack of papers, he walked in with a towel around himself from the bathroom down the hall.

"Hey."

"Um…hey. I'm Danny. From near Beckley. Shady Spring High School."

Big smile, hand not holding the towel extended: "I'm Antoine. Tony. From Northfork."

I am sure that, by now, you saw that coming. Except for passing one another a time or two, that pretty much was the extent of our roommate experience, as I had the room to myself at night for the rest of orientation. I am sure he found other accommodations more, er, *accommodating.* Antoine and I did not become friends, but we were cordial when seeing one another around campus, at least stopping to say hello. While I graduated almost two years early, things did not go as smoothly for him. I once saw him with a bandage around his head, allegedly from a confrontation with a campus security officer. I stayed on for an extra semester of graduate work before leaving Marshall (eventually finishing my graduate degree at what we commonly called "that other school in Morgantown," after a sojourn in the U. S. Virgin Islands), but didn't see him again. In fact, I supposed I forgot about him, until reading that newspaper headline.

At Northfork, the fairly diminutive Antoine (5' 8") had been a wrestler and football player at a school no longer existent today but still legendary for its basketball program. In 1975, then-Woodrow Wilson High School (Beckley) wrestling coach "Chick" Munson, when talking about the Region VIII wrestling tournament, was quoted in the *Raleigh Register* as saying, "Some of the teams that don't have too much of a chance at the team title still have some very good wrestlers. You won't find many better than Stanley Golden of Greenbrier West, Antoine

Hickman of Northfork, and Andre Hairston of Sophia." When contacted by the press just after Antoine's arrest, former Northfork principal, James Lane, said, "He was an above-average student and a nice young man, always quick with a smile, never a problem at school." But, evidently there were problems at home. By the time I met Antoine he already had a gunshot wound scar, after having been shot by his brother David during an argument.

Antoine's case was in and out of the news for several years, due to some interesting legal issues. He was convicted of first degree murder, two counts, and sentenced to two consecutive terms of life without mercy. Hickman appealed, stating his confessions were inadmissible because he was not informed of the fact that one of the lawyers present had been retained by his parents, and that he was too intoxicated at the time of his confession to voluntarily waive his rights under *Miranda v. Arizona.* He lost the appeal.

I, on the other hand, had a twenty year career with the federal court. Two boys from the coalfields, randomly thrown together, had two very different outcomes. From age 22 to his natural death, whenever that may be, Antoine will be in prison, as he has been for forty years already.

Was there any way I could have befriended him and somehow things would have changed? Probably not. But, even now, I will credit Antoine Hickman with teaching me a life lesson that has stuck with me to this day:

Always knock, even if you think the room is unoccupied.

Remembering that non-airconditioned summer of '77 orientation brings back the memory of yet another kid from the coalfields standing in those lines for classes, the only other person I recognized who was not from my own high school. I had met Ronando Holland, from Bluefield, at the State Student Council conventions at Jacksons Mill, where he had been elected state president. At Marshall, we became friends and, eventually, roommates. We were both Political Science majors (I had a second in Biology), and active in campus political organizations, he as a conservative Republican and me as a liberal

Democrat. Our political discussions would often last until my bedtime, then as now about 9:30 PM.

We were definitely wild and crazy guys.

Ronando was brilliant, and received the prestigious Truman Scholarship. He eventually went on to earn his Ph.D. at Duke. We stayed in touch as we could, but did not see one another again until he returned to Bluefield, being hired as Bluefield State's first Director of Multicultural Affairs after a stint as a Poli Sci professor at Bowling Green. One of his tasks was to try to recruit more Black students and faculty to the HBC. He authored *The Use of Black Leaders to Mobilize Population for Politics,* still used as a field guide today. (By the way, he eventually came around to something closer to my political affiliation.)

Sadly, Ronando is no longer with us. With a family history of heart disease, he died in August, 2005. He was one of the most intelligent people I have ever known, and he was a great positive influence on me.

Ronando was the son of William H. and Floristine Hopkins Woodward Holland, who married in Bluefield during 1956. Floristine was the daughter of Addison and Minnie Emma Brown Hopkins, and the granddaughter of Zackfield and Linnie Hughes Hopkins, from Franklin, County Virginia, both born well before Emancipation.

Ronando's grandfather Addison was a railroader (as well as active in Freemasonry, the First Baptist Church, and the "Colored Republican Club") in Bluefield, and involved in an unfortunate accident that took the life of J. M. Martin, a former mailman, in January 1933. J. M. was walking on the road near his Glenwood Park home, when a car driven by butcher T. B. Lewey struck and killed him, after the car was hit by one driven by Addison. Both drivers were charged with Manslaughter. Addison was initially convicted, but was later exonerated when the case was nollied and the verdict set aside. Addison died of heart disease in 1965, and Minnie of a heart attack in 1970.

Antoine and Ronando were very different people, who did not know one another until, by chance, I introduced them; they became casual acquaintances, but that's about it. That was a big crowd of eager teenagers back in 1977. Each already had a story, and all do today, some continuing to be written and some, like Ronando's, unfortunately already a closed book. The lessons? Make the best of every day, because you know neither how long you have, nor what kind of influence you can wield.

And, again, knock before entering.

Thomas Dexter "T. D." Jakes, Sr., (1957 -   ), pastor, author, Emmy winner, and evangelist. From his first "storefront" church in Smithers, he has built a worldwide evangelical ministry.

One of the most rewarding things about doing research for a book is being able to learn about people, places, and happenings to which I have previously had no exposure. As confessed elsewhere in this book, I am not that big of a sports fan, and I certainly had little knowledge about television evangelists. Being Catholic, watching a sleepy single-camera mass online during the COVID pandemic is about as far as it went. So, I looked up film clips of native Mountaineer T. D. Jakes in action, and the difference is substantial.

T. D. was born in South Charleston to Ernest Lamar and Odith Thelma Patton Jakes, whose address is found listed as 600 Page Street. He is the youngest of their three children. Ernest died of kidney failure in 1973, when T. D. was just a teenager.

The Jakes, like many other families, were descended from enslaved Americans and migrated from the deep south to the Mountain State in search of a better life. T. D.'s DNA, analyzed for the PBS program *African Lives*, indicates he is descended from the Igbo people of what is now Nigeria. Ernest Lamar Jakes was born in Hattiesburg, Mississippi to Thomas and Lorena Smiley Jakes (often written as "Jake" in the older records). Thomas was the son of Lemon Jakes, who had been born in Georgia, and married Louisa Stenny there in 1887. Odith Patton Jakes (1926 – 1999) was born in Alabama, the daughter of Richard and Susie Williams Patton. Ernest was an entrepreneur, owning a janitorial service that employed more than fifty people. Odith, as well, had the spirit, selling Avon products in addition to teaching school.

As a boy, T. D. stayed busy, selling vegetables from the family garden, delivering newspapers, and cutting grass. He showed a prodigious interest in the Bible, and was sometimes called "the Bible Boy," but was discouraged from believing he could someday be a preacher because of a slight speech impediment. Between his father's death and that discouragement, he dropped out of high school, later competing a GED. He enrolled at West Virginia State while working full time, but was unable to keep up his studies and only attended one year.

Overcoming those obstacles, he preached his first sermon in 1976 and was officially ordained in 1979. The following year, he formed his first church, in a vacant store in Montgomery and then in Smithers, with only ten members. He worked at his "day job" at Union Carbide in order to keep his church, and himself, afloat financially. His congregation began to grow, allowing him to move it first to South Charleston, and, in 1993, to Cross Lanes. While he had grown up attending the First Baptist Church in Charleston, he became attracted to Pentecostalism after being invited to sing one night at Greater Emanuel Gospel Tabernacle.

T. D. truly found his niche when he began television ministry. He, along with some other members of his Cross Lanes congregation, relocated to Dallas, Texas, where he bought property from a man who had to sell due to being convicted of tax evasion. His Potter's House Church took off, and now boasts more than 30,000 members, with a veritable multi-media empire of television, music production (under its own label, Dexterity Sounds) and even a movie production company. He has published more than twenty-five books.

T. D. met his wife, the former Serita Ann Jamison, while he was guest preaching at her church. They were married in 1981, and have five children.

James Jett (1970 -   ), football and track star. The term "all-around athlete" barely does this record holder justice.

At only 5'10" and 176 pounds, "Professional football player" isn't the first vocation that comes to mind. But for wide receiver James Jett, those were perfect numbers.

At Jefferson High School, James held five individual track titles and four state records. During his three years at WVU (1990 – 1992), he was one of the most dependable performers in the school's track team's history, earning seven All-America honors. He was the football team's starting receiver, the only freshman to play on the squad's 1989 Gator Bowl lineup, and was elected to the WVU Sports Hall of Fame in 2002.

In 1992, James qualified for the United States Olympic Track Team, running the first two rounds of the 4 x 100 relay in the Barcelona, with Team USA bringing home the Gold Medal.

The Los Angeles Raiders signed James following the 1993 NFL Draft, and, in his first season, he led the league with more than 23 yards gained per reception.   He ended his professional football career in 2002, with a career 256 receptions for 4,417 yards gained, and 30 touchdowns. While the Raiders have jumped around a bit (Oakland? Las Vegas?), he finished his career as the 8th-leading receiver in their history.

In a recent interview with Katherine Cobb, James admitted the transition from West Virginia to Los Angeles as a professional athlete was, in his words, a "culture shock." "It was crazy. There was always something going on and I don't know how I did it, but I stayed out of trouble. It probably helped me to be from a place like this (West Virginia). It's like a wide-open freeway and you just get on it. Going from college where I was broke and it was rough to getting big checks and the phone ringing off the hook was like zero to 60."

James Sherman Jett was born in Charles Town, the son of Louis Albert and Vivian Curry Jett. The family has known a great deal of loss. James's mother Vivian died at age 46, in April 1999. She had been born in Jefferson County, a daughter of James and Thelma Elizabeth Campbell Cook Curry. Vivian, known as "Bunny" to her friends, worked for the school system across the state line in Berryville, Virginia, and was a member of the U. S. Army Reserves. By that time, she and Louis had been divorced for about fifteen years. James's only full sibling, Louis Albert Jr., born in 1969, died in 2020 at the age of only 51. And, in perhaps the most difficult thing anyone can face, James and wife Amy Rose lost a daughter, Vivian Marie, at only 9 months of age, in 2009. Today, James and Amy have teen twins James Jr. and Jordan, as well as daughter Ava.

John Clyde "Johnnie" Johnson (1924 – 2005), pianist and U. S. Marine. *He's in the Rock and Roll Hall of Fame, yes, but also a Congressional Gold Medal recipient for his service to America. He was the original Mr. J. B. Goode.*

So many Black pioneers in their chosen professions are even more remarkable because of the double obstacle course of racial discrimination they faced while pursuing their dream, and Johnnie Johnson is no exception. Around 1930, his parents bought a used piano, quite an extravagance in a coal miner's home in depression-era Fairmont. In an interview with Ken Burke of the Rockabilly Hall of Fame, Johnnie said it was a "great big toy" to him, and he started banging on keys without lessons. But, natural talent soon surfaced, and he taught himself to play "by ear" along with records "I could hear what they were playing and I could get on the piano and follow them. That's the way I developed my playing until I got up where I actually knew some of what I was doing." He joined a local jazz band at 13.

Music wasn't initially making a living for him, though, and, like so many Mountaineers of that pre-WWII defense plant boom era, he moved to Detroit to build tanks in Ford's Dearborn plant, while still playing local gigs. When the pre-war turned into the hot war, he became a United States Marine, in 1943, when there were relatively few Black Marines, and, even during that existential conflict, suffered considerable discrimination due to his race. He served in the south Pacific, and was part of a Marine band called The Barracudas. After the War, he returned to Detroit determined to pursue a full-time music career, which eventually led him to St. Louis.

On New Year's Eve 1953, Johnnie's group Sir John's Trio was short a guitarist, because their regular musician became ill. At the last minute Johnnie was able to pick one up, as a single-night replacement.

That young replacement guitarist's name was Chuck Berry, and the single night stretched into thirty years. Berry was good at promotion, and eventually became the de facto leader of the group. The first song they recorded together was *Maybellene*.

It did, as you know, pretty darned well. Johnnie and Chuck were off and running on a legendary career together. *Roll Over, Beethoven, Rock and Roll Music,* and *Sweet Little Sixteen* all soon followed.

But, the biggest hit of all, the one that changed the face of Rock and Roll forever, was the one Chuck wrote as an admonition to and in admiration of his bandmate: Johnny B. Goode.

There have been many famous songwriting credit disputes over the years, and the Berry/Johnson collaboration is an example. Berry wrote lyrics, and he and Johnnie would sit down together and "work out" the music. But, Johnnie never received co-writing credit. To folks with a highly musically-trained ear, the songs are plainly written more from a pianist's point of view, rather than a guitarist's. Folks like Rolling Stone Keith Richards, for example, who said of Johnson, "Johnnie had amazing simpatico. He had a way of slipping into a song, an innate feel for complementing the guitar. He ain't copying Chuck's riffs on piano. Chuck adapted them to guitar and put those great lyrics behind them. Without someone to give him those riffs, no song…just a lot of words on paper."

Keef isn't Johnnie's only huge fan amongst Rock and Roll royalty. In 1990, Eric Clapton invited him to perform at a huge concert at London's Royal Albert Hall. The performance came close to ending in tragedy, but was a turning point in the Fairmont native's life. Like so many others in the industry, Johnnie had long been plagued by a drinking problem, to the point that it was a factor in his disassociation with Chuck Berry. In Berry's autobiography, he wrote that he had forbade drinking in the car while the band was on the road, so Johnnie complied with the rule by putting his head out the window while taking a swig or two or ten.

During that London performance, Johnnie developed a severe nosebleed, obvious to the crowd, but he continued to play and finished the gig before being rushed to a hospital. "The piano keys looked crimson, they were so red," he later said. He nearly died that night and remained hospitalized for an extended time, but the experience moved him to finally get help for his drinking, and he eventually gave it up.

That gig was part of Johnnie's "comeback," of sorts. He split company with Chuck Berry in the 1970s, and the alcoholism caused him to fade from the music scene. He was living back in St. Louis and working for a senior citizens' center when Keith Richards hunted him down for a 1986 documentary he co-produced. After the demon was back in the bottle, Johnnie's career again took off, and he played for both of President Clinton's inaugurations, and received a Congressional Citation from the Congressional Black Caucus. In 2001, he was inducted into the Rock and Roll Hall of Fame. The year before, he sued Chuck Berry to obtain credits and royalties on the songs he helped create, but the case was dismissed because too much time had passed since the songs had been written.

Johnnie played his final performance at the NCAAA Final Four activities in St. Louis on April 3, 2005, and died two weeks later, leaving his wife Frances, ten children, and many grandchildren.

His obituary from London's *The Guardian*, April 14, 2005:

Pioneering rock'n'roll pianist Johnnie Johnson, who has died at his home in St Louis aged 80, may never have been a household name, yet millions have enjoyed his music since he first stepped into a recording studio, on May 21 1955.

The occasion was Chuck Berry's recording of his first single, Maybellene. Not only was Johnson Berry's pianist, but he was also the man who discovered and, initially, employed the young guitarist.

Born in Fairmont, West Virginia, Johnson learned to play the piano at the age of seven. Never taking formal lessons, he was influenced by the jazz and boogie-woogie musicians he heard playing in bars among Fairmont's black community.

Service in the second world war with the Marine Corps in the Pacific gave him the opportunity to perform with musicians from the Count Basie and Lionel Hampton bands. Johnson settled in Chicago, Illinois, in 1946 and began playing piano professionally.

Chicago was home to a burgeoning blues scene, and Johnson played both blues and jazz in the city's clubs. However, never feeling entirely comfortable in Chicago, he shifted to St Louis in the early 1950s. There he led his own R&B band, the Sir John Trio.

When a band member became ill on New Year's Eve 1952, Johnson hired Berry to fill in. Berry quickly took over as the band's leader, his highly original songwriting and ability to blend every popular form of music, from country to Nat "King" Cole, into his own sound making the band the most popular live outfit - alongside Ike Turner's Rhythm Kings - in St Louis. Always ambitious, Berry travelled to Chicago and approached blues star Muddy Waters for advice.

Waters provided Berry with an introduction to Chess Records, and the recording of Maybellene by Berry, Johnson and rhythm section followed. The song was an immediate hit, and is now seen as one of the pivotal moments in the birth of rock'n'roll. The hits continued to flow from Berry's pen for the rest of the decade, with Johnson playing piano on most.

Johnson's pumping, two-fisted style of piano, pushing forth a dancing rhythm while capable of delivering inventive, melodic solos, became the touchstone of rock'n'roll pianists everywhere. Indeed, Berry celebrated Johnson on his most famous composition, Johnny B Goode.

Johnson left Berry's band in the 1960s, and worked with blues guitarist Albert King. Johnson led his own band in the 1970s, still pairing up with Berry on occasion and gaining a wide public profile when he appeared in Curtis Hanson's inspired 1986 documentary film about Berry, Hail! Hail! Rock And Roll. The film's band leader was Rolling Stone Keith Richards, who then hired Johnson to play on his solo album Talk Is Cheap.

Johnson, now commanding a wider audience, issued several solo albums and found his piano skills in demand with Eric Clapton, Aerosmith and other rock stars. Johnson married his wife, Frances, in 1989, and credited her with helping him overcome alcoholism.

In 2000, Johnson sued Berry, seeking a share of royalties and credit for what Johnson said were more than 50 songs the men composed together. A federal judge dismissed the suit in 2002, ruling that too many years had passed. The lawsuit contended that Berry took advantage of Johnson's alcoholism, misleading him into believing that only Berry was entitled to own the copyrights "and reap the monetary benefits".

While the men did not speak during the lawsuit, they later became reconciled, performing together at St Louis's Blueberry Hill nightclub as recently as a year ago.

In 2001 Johnson was inducted into The Rock And Roll Hall Of Fame in the "sideman" category by Richards.

Johnson is survived by Frances and ten children.

Katherine Johnson (1918 - 2020), mathematician. *One of our greatest Mountaineers received recognition late, but not too late. She and other graduates of West Virginia State benefited from an unusual pre-Civil War relationship.*

Until the movie *Hidden Figures* (2016), I had never heard of Catherine Johnson, which is a shame. We need to do much better. It makes me wonder how many other living West Virginians are true national heroes, but not known outside their own circle. Thank goodness it came in time for this noble lady to see it.

Katherine Coleman Goble Johnson was born in White Sulphur Springs just before World War I came to an end. Her parents were Joshua and Joylette Coleman. Joshua M. Coleman was born in West Virginia in 1882, is listed in the language of the 1920 census as "Mulatto," and owned his home without mortgage. He also worked as a lumberman, and, for a time, at the Greenbrier. Joylette R. Coleman was born in 1887 in North Carolina and is also listed as "Mulatto" in 1920. She was a teacher. In 1900, Joshua is listed as "Colored," living with his father

Horace and stepmother Annie Norris Coleman. Horace was born in Albemarle County, Virginia, and Annie (daughter of David Norris of Tennessee and Sallie Fleming of Virginia) in Botetourt.

There are so many things that are hard to believe from today's perspective, even things that happened within the lifetime of people still with us. When Catherine was young, Greenbrier County did not offer public education to African-American students beyond the eighth grade. Catherine showed such skill in math (something she and I do not share, by the way) that her parents made the decision to send her, at only thirteen years of age, to attend high school in Institute, which had one for Black students on the campus of what later became West Virginia State College.

Now known as West Virginia State University (WVSU), the school is one of two Mountain State colleges with "Historically Black Colleges and Universities (HBCU)" status. The other is Bluefield State. The land upon which it stands has an interesting history itself. The site was, at one time, a thriving Native American settlement. The entire area was deeded by King George III to a young American soldier for his service in what we now call the French and Indian War. That was common practice: kick the natives off the land (or not) and give it to soldiers instead of money.

That young soldier was named George Washington, and he eventually sold it. The land became part of a large plantation, worked by slaves. The roots of African-American education at the site extend prior to the end of the Civil War, to the time it was bought by slaveowner Samuel I. Cabell (1802 – 1865). Some sources state, incorrectly, I believe, that he was the son of William H. Cabell (1772 – 1853), the fourteenth governor of Virginia, after whom Cabell County is named, but that's a different story. Samuel did something very controversial at that time. He married (a perpetually "common law" marriage, evidently, because his wife filed to change her name after Samuel's death) one of his slaves, Mary Barnes. She bore him thirteen children. He granted all the children their freedom from slavery, and sent some of them to a private school in Ohio. He bequeathed them his considerable estate when he died. At the same time, he continued to hold other enslaved people as property, working his plantation, and was an ardent Confederate supporter, which seems so incongruent to us today.

How he died is part of the saga. Taking a Black woman as his wife and acknowledging their children as his rightful heirs did not sit well with many in the area, and he was in conflict with neighbors and local officials over it. On the other hand, he was a Rebel, and, when the war ended, there were scores to settle. The West Virginia Culture website quotes a newspaper of the day, *The West Virginia Journal*, in its July 26, 1865 entry:

The community here was thrown into considerable excitement on last Thursday evening, by the report of the death of Samuel I. Cabell, a bitter and open rebel who lived some nine miles below Charleston. Seven have been arrested. Their names are Allen Spradling, Andrew Jackson Spradling, Mark L. Spradling, Stark B. Whittington, Lawrence Whittington, William Whittington, and Christopher Williams. The rumors of the causes leading to this crime are so contradictory that it is impossible to give any reliable statement of the facts; but if, as the friends of the deceased maintain, the act was a premediated murder, the guilty party should be punished to the full extent of the law. We have already held up the law as the true guide, and nothing can justify its violation. If, on the other hand, it is held by friends of the prisoners that they had been subjects of repeated insults on account of their loyalty to the Union, and that they went to his house for the purpose of telling him they would put up with them no longer, when, getting excited, Cabell jumped over the fence flourishing his knife, and he was shot in self-defense. We can express no opinion, however, until the evidence is revealed.

We do not have extensive official court records, other than that the seven were tried and acquitted. From the next issue of *The West Virginia Journal*:

It was established, we believe, that it wasn't a premeditated murder. The charge that the "Union League" is responsible for Cabell's death contains about as much truth as that the Union men of this country are blood-thirsty, etc. The society spoken of is distinctly a Union society. Its purposes are lawful and its members law-abiding.

Samuel and many of his kin are buried in a family cemetery on the grounds of the University. Several of his and Mary's descendants became successful, and some moved back onto their ancestral home plantation. It became a settlement where African-Americans could live in peace. When the state looked for a town in which to build the "West Virginia Colored Institute" in 1891 (not until, it should be noted, pressure from the federal government required it), several other towns didn't want it. The Cabell settlement welcomed it, and Cabell's daughter Marina sold thirty acres to the state for the "Colored Institute."

By the time adolescent Katherine arrived as a boarding high school student, the name of the school had become the West Virginia Collegiate Institute. After *Brown v. Board of Education of Topeka* in 1954, it was the subject of "reverse integration," and, over time, transformed from primarily a residential student population to include many white commuter students. She graduated from the high school and from the college, summa cum laude, in Mathematics and French, in 1937.

For educated African-American women at the time, teaching was the most common career. Katherine taught for a while at a Black public school in Marion, Virginia. In 1939, she became the very first African-American student to attend graduate school at WVU. Having started a family, though, she did not complete the program. She married James Goble that year, and they had three daughters. Only a few years later, Katherine became a single mother when James died of a brain tumor. In 1959, she married Korean War veteran James Johnson.

In 1953, she was hired by the National Advisory Committee for Aeronautics (the precursor of NASA), then located near Langley AFB in Hampton, Virginia. She became part of a pool of mathematicians, women who spent all day doing complex calculations.

A segregated workplace at the facility back then was not only legal, it was mandated. Katherine and her collogues had separate work areas, dining facilities, and restrooms. The racial segregation ended when NACA became NASA, but unofficial racism and sexism persisted. She dealt with it by simply being the best at what she did.

In 1961, it was Katherine Johnson who calculated the trajectory and launch window of Alan Shepard's space flight, the very first for an American. The following year, for John Glenn's first orbit around the

Earth, those calculations were made by a newfangled computer, but they were given to Katherine to verify first. "Get the girl" to verify these calculations, John Glenn supposedly demanded of the male engineers working on the project that would carry him around the planet. Such was her stature with NASA. When America's crowning space achievement (to date) came and Apollo 11 went to the moon and back, Katherine was once more involved with the trajectory calculations.

She quietly retired in 1986. Her legacy at NASA and her published scientific papers (twenty-six in total, unless she had another one up her sleeve post-hundredth-birthday. It wouldn't surprise me), brought her accolades in the scientific community, but it wasn't until *Hidden Figures: The American Dream and the Untold Story of the Black Women Who Helped Win the Space Race* (2016) by Margot Lee Shetterly, and the almost simultaneous movie adaptation *Hidden Figures* (starring Taraji P. Henson as Katherine, Octavia Spencer as Dorothy Vaughan {also a West Virginian. See her story in the LIVED section}, and Janelle Mona'e as Mary Jackson) that the White Sulphur Springs native became a nationwide celebrity. In 2015, she received the Medal of Freedom, the highest civilian award the President can bestow, from President Barack Obama. And on the former Confederate Mr. Cabell's land, now a college campus, stands a beautiful life-sized bronze statue of Katherine Johnson. She died at a retirement home in Newport News, and the age of 101. On February 20, 2021, the 59th anniversary of John Glenn's first earth orbit, NASA launched a supply vessel carrying four tons of cargo to resupply the International Space Station. The Northrop Grumman Cygnus capsule was christened the S.S. Katherine Johnson.

When young, many of us think we will see a steady arc of progress throughout our lives. I have seen that's not the way it works. Instead, it's fits and starts, gain a yard, lose a foot, gain another inch, and each is hard-earned, not given. Women having more equal opportunity in mathematics and science is one of the successes, I think, and I am confident it will continue. For example, in 2018, a third grader named Na Kia Boykin made a perfect score of 600 on the Mathematics Standards of Learning test at Palmer Elementary School in Newport News, Virginia. "I like math because I can look at a problem and figure it out," she told the local newspaper. "You can just look at the problem and do it. You use the numbers, and you use your brain. It's a good challenge." Well said.

In fact, Na Kia was not the only girl at the school to achieve the perfect score. She was, though, the only one whose great-grandmother is Catherine Johnson. We will stay tuned, Na Kia.

Mary Jane Trust Lawson (1865 – 1933), midwife, and ***James Harrison Lawson (1857 – 1938), miller and merchant.*** *Having been born into slavery, they became another early-twentieth-century "power couple" in the Kanawha Valley, who raised an accomplished tribe of "firsts."*

Midwifery has made a bit of a comeback in modern times. There is research to show that the strictly clinical hospital approach to birthing popular when I made my entry into the Mountain State is best for no one. Sweep the mother away, sedate her heavily, whisk the baby away with no skin contact, leave dad smoking cigarettes in the waiting room, leave mom in the bed without getting up for three days? No longer "best practice." (Two other family things not likely to happen now: My family did not own a car when it was time for my mother to be taken to the Beckley Miners Memorial Hospital, now known as Beckley Appalachian Regional Hospital, so she and the about-to-be-born Danny were driven by my uncle in his Studebaker, a conveyance I doubt many expectant mothers use today. And, my youngest uncle, born in my grandparents' Monroe County farmhouse, was delivered by the local doctor making a house call. As was common in that agricultural area at the time, the doctor's fee was paid with two young pigs instead of hard-to-come-by cash.)

Mary Jane Trust Lawson was an accomplished midwife in the Kanawha Valley in the day when the at-home service was the default. She was born in Putnam County in 1865, but I am not sure of what month, so whether or not it was before or after Lee's surrender, I don't know. But, of course, slaves were not necessarily freed in the new state of West Virginia by that time. Her parents, Peter and Ruth Jane Hines Trust, "officially" married as free people in Buffalo in 1868, and were definitely born into bondage, even if Mary Jane was not. Peter died in Buffalo in 1895, and Ruth Ann in 1933, in Charleston. James was born on a plantation near Richmond, where he and his parents Edmond and Courtney were owned by the Craig family. He settled in Buffalo after the War ended, and he and Mary Jane were married in Gallia County, OH in 1884.

Now, in some ways, their story is not extraordinary. They worked, got ahead, raised a family. James worked as a miller at the Elk Milling Company on Bullitt Street in Charleston. That whole area (Bullitt, Piedmont Road, Slack Street) is now often considered the "back side of town," separated by the Interstate, but was contiguous with downtown and the East End before the highway changed things in the 1970s. The entire corridor, parallel with the river and stretching along the base of Charleston's northeastern hills, was filled with commercial, warehouse, and industrial properties, with easy access to the Elk and the railroad. The mill had been built by coal baron James Kay, who had also built the self-named Kaymoor coal camp in Fayette County, and used the mill, at least at first, primarily to supply his coal company stores there and up and down Cabin Creek. When James went to work at Elk Milling, he was its first Black miller.

Likewise, Mary Jane was the first Black Licensed Midwife in the County. In addition to making house calls, she worked at the original Charleston General Hospital, then located up the hill on Farnsworth Drive toward the cemetery. She and James eventually bought a home on Piedmont Road, that, like many others in that area, was destroyed to build the Interstate. While there are no headlines to be found in newspaper archives on this family, they carved a successful life out of the War's aftermath despite the legacy of slavery and Jim Crow, and passed along a strong sense of achievement to their offspring, including Frank (1885 – 1934 married Hattie Cross), Sallie (1890 – 1965, married Arthur Goodman), Hattie (1892 – 1968, unmarried), Ruth (1893 – 1972, married C. W. Lewis), Joseph, (1900 – 1964, married Ludelia Johnson), Mary Elizabeth (1906 – 1991, married Julius Thomas Jackson), Talma Katherine (1910 – 1985, married Benjamin Wynn), and several others, fifteen in all. We find James and Mary Jane's children, grandchildren, and great-grandchildren working in companies and industries across the Kanawha Valley for the next century.

We learn from examples of the exceptional, but we survive and progress from the quiet, hard work of those who go about their business with diligence.

Lou Myers (1935 - 2013), actor. *After a long film and stage career, he got to portray a grumpy old man on a hit television series.*

Many great actors who make a good living in the business aren't household names because they work mostly on stage (and many of us aren't really part of that world, even enjoying *Hamilton!* as we might), while having an occasional television or movie role to fill in the gaps. But, then, later in life, they may have a role that makes us say, "Oh, I know that person!" Such it was with Louis "Lou" Myers, most recognizable as Mr. Gaines, the owner and manager of the Hillman College restaurant The Pit in the 1987-1993 *The Cosby Show* spinoff *A Different World*, sharing the screen with Jasmine Guy, Kadeem Hardison, and Sinbad.

As we have seen, tracking down family history information is often difficult, but, particularly with entertainers, the layers of "modification" for the press and portfolio sometimes add even more obstacles. For example, in some bios Lou's birth year is given as 1945, but it may actually be 1935. You can find his middle name listed as "Leabengula," and his birthplace as Cabin Creek, but he more than likely made his debut in Chesapeake, and, for that middle name, well...

Lou's father, Otis Lewis Myers, was born in North Carolina in 1912, the son of Buren and Laura Atkins Myers. He was a coal miner living in Charleston when he died of cancer in 1945.

Lou graduated from West Virginia State and served his country in the military, developing a love for travel and getting to know other cultures (including their languages) that served him well in his later career.

On stage, Lou had parts in some of the biggest shows, including *The First Breeze of Summer, The Piano Lesson, The Color Purple,* and *Cat on a Hot Tin Roof.* Some of his movie roles included parts in *How Stella Got Her Groove Back, Volcano, Tin Cup,* and *The Wedding Planner,* and he was seen on television in *ER, JAG, NYPD Blue,* and many other shows. Also a singer and piano player, he toured the world in his own jazz and blues show called *Negro Music in Vogue.*

Somehow, between acting roles, Lou found time to serve as the Performing Arts Director of the Marcus Garvey Performing Arts Center in New York City, and earn a Master of Fine Arts degree from New York University. He spoke several languages fluently.

Even while performing in New York and globetrotting with his music tour, Lou never forgot West Virginia. In 1974, he returned to star in the John Henry Memorial Authentic Blues and Gospel Jubilee at Camp Washington Carver in Fayette County, sharing the stage with, among others, Taj Mahal.

Lou began a nonprofit organization called Global Business Incubation Incorporated to help urban small businesses get started. He had returned to Charleston area to live as his acting career wound down. In late 2012, he began to suffer heart and lung difficulty, and was hospitalized several times before passing away from pneumonia at CAMC in February 2013. He was survived by his son Melvin and his mother Dorothy, age 95 at the time.

Dr. John Clavon "Jack" Norman, Jr. (1930 – 2014), thoracic surgeon and artificial heart assist device pioneer. *He was an exceptional and innovative physician from an accomplished Charleston family.*

In some families, exceptional achievement isn't exceptional. It's the norm. That describes the Normans from Charleston. John Norman Sr. was an architect and structural engineer. His wife, Ruth Stephenson Norman, was an educator, community leader, and radio personality. Son Jack was one of the country's foremost heart surgeons and transplant researchers.

Like many African-American Mountaineer stories, this one begins elsewhere. John C. Norman Sr. (1892 – 1967) was born in New Jersey. His parents, Sandy and Sally Hunt Norman, died when John was young, so he was raised by his grandmother, Lucy Hunt, in North Carolina. He served our country during World War I in the U. S. Army Cavalry Engineers. After the war, he studied architecture and engineering at Carnegie Technical Institute in Pittsburgh, moving to West Virginia in 1919. He set up a practice that became quite successful, taught part-time at West Virginia State, and was West Virginia's first fully licensed African-American architect. Some of his projects include the Charleston Municipal Auditorium, Orchard Manor, and Cabell Junior High School, as well as many high-end private homes near the State Capitol on Elizabeth and Quarrier Streets, and in South Hills.

John Sr. married Ruth Lydia Stephenson on August 2, 1924, in Charleston. She was a Charleston native, the daughter of Charles H. and Nannie Preston Stephenson. She became Charleston's first graduate of Howard University in Washington DC, in 1919.

John Jr. graduated from Garnet High School just after the end of World War II, and entered Howard University, later transferring to Harvard. He graduated magna cum laud and Phi Beta Kappa in 1950, and stayed in Cambridge for medical school, finishing in 1954. Joining the U. S. Navy, he served as ship's surgeon on the aircraft carrier Saratoga for two years, then completed cardiac surgical training at the University of Michigan before returning to Harvard as a medical school professor and practicing at Boston City Hospital.

While he conducted high-level medical research at the country's most prestigious university, he never shirked community involvement. In 1969, he published an article titled *Medicine in the Ghetto* in the *New England Journal of Medicine*, calling attention to the inequities in healthcare delivery across racial and community lines that, unfortunately, still exist today. Over his career, he authored more than 500 scientific papers and eight books.

There are many medical advances we think of as commonplace today that were unheard of only a few years ago, and it's easy to forget how much research, how much trial-and-error, went into their making. We hardly think twice about pacemakers and "heart assist machines" used during surgery, but they are relatively new developments. Beginning in 1972, Dr. Norman conducted research at the Texas Heart Institute in Houston. One of the results was the world's first successful abdominal left ventricular assist device, or ALVAD, which could be implanted in cardiac failure patients after surgery. In addition to saving lives, his research paved the way for improvements in artificial heart devices.

Dr. Norman felt the state calling him back later in life. He returned in 1986 to serve as chairman of the surgery department at Marshall's School of Medicine.

Some of Dr. Norman's research involved transplant tissue, and, though it may sound strange to the layman, led to advances in anti-rejection therapies. For example, he successfully transplanted a spleen in a dog, for the first time. He extended the life of a patient suffering liver failure by using liver tissue from a pig, advancing knowledge that led to porcine-to-human heart valve replacements being now relatively common.

Dr. Denton A. Cooley, founder of the Texas Heart Institute, wrote this tribute for the National Institute of Health. It was published on the NIH website on Dec. 1, 2014.

The Texas Heart Institute community is saddened by the loss of John C. Norman, MD, who died at age 84 on 23 August 2014. He was the first director of the THI Cullen Cardiovascular Surgical Research Laboratories and was the founder and first editor-in-chief of this journal.

John Clavon Norman, Jr., was born on 11 May 1930, in Charleston, West Virginia. His father was an architect and structural engineer, and his mother was a high school English teacher. As one of West Virginia's first licensed black architects, John C. Norman, Sr., erected hotels, high schools, theaters, hospitals, and churches around the state; during World War II, he also worked on classified construction projects related to the war effort.

From childhood, John, Jr., was a self-described "perpetual overachiever." He was valedictorian of his high school class and entered Howard University at age 16. He subsequently transferred to Harvard, from which he graduated magna cum laude and Phi Beta Kappa in 1950. Four years later, he received his MD from Harvard Medical School. At that time, few blacks were admitted to white medical schools. "It was very difficult for any member of any minority to forget that some avenues had been closed to them because of their race," he later explained to an interviewer. "I had to be a pathfinder. And once you train yourself to run, you keep running.

Dr. Norman completed his internship and residency at Presbyterian Medical Center and Bellevue Hospital, in New York. Subsequently, he joined the U.S. Navy and served on the aircraft carrier Saratoga (1957–8), attaining the rank of lieutenant commander. Afterwards, he finished his cardiac surgical training at the University of Michigan, then spent a year at the University of Birmingham, England, pursuing a National Institutes of Health fellowship.

On returning to the United States, Dr. Norman became an associate professor of surgery at Harvard Medical School and joined the surgical staff at Boston City Hospital in 1964. He also became involved in several medical research projects involving organ transplants. In 1967, he successfully transplanted the spleen of a healthy dog into a hemophiliac beagle. He and his team later used a pig's liver to keep a patient alive for 18 days. During this period, Dr. Norman began to focus on developing a partial artificial heart, or left ventricular assist device (LVAD), which could temporarily sustain patients whose hearts failed after open heart surgery.

I first met Jack Norman in 1971, when we both were flying home from Russia after attending a medical meeting. On the airplane, the two of us happened to sit next to each other. Being familiar with his work, I told him about my eagerness to develop a research laboratory. We talked for several hours, and I decided that I needed this brilliant mind. I asked if he would be interested in creating, designing, and staffing a laboratory at THI. Dr. Norman later stated in a Texas Monthly interview, "By the time we were over Warsaw, we were talking business. By Paris, we were coming to terms."[2]

Accordingly, in 1972, he moved to Houston and established THI's Cullen Cardiovascular Surgical Research Laboratories, of which he became the first director. He also became a clinical professor of surgery at the University of Texas at Houston and San Antonio. At THI, he focused on developing and testing mechanical devices for cardiac assistance or replacement. He also investigated potential materials for these devices, as well as alternative power sources, including plutonium. Between 1975 and 1978, he and I used a pneumatic, abdominally positioned left ventricular assist device (ALVAD) for the temporary support of 22 patients who could not be weaned from cardiopulmonary bypass after heart surgery. In February 1978, we implanted the ALVAD in a 21-year-old man who developed "stone-heart" syndrome after double heart-valve replacement. The device functioned as a total artificial heart for nearly 6 days until the patient underwent a transplant. Unfortunately, he died of infection 15 days later. This was the first case in which an LVAD was used as a bridge to cardiac transplantation.

In 1973, in connection with a THI symposium called Coronary Artery Disease: Concepts and Controversies, Dr. Norman began to collect articles for a proposed medical bulletin, of which he would be editor-in-chief. The first issue of Cardiovascular Diseases: Bulletin of the Texas Heart Institute was printed in January 1974, contained 10 short articles, and was mailed to 2,000 physicians. By the end of the 2nd year, manuscripts began to arrive from outside the Texas Medical Center. The bulletin gradually grew into an international publication, and in 1982 its name was changed to the Texas Heart Institute Journal. Today, its archives at PubMed Central are visited by at least a million individual viewers per year.

In the early '80s, Dr. Norman felt that much of his work had been accomplished at THI. To be nearer his home, he accepted a position on the surgical staff of Newark Beth Israel Medical Center in New Jersey and became a professor of clinical cardiothoracic surgery at the University of Medicine and Dentistry of New Jersey. In 1986, he returned to West Virginia to head the surgery department at Marshall University School of Medicine. Later, he served as senior scholar-in-residence at the Humana-Reese Hospital, in Chicago, and as director of clinical investigations at Whalen Biomedical, Inc., a research and development company in Lexington, Massachusetts.

Over the course of his career, Dr. Norman wrote or edited several medical textbooks and more than 700 articles concerning his research and clinical work. He was a Nieman Foundation lecturer at Harvard, a consultant to the medical science grants review committee of the National Institutes of Health, and an advisor for the National Science Foundation's grants review section. He testified before the House Ways and Means Committee on the adequacy of funding for the National Heart, Lung, and Blood Institute. In 1971, he was named West Virginian of the Year by the Charleston Gazette-Mail. For his research breakthroughs, he received the 1985 Congressional High Technology Award.

Those of us who worked with John Norman knew him as a brilliant thinker, researcher, writer, and procurer of government funding. He was an excellent mentor and teacher, who could be exceptionally charming and witty. However, he was also a complex, rather eccentric man, a workaholic and demanding taskmaster who expected his research team to work long hours. During his time at THI, he had no local residence but lived in the windowless laboratory and slept in a hospital room at night. For days on end, he neither left the hospital nor was aware of what the weather was like outside. Visitors to his office were often greeted by his harlequin Great Dane, Yonnie, who roamed the laboratory freely—hospital rules being more lax at that time than they are today.

After leaving THI, Dr. Norman stated in a letter to his former coworkers, "I do not believe everyone realized my true feelings towards the lab and the wonderful people there . . . [they] came to constitute my little world on which I became so dependent. My heart will always be in Houston. Think of me kindly, as I do of you."

Dr. Norman's survivors include his wife, Doris; their daughter, Jill Caryn; and 2 grandchildren. I extend my sympathies to his family and gratefully acknowledge his many contributions to the Texas Heart Institute.

Fittingly, a two block section of Lewis Street in Charleston was renamed John Norman Street in 2016, in recognition of both John Sr. and John Jr., pioneers in their fields.

Lavinia Norman (1882 – 1983), educator and Alpha Kappa Alpha founder. *She saw a century of change, and service.*

I was not a member of a fraternity during my college years at either Marshall or WVU, but I was sometimes impressed with the level of devotion I saw, particularly in the Black fraternities and sororities. The very first intercollegiate historically African-American Greek-lettered sorority, Alpha Kappa Alpha, was founded on January 15, 1908, and one of its 16 founding members was a young student from a large family in Fayette County.

The 1900 census for the Montgomery area shows us the family of Thomas H. Norman, 45, and his wife Josephine, also 45. It was a full house. Their quiver was full, as the saying goes, of daughters, with no fewer than 14 of them in the household, as well as one granddaughter and, low and behold, a one-year-old grandson. Thomas was a postal clerk, and Josephine, I am sure, had her hands full otherwise. When an opportunity for a position with the post office in Washington, DC became available, the family relocated to the city, and Lavinia entered Howard University in 1901, graduating cum laude with an A.B. degree.

Along with students Margaret Flagg from North Carolina and Ethel Hedgeman from Missouri, Lavinia drafted the AKA constitution in 1908. As a senior, she succeeded Hedgeman to lead the organization. As with many of us, the pull of the Mountain State was strong enough to call Lavinia back home. She took a teaching position at Huntington's fabled Douglass High School, and taught English, French, Latin, and Drama for almost four decades. During that time, she also completed a second degree at West Virginia State College.

Lavinia moved back to Washington after retiring, and was active in the AKA right up until the organization helped her celebrate her 100th birthday.

Today, AKA has more than 300,000 members in 1,024 chapters across the United States, and in several other countries as well, and serves as a legacy for the young lady from the crowded house in Montgomery. Amongst its first 20 members, and considered a Founder along with Lavinia, was Sarah "Sadie" Meriwether, who late married Charleston lawyer T. Gillis Nutter, and helped found the chapter at West Virginia State.

Christopher Payne (1845 – 1925), minister, legislator, journalist, and diplomat. This "servant" to the Confederacy became the highest resident U. S. authority in what is now the U. S. Virgin Islands.

Have you ever visited St. Thomas, in the Virgin Islands? I actually lived there for a time, just out of college. What I did not know then was that the island is the final resting place of a fellow West Virginian, who was America's Consul General there.

So many times throughout this work we will make reference to the influence of the church, and to what were officially known as "Free Blacks" before Emancipation. The story of Christopher Payne, the very first Black person elected to the West Virginia legislature, incorporates both elements. He was born in Monroe County while our state was still part of Virginia. His parents were both born into slavery, but were, by the time of his birth, both free. Thomas Payne was a cattle drover, but, sadly, died of smallpox when Christopher was only two years old.

The story of Christopher's mother, Barsheba (sometimes shown as "Bashaby" in the records) gives us a window into a side of history many choose to gloss over. She was the daughter of white slaveholder (and veteran of the Battle of Point Pleasant and Revolutionary War) James Isaac Ellison Jr. (1757 – 1839) and his slave Fanny.

Ellison was the son of early Monroe County immigrants from New Jersey, James and Anne English Ellison. After his days of soldiering were over, James "converted" at the very first service of the Greenbrier Baptist Church on July 25, 1783. He became a Baptist preacher and helped found churches in Lewisburg and Red Sulphur Springs. His son, James III, was also a preacher and moved west to what is now Wyoming County, and Ellisons can still be found throughout the region. One of my sons-in-law happens to be one, as a matter of fact. Now, preacher that he was, James apparently was not immune to the temptations of the flesh, because, around 1817, the 60-year-old slaveholder impregnated the (probably around 19-year-old) Fanny.

We know that literally "happened all the time" in those days. Particularly after DNA all but proves that Thomas Jefferson sired a fairly large brood of children by one of his teenaged slaves, some revisionist historians try to make it into something is wasn't: a widespread form of romanticized, caring relationship.

It was rape. The slaves did not have the option of refusing. No matter how Jeffersonian you want to be about it, the fact remains. Call it what it was.

What was the Baptist preacher's continued relationship with Fanny like? What did his wife Elizabeth think of the whole affair? We can only conjecture, But, James did teach Barsheba to read and write, a rare thing at the time, made even more so because it was illegal.

James wrote his will on December 22, 1838, leaving his wife Elizabeth a life estate in all his property, with the direction that, upon Elizabeth's death, Fanny and her (as well as his) daughter Barsheba were to have "their freedom together with the use and sole control of the dwelling house I now live in, including two acres of land, the garden spring, and as much of the best ground near the house as can be included in a respectable form, and also the privilege of firewood and pasture for a cow on the place that I live in forever, provided they continue to live on it, but no power to sell or convey to any person or any way." As well as the house and land, they were to have, after the death of Elizabeth, "one featherbed, bedstead, and furniture, one yearling heifer and heifer calf, one ewe and lamb to each, and to Barsheba I give my loom and weaving utensils, to each I give a trunk now called their own."

James is buried in the Ballard Baptist Church cemetery, where my own great-grandmother Nancy Wood Sheaves rests.

So, Fanny and Barsheba remained slaves, but became both free and property owners, albeit without selling or inheritance rights, when Elizabeth died in 1841. All of those machinations, along with free Black cattle drover Thomas's early death, brought us to the rather unlikely census of 1860, with the rather prosperous Free Black family of Grandmother Fanny, mother "Bashaby," and young Christopher living near Peterstown. Fanny is listed as Black, while Barsheba and Christopher are counted as being Mulatto.

Of course, just after that 1860 census was complete, all hell broke loose in America. Those who wanted to protect White Supremacy chose not to accept the results of a free and fair election, and were willing to wreck violence against their fellow Americans over it.

Why, who could ever imagine that happening today? Sigh...

His mother taught young Christopher to read and write as well, of course. Christopher worked as a farmhand near Hinton, and was then, age 12, forced into servitude by the Confederate Army as an "orderly," probably at the Red Sulphur Springs Confederate Hospital. In other words, enslaved by another name.

Christopher was able to return home, and to his work as a farm laborer, not long before the war ended. The farm was owned by Vincent Sweeney, and there he met one of Sweeney's slaves, Ann Delilah Hargo, who was a decade older than Christopher. She was freed when the new state of West Virginia abolished slavery on February 3, 1865, and they married in early 1866, eventually having eight children. After Appomattox, when it became legal to do so, Christopher continued his education by going to school at night, and obtained a teaching certificate in 1868, becoming one of the first Black teachers in what is now Summers County. He had his own conversion experience in 1875, and was ordained a Baptist minister two years later, founding the Second Baptist Church in Hinton. He receive a Theology degree from Richmond Theological Institute, and, along the way, founded three newspapers, including the *West Virginia Enterprise* (beginning in 1885 and published weekly in Charleston) the only Black newspaper in West Virginia at the time. The others included *The Pioneer* and the *West Virginia Eagle,* both published in the late 1890s – early 1900s, in Montgomery.

Our state, like many others, has gone through political shifts over the years, as have the major political parties. The Republican Party was founded as an Abolitionist party, and Blacks were, understandably, mostly Republicans until things began to shift with Franklin D. Roosevelt. Even back then, though, it was not common for a Black man to be chosen as a delegate to the Republican National Convention. Christopher was chosen as an alternate in 1884, and a full delegate in 1888, when Benjamin Harrison was nominated. Successful in unseating the incumbent Democrat Grover Cleveland, Harrison appointed Payne as Deputy Collector for the Internal Revenue Service in Charleston (everyone's favorite government official, right?). In 1896, he was the first Black elected to the West Virginia Legislature, and received his law degree in 1889.

Harrison was defeated for re-election by Grover Cleveland, who thus became the only (to date) American president to serve two non-consecutive terms in office. The GOP regained the White House in 1897 when William McKinley defeated Democratic populist William Jennings Bryan, eventually bringing former New York Governor Theodore Roosevelt to the office of Vice President in his second term.

That term didn't last long, though, because McKinley was assassinated, propelling Rough Rider Teddy to the White House.

Christopher Payne was already known to Teddy Roosevelt, not just as a loyal Republican politician, but as one who had raised a volunteer Black regiment to serve in the Spanish-American War. As today, loyalty often is rewarded when appointments are made, and our former West Virginia farmhand became the United States Consul General to the Danish West Indies in 1903. Those popular cruise stop Caribbean Islands, St. Thomas, St. John, and St. Croix, were later purchased from Denmark and became the U. S. Virgin Islands.

When the tropical paradise (where this writer briefly lived) became part of the United States, there was no longer need of a Consul, but Christopher stayed on as a prosecuting attorney and judge on St. Thomas. He remained there the rest of his life.

The next time your Fun Ship pulls into port in St. Thomas, between shopping for jewelry and drinking Pina Coladas, think about the extraordinary life of Christopher Payne. But, unfortunately, you will not be able to visit his grave to pay respects, because its location has been lost.

And that historical marker tribute to Christopher Payne near Montgomery that begins, "Born in slavery in Monroe Co.?" As we have seen, not quite, with all due respect. He was born a free man, and truly an exceptional one.

Doris Marie Payne (1930 -), *international jewel thief. The Pink Panther thief has nothing on Doris, who began her career in a southern West Virginia company store.*

Doris Marie Payne was born in the coal camp of Slab Fork, Raleigh County, in 1930. She once, as a young teen, pocketed a watch at the company store. She returned the watch, but learned a valuable (to her) lesson from the experience: Look like you have every right to be doing what you are doing, and few people will question you.

Her official criminal record dates back to 1952. Her usual MO is to enter an exclusive jewelry store, elegantly dressed, and ask to see several expensive items. Through conversation and drawing the attendant's attention away for a split second, she pockets a choice piece or two and walks out, often leaving the attendant quite charmed until inventory time. London, Paris, Athens, Tokyo, New York, Los Angeles...Doris has traveled far from Slab Fork. Perhaps her most fabled alleged heist was 40 years ago, when a half-million-dollar 10-caret diamond ring was stolen in Monte Carlo. Doris fleet-footed it across the border to France, but was detained in Nice and extradited back to Monte Carlo. She was held for almost a year, but finally released; she could not be prosecuted because of "lack of evidence." The "evidence" lacking was the ring. It was never recovered. Score Doris.

Having worked for the federal court for twenty years, I am reluctant to not use the term "alleged" when discussing crime, but Doris has pled guilty to many of her offenses, including one involving a $22,000 diamond ring in Palm Desert, California in 2013.

That's right, count it up. She was eighty-three at the time. The little coal miner's daughter from Slab Fork with nimble fingers has been one of the world's most successful and prolific international jewel thieves. *Variety* reported in 2013 that a movie deal was in the works, with Halle Berry playing Doris Payne. That plan apparently fell through, but a subsequent documentary, filmed with the cooperation of Doris herself, has been made.

I thought I was finished with this piece (first published in *Fresh History, Brewed Daily: Raleigh County (WV) People – Places – Happenings, 1750 – Present* and in *Volume I* of this series), in early July 2015, but Doris apparently believes that being active well into one's eighties is a good thing. It seems Doris was released from prison for the Palm Desert ring heist early due to overcrowding. The very ordinary looking eighty-four-year-old fell off the radar until July 11, 2015, when she is alleged (now is the time to use the word!) to have visited the David Yurman jewelry store at the South Park Mall in Charlotte, and walked out with a $33,000 ring.

And then, she was arrested on larceny charges involving a $2000 necklace in Atlanta on December 13, 2016.

Still adorned with the electronic monitoring "ankle bracelet" from her conditional release, she was arrested on July 17, 2017, for stealing less than $100 worth of goods from Wal-Mart, also in Atlanta. But, according to Doris, she simply forgot to pay before she walked out. "Thieving was the farthest thing from my mind," she is quoted as saying by NBC News. The almost-nonagenarian said she had taken some medicine, and "It causes me to forget."

Who knows? Let's face it. Wal-Mart is not on the list of her usual targets.

Doris, Doris. You have my thanks for allowing me to keep the *(or Notorious)* part of the title for this volume, from the original!

Note: I included Doris in the BORN section because all biographical information I can find states just that. But, in the 1930 Slab Fork, Raleigh County census, baby Doris, daughter of Dave and Clemmie Payne, was listed as having been born in North Carolina, like her parents. If that was, indeed, the case, she became a Mountaineer before her first birthday, so we will cut Doris some slack. In the 1940 Slab Fork census, 10-year-old Doris is still listed as having been born in the Tar Heel State, along with siblings Albert, Clarence, Louise, David (all older than Doris) and 4-year-old John.

Maceo Pinkard (1897 – 1962), composer. *Sweet Georgia Brown. There…now it will be in year head all day!*

It was known as the Harlem Renaissance. During the 1920s and early 1930s, before the Great Depression and then World War II brought an end to almost everything but bare existence, the New York City neighborhood was the center of a great intellectual and cultural revival of African-American music, dance, art, fashion, literature, theater and even politics. This flourishing activity had worldwide influence, and still does today. In fact, some cultural historians argue that it never really ended, continuing to influence us today, with the legacies of such active participants as Claude McKay, Hubert Harrison, Zora Neale Huston, Langston Hughes, Alain Locke, Jelly Roll Morton, Fats Waller, Ethel Waters, James P. Johnson, right on to Duke Ellington, the Zoot Suit, Josephine Baker before she relocated to Paris, and Louis Armstrong.

In the midst of this heady time was a young man originally from Bluefield, West Virginia named Maceo Pinkard.

Little Maceo, age two, is found living with his parents on High Street in Bluefield in the 1900 census. His father, G. Pinkard, was a coal miner born 9possibly enslaved) just before the Civil War, and his mother Mary E., a few years after. Both parents were from Virginia. Three other children were there, as well as two boarders. They owned their home. Things had changed by the following census, in 1910. Mary was listed as the head of the household, now on Stewart Street, and the owner of a restaurant. Maceo graduated from the Bluefield Colored Institute, which became Bluefield State College, in 1913. He formed his own orchestra right out of school and began touring the country. In 1914, he had a hit with *I'm Goin' Back Home,* a song about a man returning home to "Dixie Land" and telling his girl, "Now you can stay up here and have all I've seen," but he intends to return to "the best old land" where "the band will play some rags."

The place that caught young Maceo's eye was, perhaps surprisingly, Omaha, Nebraska. He settled down briefly and founded a theatrical and publishing agency. The Big Apple and the Harlem Renaissance beckoned, though, and he was in New York City before 1920.

But, Maceo's truly immortal tune is 1925's *Sweet Georgia Brown.* As a Baby Boomer, my introduction to the irrepressible song was, of course, as the theme of the Harlem Globetrotters, who toured and showed up on television and even had their own cartoon when I was a lad. Some may think the song was written for them, but far from it. It's been recorded over the years by a true 'Who's who" of American singers, including Black artists such as Louis Armstrong, Ray Charles, Charlie Parker and Pearl Bailey, as well as White artists such as Bing Crosby, Chet Atkins, Mel Torme, Harry Connick, and even the Beatles.

Maceo had a good eye for talent, as well as a good ear. As the story goes, he was hanging out at a nightclub called Barron's when he met a young man trying to break into the business. Maceo was impressed with him, and used his own contacts to introduce him to music publishers he knew down town, in the Tin Pan Alley heyday. He arranged a meeting with Irving Mills, of Mills Music. That young man was Edward Kennedy Ellington, from Washington DC...more commonly known as Duke.

Maceo married Edna B. Alexander in 1911. Maceo and Edna were living at 121 W. 53rd Street when he died. From the *Chattanooga Daily Times,* July 20, 1962:

NEW YORK – Maceo Pinkard, 65, the song writer who wrote "Sweet Georgia Brown," died Thursday after a short illness. A music publisher as well as song writer, Pinkard headed his own firm, Pinkard Publications, Inc.

A native of Bluefield, W.Va., Pinkard turned to music early in life. He was a pianist with his own orchestra and just before World War I operated a theatrical agency in Nebraska.

His first published song was "When He Sand That Baritone" in 1915. His last was "Let's Have a Showdown" in 1959. Among his best known hits was "Gimme a Little Kiss, Will Ya, Huh?"

He leaves his widow, Edna.

His death was reported in the *New York Times,* and in the major papers in Chicago, Los Angeles, San Francisco, Boston, etc. Ironically, the only mention I find in a West Virginia paper was in the *Raleigh Register,* (Beckley) July 20, 1962:

NEW YORK - Maceo Pinkard, 65, composer of "Sweet Georgia Bowen" and other hit songs, died Thursday.

That's it. The whole thing. No mention of being a native West Virginian from the next county. A prophet in his own country, as they say. The Bluefield coal miner's son was posthumously inducted into the Songwriting Hall of Fame in 1984, along with Neil Diamond and Henry Mancini. Not bad company, hm?

Ernest Porterfield (1843? – 1921), police officer. *We wish we had the whole story of Charleston's first Black police officer.*

Researching and writing this book has been enlightening and inspirational, but, with this entry, frustrating. The story of Charleston's first Black police officer tantalizes, but we only have a tiny fragment of a saga that I am sure is historical novel-worthy.

What we know: According to its webpage, there was an organized police force in Charleston even before the Civil War, but it did not operate under a formal set of rules until 1873. The pay for the half-dozen-man force was $30.00 per month, about the same as the teachers at the Union School, the city's first supported by taxes. On June 11 of that year, Charleston Mayor Charles P. Snyder and the city council appointed Ernest Porterfield as the city's first Black police officer. In fact, he was the first to receive any public job from the city.

And then...within an hour, the rest of Charleston's police force resigned, rather than serve with an African-American. This included the chief, a man named Rand.

And then (Yes, I am hearing *Along Came Jones* by *The Coasters* in my mind while writing this)...the mayor accepted their resignations and hired a new police force instead of firing Porterfield, to almost everyone's surprise.

Don't you wish we had more? I know I do.

The players:

Charles Philip Snyder (1847 – 1915), was the Democratic mayor. He was a lawyer by trade, had been born in Charleston, and later served in Congress.

Police Chief Rand: We have a few possibilities. A well-to-do merchant originally from Vermont, William J. Rand, and his wife Ellen are living in the Courthouse section of Charleston in 1860. In 1873, he would have been 64. His son Noyes is listed as a bookkeeper in 1870, and an older Noyes Rand had been a captain in the Confederate Kanawha Riflemen during the Civil War. Had one of them been appointed Police Chief? Or William's brother Christopher Columbus Rand, who also had sons old enough for the job in 1873? All were, in today's words, "connected," and could have been appointed to a public position.

And, the star of the show, Ernest Porterfield: We have a candidate, but, as with history in general and Black history in particular, the document trail is sometimes sparse, contradictory, and confusing. Here's what we do have:

Ernest Porterfield, the only one found in records of the area at the time, was born in what is now West Virginia, the son of Eli and Charity Porterfield. According to the census, they were a mixed couple, Eli being White and Charity, Black. Ernest is found in the 1870 census, listed as "Mulatto," running a boarding house. In 1871, he married Nancy Powers, whose mother was also named Nancy, in Kanawha County.

Now, the police officer appointment took place in 1873, but we do not know if Ernest stayed on the force. In fact, we know almost nothing else. By 1880, Ernest Porterfield and his wife Nancy were living on Hansford Street in Charleston, and Ernest's profession is that of Drayman.

What? The term is new to me as well. A Drayman is a delivery person, generally back in those days one who drove large flatbed wagons. Among other things, barrels of beer were often hauled in that fashion. The next time we see him, though, in 1900 (the 1890 census, unfortunately, is lost) living on Bradford Street, his job is listed as "Excavating." Did he have a crew, or was he a lone ditch digger? We don't know. He did own his house instead of renting it, though.

Neither Ernest nor Nancy show up in 1910. In 1912, an Ernest Porterfield was appointed treasurer of the local Black Knights Templar, though I believe that to be a different gentleman, generally known as "Fleet" Porterfield, very active in secret societies. There is no death record for Nancy, but that's not at all uncommon from that era. Things take a sad direction for Ernest, though. He died of heart disease in November 1921, in the state mental hospital in Weston.

So many unanswered questions. Maybe reading this will inspire someone living in Charleston to become a history detective!

Marie E. Redd (1954 –   ), first African-American West Virginia State Senator. *Criminal justice and community development continue to be her mission, even outside the Legislature. While our first African-American House of Delegates member came before the Great Depression, it took more than seventy years longer to integrate the Senate.*

Forgive me for being snarky, but people who switch political parties just because they see how the wind is blowing irk me. One chooses one's politics due to policies and ideals, not popularity.

Yes, I know it's nothing new. Winston Churchill did it…twice. He began in politics as a Conservative (commonly known in Britain as the Tories), but left to become a Liberal in 1904. When the wind shifted, so did he, rejoining the Tories in 1925. "Anyone can rat," he supposedly said, "but it takes a certain amount of ingenuity to re-rat."

If switching parties for political gain is, to use the British term, a "rat," then the voters of West Virginia's Fifth Senatorial District, home of the first Black state senator, were victims of just that, by Evan Jenkins.

Marie Redd's interest in politics started early. She told the African-Americans in West Virginia Oral History Project, "Huntington High integrated back right after Brown. It was just about after *Brown v. the Board of Education* ruling in 1954. (While a student there) I ran for student council. I can't remember what year that was. I was a junior or senior. I got the office and I said prayers on certain days, and then prayers before assemblies. But I was a member of the student council."

A native Huntingtonian, Marie received her first degree in Criminal Justice in 1989, and a MS also in Criminal Justice in 1995, both from Marshall. She has worked for IBM, as an Associate Professor at Marshall, and as a legal advocate for her husband William's law firm. She is active in Alpha Kappa Alpha, and the First Baptist Church in Huntington.

In 1998, Marie successfully ran for the West Virginia State Senate, from the 5th District containing Cabell County and a small portion of Wayne County. She defeated incumbent Republican Dr. Tom Scott in the general election.

Dr. Scott, in his late 70s, definitely carried baggage. At one point later, the West Virginia Board of Medicine ordered Scott to be publicly reprimanded for his conduct concerning sexual advances toward a female. He was ordered to complete a Board-approved ethics course. The West Virginia Mutual Insurance Company denied Scott coverage as a result, and he sued the company. It was all a pretty big mess. Marie Redd had a lifetime of experience in the District, and broad community support. But, the going was not easy. After Marie's election, columnist Dave Peyton of the *Huntington Herald-Dispatch* wrote, "The State Senate tends to be horribly chauvinistic and, yes, a bit racist. It's the very model of an old White man's club." Despite the obstacles, she was an effective senator and served with distinction. On the face of it, she should have been a shoo-in for re-election.

On the face of it.

Here we credit Lynne Marsh for an in-depth analysis of why Marie Redd is not still in the Senate today. As part of her W. Page Pitt School of Journalism and Mass Communication Master's Thesis *Race for the Senate-A content Analysis of the Campaign Coverage of West Virginia Senate Candidates Marie Redd and Tom Scott in 1998 and Marie Redd and Evan Jenkins in 2002* at Marshall, she extensively researched and wrote about how the media treated the candidates differently, giving us a detailed slice of political reality. {Marsh, Lynne, "Race for the Senate—A

Content Analysis of the Campaign Coverage of West Virginia Senate Candidates Marie Redd and Tom Scott in 1998 and Marie Redd and Evan Jenkins in 2002" (2004). Theses, Dissertations and Capstones. 118. https://mds.marshall.edu/etd/118}

For example, two months before the 2002 primary, the *Huntington Herald-Dispatch* ran a lengthy column by Evan Jenkins, titled *"Huntington Deserves a Big Slice of State Pie.* "We have critical needs in our region that require strong leadership to fight for our fair share," he wrote.

Talk about free political advertising.

Overall, Marie's gender and race were frequently the attention of the media's mentions, which were often at a low-profile placement, while accomplishments and policies were featured less. Lynne's thesis (available to read online at the marshall.edu address given above in the citation, by the way; I recommend it) does a thorough job of describing the history of similar goings-on with Black political candidates over the past half century.

So, Jenkins, a lawyer who had made a successful career working for business interests as the Executive Director of the West Virginia State Medical Association and the West Virginia State Chamber of Commerce, beat Marie in the 2002 Democratic primary. He went on to win the election against the (very) perennial Dr. Scott, and again defeated Marie in the 2006 Democratic primary.

Then, in July 2013, Jenkins announced he was switching to the Republican Party, and would run against Beckley native and long-term Congressman Nick Rahall. He stated, "West Virginia is under attack from Barack Obama…"

Jenkins defeated Rahall, 55% - 45%, the second-largest margin of defeat for a House incumbent in the 2014 election cycle. In 2018, he decided to run for the United States Senate seat held by Joe Manchin, but was defeated in the GOP primary by Patrick Morrisey, who subsequently lost to Manchin in the general election.

"West Virginia is under attack from Barack Obama..." Really, Mr. Jenkins? Beating us over the head with dastardly things like lower unemployment, lower deficits, and greatly expanded healthcare coverage, was he? While in office, Jenkins voted to repeal the Affordable Care Act, which has given West Virginia its highest percentage of its population covered by health insurance in our history.

Jenkins, of course, was later appointed to the West Virginia Supreme Court of Appeals by Jim Justice, and is now Chief Justice.

You know, the same Jim Justice first elected as a Democrat, and then...well, they are birds of a feather. Birds, or, let's see, we made reference to some other animal earlier, in regard to party switching, didn't we?

Politics is a dirty business, folks. Vote, and make sure everyone you know does as well. If we want positive change, it's our only real weapon.

In the meantime, Marie isn't finished. She ran for Cabell County Commission, but was defeated by Republican Nancy Cartmill. We will see what is next in store for her.

Marie and William have two grown children and three teenage grandchildren. There's the future. We are ready for a new crop of pioneers.

George Spencer "Spanky" Roberts (1918 – 1984), aviator. *A member of the famous Tuskegee Airmen, Spanky served our country in three wars.*

There have been so many instances of important stories from our history going untold, practically forgotten until someone restores them to the public eye. The heroic tale of the Tuskegee Airmen is, sadly, one that I was not taught in history classes. I had never heard of them until the 1995 HBO film *The Tuskegee Airmen,* starring one of my favorite actors Laurence Fishburne, was produced. But, I still didn't know that one of the Airmen was a Mountaineer until even more recently.

Before we turn to Spanky's roots, let's look at the Airmen's place in history. Tuskegee, Alabama is extremely important in African-American history for several reasons, with even more connections to the Mountain State. First, it is the home of Tuskegee University, which had its origin as Tuskegee Normal School, established to educate Black teachers, in 1881. It's founding was the result of a "Devil's bargain" of sorts. A former Confederate colonel, W. F. Foster, was running for the state senate. Old Jim Crow's grip was strong even then, but not yet strong enough that Foster didn't need some Black votes to win, so he struck a deal with local leader Lewis Adams, a former slave. There is evidence that Foster first offered an outright personal bribe for Lewis's endorsement, but, instead, Lewis demanded that Foster support building a school for Blacks. Foster won, and the state allocated $2,000 for teachers' salaries, but not a cent for land, buildings, or equipment, in hopes that the salary money would run out without a school actually being established, and that would be the end of that.

Their plan didn't work, because Lewis found the right man to appoint as the school's first principal, a former slave who grew up in Malden, West Virginia named Booker T. Washington. He began teaching in a church and a tumble-down outbuilding. He raised enough money to buy a plot of land, and, during the first years, helping to literally build the school, sawing boards and laying brick, was part of tuition. For the agriculture department, he brought on botanist and former slave George Washington Carver (I know we think peanut butter first, but his work on soil depletion and crop rotation was, in the long run, even more important. {I first wrote "his ground-breaking work on soil depletion," but thought better of it during the editing process...sorry!}). Washington was a brilliant fundraiser, securing grants from Andrew Carnegie, Collis P. Huntington, and John D. Rockefeller among others.

Sadly, though, the name also represents a dark chapter in our history, the infamous Tuskegee Syphilis Study. In 1932, the United States Public Health Service recruited 600 Black men, almost all impoverished sharecroppers, from Macon County to study the effects of syphilis left untreated. Of the subjects, 399 tested positive for latent syphilis, while the other 201 served as the control group. The men, of course, were not told the purpose of the study, but, instead, only promised "free healthcare."

Some "healthcare," indeed. Some participants were treated with ineffective methods, while others were given placebos. Even when penicillin, and actual cure, became widely available in the mid-1940s, the Health Service withheld the treatment. When some of the participants were drafted during World War II and tested positive for the disease during their examinations, the Health Service stepped in and kept the military from treating them, pleading that the study was too important to be derailed for something as pedestrian as treating a soldier defending our country with life-saving medication.

The almost unfathomable part is that the study, funded by our tax dollars, went on until 1972, and only ended then because of a whistleblower, a Health Service sociologist named Peter Buxtun, still only in his 20s at the time. By the time it ended, only 74 of the participants were still living. Of the 399 positive test subjects, 28 had died of syphilis, 100 of related complications, 40 of their wives had been infected, and they had fathered 19 children born with congenital syphilis.

I became a teenager in that year, 1972, and this was still going on in the United States of America, using money my Dad paid in federal taxes from what he made working in 32-inch coal in Jonben, West Virginia. That's still difficult to process.

But, on to the Airmen.

During World War I, Blacks were not allowed into the U. S. Army Air Corps, the predecessor to the Air Force. It was a purely racist policy. One Black American, Eugene Bullard from Georgia, went so far as to join the French Foreign Legion, and from there the French Air Service, during the War to End All Wars. But, as it became plain that we would eventually be fighting Hitler and success or failure would largely depend on air power, more pilots were needed. Tuskegee already had a pilot training program and nearby Army airfields, so was the logical place to begin recruitment.

Even then, it seems some of the powers that be were against the idea, and they succeeded in making the admission standards almost ridiculously high, seemingly in hopes of using the "See, I told you so" strategy to kill the project. What that did, instead, was bring together a group of men with exceptional ability. The first combat-ready airmen were made part of the 33rd Fighter Group in North Africa in the spring of 1943, and more followed throughout the war. What also followed throughout the war was racial discrimination, in everything from housing and promotions to pay and privileges. But what can't be questioned is the record the Airmen chalked up despite those obstacles, including Distinguished Unit citations, Silver Stars, Distinguished Flying crosses, Bronze Stars, Air Medals, and Purple Hearts. Even with that record, the Airmen continued to battle systematic in-house military discrimination. One example: while assigned to a post in Indiana, some of the Airmen officers were arrested for entering the Officer's Club, which was all-White. They simply went inside. And with what were they charged? Mutiny. They were eventually released, with one Airman receiving a token fine. During the proceedings, they were represented by a young lawyer in what was his first significant case. You may recognize his name: Thurgood Marshall.

The game-changer came in 1948, when President Truman signed Executive Order 9981, desegregating the military. Integrated into general units, their abilities could not so easily be denied, and, much later than deserved, the unit received a collective Congressional Gold Medal in 2007.

George Spencer "Spanky" Roberts was, according to biographies, born in London, Kanawha County, to Spencer and Estella Patterson Roberts. The first record of him I found, though, is as a one-year-old living with his parents in Elkins, Randolph County. The elder Spencer was born in Kentucky, and Estella in Kanawha County. They married in Elkins on November 28, 1917. Perhaps Estella went home to her family in Kanawha County to have her baby? The 1920 census shows the young family living in a rented house, and Spencer's (who was only 22 at the time) occupation as "Private Family Chauffeur." By 1930, the family is living in Fairmont, and Spanky is, incorrectly perhaps, listed as an 11-year-old grandson to a couple only 37 and 38 years old. They are still in Fairmont in 1940.

After graduating from Dunbar High School in Fairmont, Spanky attended West Virginia State College in Institute, graduating with a degree in Mechanical Arts. He received his pilot's license through the Civilian Pilot Training Program, and entered the aviation cadet training program with the very first Tuskegee Airmen class, July 1941. He entered as one of a class of thirteen; only five graduated. Such was the program's high standard. But graduate he did, becoming the very first African-American military pilot from West Virginia.

How did Spanky celebrate graduation day, March 7, 1942? By marrying his fiancée, Edith. Housing that would accept Black renters was so limited in segregated deep-south Tuskegee then that the newlyweds could not find a house to rent, and had to move in with another Black family. While on alert, the airmen were ordered to not leave the base, so he even missed the birth of his first child.

Their first overseas mission sent them to Morocco, where they were trained to fly outdated P-40 Warhawk planes by British Royal Air Force pilots. Spanky eventually piloted the newer, faster P-51 Mustang. He ended up flying more than 100 missions against the enemy in Africa, Europe, and the Middle East. After the integration of the armed forces in 1948, he became the first Black officer to command a racially integrated unit, at Langley Air Force Base, in 1950. After the war, he returned to Tuskegee to became the senior Air Corps ROTC instructor, and served in the Korean Conflict, both in Korea and on Okinawa. During the next war (there seems to be an endless string of them, doesn't there?), he served as Deputy for Logistics for pilots in Vietnam. He had attained the rank of Colonel when he retired in 1968, having given so much to protect our country.

Seeking a considerably quiet life, Spanky went to work for Wells Fargo in Sacramento, California, and re-retired in 1982. He is buried in Mount Vernon Memorial Park, in Fair Oaks, California. He was survived by Edith, four children, and three grandchildren, and was an elder in his local Presbyterian Church. We hope those years with family in California were filled with peace and love, because he certainly deserved it.

When the space shuttle Challenger lifted off with Lt. Colonel Guion S. Bluford, the first Black American assigned to a space mission, lifted off, NASA assigned Colonel Roberts a front-row seat in the VIP spectators' box, which he called a "terrific honor."

The honor is ours, Colonel.

Major General Charles Calvin Rogers (1929 – 1990)., Congressional Medal of Honor recipient. *From humble beginnings, this Great Warrior was also a spiritual leader.*

A farm boy and coal miner's son from the New River became the most senior Black soldier ever awarded the Congressional Medal of Honor.

General Rogers was born in Claremont, a coal camp no longer existent. His father Clyde was a coal miner, farmer, and veteran of World War I, serving as a mail clerk. Clyde and his wife Helen Ford married in Fayetteville in 1921, he the son of John and Gertrude Rogers, and she the daughter of Fred and Lizzie Ford.

For a time, a younger lad lived on the next farm over: Joseph Turner, who would also reach the rank of general. Young Charles attended segregated Du Bois High School in Mount Hope, where he was the student council president and captain of the football team. He entered the ROTC program at West Virginia State College, graduating in 1951 and entering the United States Army as a Second Lieutenant. By executive order of President Truman, the armed services began integrating, and his first unit, in Germany, did so six months after his arrival.

Already a Lieutenant Colonel when the Vietnam War drastically escalated in 1968, he was assigned an artillery base within sight of the Cambodian border.

On Halloween night, 1968, Rogers saw a significant convoy of North Vietnamese suppliers and fighters from his helicopter vantage point. But, the rule of engagement at the time prohibited him from taking actions, because the convoy had not yet reached the border. All he could do was wait until the fighters crossed from Cambodia into Vietnam. The Viet Cong, of course, had no such restrictions, and rained rocket and mortar fire down on his base.

The convoy turned out to be bigger than intelligence had led the Americans to believe, and soon their position was practically overrun by the enemy. Charles Rogers ran into the breech to organize his troops' resistance, and was himself struck by shrapnel. Picking himself up, he rejoined the fight until hit a second time, by a bullet in the face.

Still, even after two wounds, he led a second counterattack. At dawn, while helping man a howitzer, he was struck a third time.

"A rocket hit and exploded nearby, and the next thing I knew, I was sailing through the air," he later said in an interview with the *Charleston Gazette*. His leg had been split open almost its entire length.

Later in the day, air support arrived and repulsed the attack. Twelve American soldiers had lost their lives, and sixty-eight, including Charles, had been wounded. When he received the Congressional Medal of Honor from President Nixon on May 14, 1970, he became the highest-ranking Black soldier to do so..

General Rogers admitted he had seen institutional racism throughout his Army career, but felt things improved over his tenure. After he retired in 1984, he became an ordained Baptist minister and lived in Germany, serving American troops. He died there of prostate cancer in 1990, and now rests in Arlington National Cemetery.

On all fronts, Charles fought the good fight.

Ruben (1938 – 1988) and **Ephraim (1937 – 2012) Siggers, rock and roll artists.** *They represented the Mountain State well during the days of matching blazers and Doo-Wop.*

Throughout this work, we see the strong influence of the church in the Black community, and, just as today, one of the most important elements of the church is its music. It's hard to think of a Black artist prior to, say, the 1970s, who didn't begin his or her musical career in the choir. We also mention how many Black families trace their West Virginia heritage back to a coal miner ancestor who came here to make a living during the "boom" years, when the industry had an insatiable thirst for labor.

The Siggers family fits the mold. Ephraim Siggers "the first" was born in Alabama around 1878, but came with his wife Julia Polk Siggers and family to Pond Fork, Kentucky prior to 1920. He died in a roof fall ("Crushing injury to chest and head, fractured skull") in 1930. Julia brought the family to Institute to work as a domestic, but only lived two more years.   Their son Ephraim Jr. was loading coal on Cabin Creek by 1940, and the census finds him living with his wife Annie Robbins Siggers, and their two small sons, Ephraim (the third Ephraim in a row, but who was known as Ephraim Jr., or, more commonly, "Sig.") and Rubin (named after his paternal uncle), aged two and one, respectively. Annie had musical interests herself, and the family owned a piano. She also eventually served as a "local correspondent" for the Black newspaper the *Pittsburgh Courier*, which served the entire region.

Though it was still common even then for young men to leave school at a very early age to make money in the mines, Sig and Reuben went to Booker T. Washington High School in London, constructed in 1925 as a segregated Black high school, but converted to a junior high school when desegregation came in 1956, and later elementary school, which closed in 1986. The brothers were both stricken by the muse of music, Sig for the trumpet and Reuben with the piano. They eventually joined with area musicians Billy Jo Mimms (sax) and Bernard Byars (vocalist) and also worked with drummer Robert Mosley, guitarist Bill Tyler, and saxophonist Bill Scott.

In addition to playing local and regional venues, Ruben Siggers & His Fabulous Kool Kats (Reuben sometimes dropped the "e" in the spelling for the band name) cut a record in 1958, *Those Love Me Blues*, and *Please Pretty Baby* on the flip side. (It just occurred to me that the term "flip side" may need explaining to some, and the thought made me feel really old). Just Google their names, and you can hear the songs today, on several different platforms. Sweet!

Several things intervened to break up the Kool Kats. Reuben went on to college at West Virginia Institute of Technology and received his teaching degree. Sig was drafted into the Army. Reuben took a music teaching position at Gary High School in McDowell County. But, eventually, the muse won out and he left the classroom to pursue a musical career once more.

I found this fabulous article about Reuben in the *Pittsburgh Courier,* but, because the paper served the West Virginia African-American community, let's say a few words about it first. It began publication in 1907 and continued until 1966, becoming one of the leading Black newspapers in the country. Its founder, Edwin Harleston, had worked as a guard at the H. J. Heinz Company food packing plant, and began printing a 2-page paper at his own expense, usually 10 copies, selling them for a nickel a piece. It was closed down by purchaser John H. Sengstacke in 1966, but the next year, he re-opened it as the *New Pittsburgh Courier,* and it's still in print today.

Here's the article:

A Rising Star: Keep an Eye on Reuben Siggers
By Hazel Garland, Pittsburgh Courier, February 13, 1965

Just who is this Reuben Siggers?

Now that is a question that anyone might ask. But, if you haven't heard of the rising young musician, you will before very long because this ex-Courier newsboy and former school teacher seems destined to be the next bright star to shine in the exciting firmament of the entertainment world.

Young Siggers is no optimist, but he does have a lot of confidence in his ability to make it as an entertainer. But what is better still, he has that all-important talent to back up his claim.

Born in Montgomery, W. Va., Reuben is the son of Mr. and Mrs. Ephraim Siggers. His mother, a former correspondent for The Courier, encouraged her son's interest in music early in life. She gave him first piano lessons at the age of 10, and he has been going strong since.

Reuben organized a band, "Little Reuben and His Fabulous Kool Kats," soon after he graduated from high school. The group traveled over an eight-state area where they received popular acclaim by their fans.

Money earned from the band helped defray Reuben's college expenses and, in 1961, he graduated with a Bachelor of Science degree in Music Education from West Virginia Institute of Technology.

Reuben was forced to disband his "Kool Kats" when he finished college in order to accept a teaching post in Gary, W. V. He taught there until June, 1963, when he made his decision to return to his first love, entertaining the world of show business.

He plays both organ and piano as well as sings. Reuben patterns himself after Earl Grand, one of the first to play the organ and piano simultaneously while singing his own vocal refrains. Reuben sings in the manner of Ray Charles, however, on the gospel side with a lot of "soul." Reubens idol is Ray Charles and he thinks the blind singer is the greatest.

On the piano and organ, Reuben is at his best. He plays everything from Bach to the Beatles and does it all with lots of soul.

He appeared on television with the Four Freshmen and television personality Dave Garroway during West Virginia's Centennial celebration. And when the great Count Basie brought his band to play for Reuben's alma mater's Homecoming Ball, the Count asked Rueben to play for him after the dance. He did so for 45 minutes and the bandleader was impressed to no end with Reuben's performance.

In 1962, Reuben won a scholarship to Berkeley School of Music in Boston. He won the award in a world-wide contest sponsored by Down Beat magazine, the publication known as the musician's Bible."

Since his return to show business, Reuben has been performing as a single. He recently completed a tour of cities in Illinois, Indiana, and Ohio.

Reuben isn't the only musician in the Siggers family. He has an older brother, Ephraim Jr., who played trumpet in a band while in the Army. He later performed with Reuben's Kool Kats. A sister, Paulette, plays piano and sings, but is now a co-ed at West Virginia Institute of Technology where she is majoring in social studies.

Like most Negro singers, Reuben has his roots in the church. He sand gospel songs at various churches in his area while in high school and college. While he likes to read as a hobby, most of his time is devoted to his great love,…music. He does a lot of composing and arranging.

In college Reuben was active in dramatics and won several awards for his work. He was active in all phases of college life and served on the student council at the college, which has always been integrated.

Yes, keep an eye on Reuben Siggers. This boy is going places fast.

Pretty good press, eh?

Reuben made a living doing what he loved, and seems to have been particularly popular in New England. He died in 1988. Sig died in 2012. From the *Charleston Daily Mail*:

Charleston Daily Mail [WV] March 15, 2012

By God's will, Ephraim O.C. "Sig" Siggers, a longtime resident of Institute, went home to be with the Lord on March 12, 2012, at Hospice Care after a long battle with cancer. His heart was filled with love, joy, faith and happiness until the last seconds of his life.

Sig had lifelong ties to many friends and family throughout West Virginia. He especially enjoyed spending time with his grandchildren. A very loving man, he was born May 15, 1937, in Montgomery to Annie and Ephraim Siggers. He attended Washington High School in London, and at an early age could accomplish anything he set his mind to. One thing in life that he loved was music. As a teenager, he and his brother, Reuben, decided to start a band called the Kool Kats.

Sig continued to keep music at the forefront of his life, passing the gift on to his children. He was later drafted into the United States Army, where he served his country well. During his time in the military, Ephraim became a member of the military band, where he had the opportunity to travel to many countries, including Germany. After serving his country, Sig continued his walk in life, as many people do, and became an active work force member. He contributed 18 years to True Temper before spending the remainder of his working years at Union Carbide, as a coal operator, where he retired from in 1988.

Although life seems too short to many, those who were touched by Sig understand that the quality of existence far exceeds the quantity of time. He was preceded in death by his mother, Annie Siggers; father, Ephraim Siggers; and brother, Reuben Siggers.

Those left to cherish his memory are his daughters, Maria Antionette (Kevin) Wright, Angela Michelle (Donald) Cunningham and Luella Michelle Lopez; his grandchildren, Curtis Siggers, Joseph Siggers Myles, Aquila Cunningham, Donald Cunningham Jr., Alfred Lopez and Steven Lopez; his sister, Paulette Siggers Brown; four great-grandchildren; two nieces; and a host of relatives and wonderful friends.

The family would like to thank the Kanawha Hospice Care Center at Thomas Memorial Hospital for taking such wonderful care of Sig in his final days. They treated him as if he were a part of their family, and the family will never forget the kindness and warmth they showed him. They truly made him feel comfortable and rested for his journey home.

In lieu of flowers, the family humbly requests that donations be made on Sig's behalf to the Kanawha Hospice Care Center, 1606 Kanawha Blvd. W., Charleston, WV 25387-2536.

Funeral service will be held at noon Saturday, March 17, at Institute Church of the Nazarene with the Rev. James Patterson officiating. Burial will follow in

Kanawha Valley Memorial Gardens, Glasgow.
Visitation will be held one hour prior to the service at the church.
Preston Funeral Home, Charleston is in charge of the arrangements.

Ephraim married Carol Winston on Dec 15, 1965 in Hansford, Kanawha County, WV, performed by Rev. E.L. Farmer.

When you think about the life the Siggers family endured when they first traveled from Alabama to the coal mines of eastern Kentucky, and then to West Virginia after that dangerous job took the life of its breadwinner, it's sobering. But, the amount of accomplishment and joy they brought through their music is inspiring.

Arthur Eugene "Art" Simmons (1926 – 2018), jazz pianist. *From playing marbles in the dirt of a Raleigh County coal camp to playing jazz with Charlie Parker in Paris, Art knew what it meant to be cool.*

Once again, we see that the church has always been a huge influence in Black families. Many of our subjects were the sons or daughters of preachers. And, one of the most influential elements of the church is its music. That's what set the course of Art Simmons's life.

The 1930 Raleigh County census shows us the young family of Albert (born in North Carolina) and Hettie (born in Virginia) Simmons living in what is designated "Town. Colored Section – Goose Hollow." Albert's occupation is listed as a fireman in the mines, but he was also a preacher. They had three children at the time: Arthur, 4; Kermit, 2; and baby Doris. An interesting question in the 1930 census was whether or not the family owned a "radio set," and the answer was yes. There was probably little thought that young Art's music would someday be racing over the airways. But, this was the time he began learning to play the piano, studying with Mrs. Bessie Smoot in Beckley.

Art graduated from the segregated Stratton High School in Beckley at 16 and began studying classical music at Bluefield State. As in so many other lives, the War intervened, when Art was drafted into the Army in February 1944. Uncle Sam, thankfully, recognized Art's skill and talent, and the young jazz man conducted the 17ᵗʰ Special Services Band, traveling throughout Europe and Africa to entertain the troops after the War ended.

His career was going so well that he decided to stay on in Europe after leaving the Army, and moved to Paris in 1949, studying at the Paris Conservatory. He played with Charlie Parker at the Paris Jazz Festival, recorded his first album in Switzerland, and formed his own trio at the Paris Ringside Club. Over the next years, he played, and even toured with, everyone who was anyone in jazz when they came to Europe, including Dizzy Gillespie, Quincy Jones, and even Billie Holiday.

Have you ever thought about to where you would like to retire? It may sound strange, but, after having been a fixture of the Paris jazz scene for decades, Art retired and moved back to Beckley in the early 1970s. Ever a preacher's son, he became involved with the Heart of God Ministries on South Kanawha Street, which is where I once met him. He was playing the piano.

Robert Page Sims (1872 – 1944), academic and educator. *A confidant of W.E.B. Du Bois, he connected Storer and (what is now) Bluefield State.*

Born in the eastern panhandle, Robert Page Sims's influence was felt all around the state, since he taught in Huntington for a time, and became a significant figure in the history of the "Bluefield Colored Institute" on our southern border, the school that eventually became Bluefield State College. In this regard, he followed the travels of his mentor Hamilton Hatter, also an eastern panhandle educator who made his way to Bluefield.

He was the son of Charles and Lucy Page Sims, of Myerstown in Jefferson County, which today is pretty much an area near the Shenandoah River just south of Charles Town instead of an actual settlement. His mother died when he was young, and he grew up with an aunt. By age nine, though, he and his 12-year-old sister Lizzie were listed as "mulatto" servants in the household of John H. and Sarah Ware, a White farm couple in Osborn, Jefferson County.

Robert attended the local "Colored" school, and then Storer in Harpers Ferry. From there, he went to Hillsdale College in Ohio, graduating in 1887; he was also a football player. He first taught at Virginia Seminary in Lynchburg, but soon went west to the railroad/riverboat boom town of Huntington, where he taught for three years at the Douglass School. He later completed post-graduate work at the University of Pennsylvania.

He found his true calling as a college professor and administrator in Bluefield, though, arriving around the turn of the century and remaining the rest of his career. In 1906, he became president of the institution, and kept that position for the next thirty years, keeping active at the school even after his retirement in 1936.

Through his work with the Pan-American Congress he became acquainted with Du Bois, and he attended the international meeting of that organization in London, England in 1921. He and his wife Stella James Sims, also a teacher, had six children.

Ada Beatrice Queen Victoria Louise Virginia "Bricktop" Smith (1894 – 1984), all-around entertainer and self-described "saloon keeper." *Much like Sammy Davis Jr., she could do it all, from Paris and Rome to Mexico City. Talk about a "friends list!"*

Among these many stories of perseverance and achievement in the Mountain State and the greater United States there are tucked a few tales of the great worldwide Black entertainment renaissance of the 1920s. Maceo Pinkard from Bluefield, as we have seen, was part of that movement, and Ada "Bricktop" Smith from Alderson definitely was as well. In fact, as a promoter and impresario, her influence was perhaps even more profound, impacting the likes of her close friends Cole Porter, Josephine Baker, and Duke Ellington. Her wider circle of friends included F. Scott and Zelda Fitzgerald, the Duke and Duchess of Windsor and, later Mya Angelou.

She once threw John Steinbeck out of her establishment for not acting like a gentleman. He apologized by sending her a taxi cab filled with roses. In Fitzgerald's most famous short story, *Babylon Revisited,* Charlie longs to recapture lost life with a visit to Chez Bricktop.

That's quite a journey for a girl born on the banks of the Greenbrier River, the daughter of a former slave, don't you think?

Ada was born in Alderson, in a tiny apartment over a café. Her father, Thomas Smith, a barber, was of very dark complexion, while her mother Hattie, a cook, was very light-skinned, and could have, in Ada's words, "passed for White." Yet, though emancipation came when she was a toddler, Hattie had been born into slavery, probably the biological daughter of a red-haired Irish-American slave owner. That brownish-red hair was passed on to Ada, hence the name "Bricktop."

Tragedy struck the family when little Ada was only four years old, when Thomas died suddenly. Without a support system in Alderson, Hattie moved with her four children to Chicago, where her brother had built a successful life as a White man. In the integrated Southside area, Hattie opened a boarding house. It just happened to be down the street from the Pekin Theater with its thriving Black arts scene, and so attracted many musicians and other performers, setting Ada on her life's path. At sixteen, she began touring the Midwest with a Black Vaudeville show, and later returned to Chicago as a singer in upscale saloons, including one owned by world-champion boxer Jack Jackson.

As with most successful Black entertainers of the day, Ada eventually worked in Harlem. While living there, she arranged to meet her mother Hattie in Washington DC, while Hattie was on a trip "back home" to Alderson. While they were there touring the city, Ada happened to meet Sammy Richardson, one of the most successful Black entertainers in Europe at the time, and he invited her to perform at one of his venues in Paris.

Arriving in the City of Light tired and seasick, she was sorely disappointed when she saw her new performance stage, a dingy little saloon called Le Grand Duc. She broke into sobs and wanted to go directly back to the steamship bound for America. It so happened, though, that a waiter working there that day was also a Midwesterner, a sympathetic listener, and had a comforting manner. He persuaded her to give it a chance.

You might even have heard of that waiter. His name was Langston Hughes. He confided in her that he really wanted to be a successful writer someday. We know how that worked out.

And, that dingy little saloon where Ada became the star attraction whom all the patrons wanted to befriend, somehow, became the dark and smoky meeting place of F. Scott and Zelda Fitzgerald, Ernest Hemingway (whom she really didn't care for), Pablo Picasso, John Steinbeck, Man Ray, Cole Porter, a veritable *Movable Feast* and *Midnight in Paris* on the banks of the Seine presided over by the lady from the banks of the Greenbrier. She soon parlayed her popularity into her own establishment, the Chez Bricktop.

Of course. What else would you call it? Her crooning, cocktail-mixing, black-bottom-dancing persona brought the place notoriety and success. It became the place to go in Paris. She often introduced visiting Americans to one another, as she did Duke Ellington and Franklin D. Roosevelt Jr., both on their first trips to Europe, after which they became lifelong friends.

But, the good times didn't last. The worldwide depression hit, and then an even darker menace: the rise of Hitler. Chez Bricktop closed in 1936, though Ada still made a comfortable living as a performer. Though she, by then, considered herself thoroughly Parisian, it was clear the city was about to become a very dangerous place for Black Americans. Travel was already being restricted, but her friend, the Duchess of Windsor, secured Ada a ticket on one of the last ships to leave France before the German invasion.

Wartime America and her style of entertaining just didn't mix, so she opened a saloon in Mexico City. After the War, she was anxious to return to Paris, but found it a very different place, pillaged and dour by the devastation the war had brought.

And, sadly, she found the American occupation brought something else: a degree of racism she hadn't experienced during the Jazz Age.

She decided to try Rome, and found it suited her more than post-war Paris. Having converted to Catholicism while living in Mexico, she was enthralled by its history. Now middle-age, she again found success as a club owner, and endeared herself to the Romans by working tirelessly for children's charities in the Eternal City. While in Europe to receive the Nobel Peace Prize, Dr. Martin Luther King Jr. came to visit her.

In retirement, Ada made amends with America, and moved to Manhattan. She was still active with friends right up until she died peacefully in her sleep at almost ninety.

For a history geek, it's fun to think about that "if you could spend one day anywhere at any time, where and when would it be?" game. So many possibilities. But, if I decided to not give in to my uptightness and have fun instead, it might be seated at Chez Bricktop, with the proprietor, a fellow southern West Virginian. Maybe I could talk some sense into Steinbeck and get him to act more like a gentleman.

You can read about Ada in her autobiography, *Bricktop by Bricktop* (Welcome Rain Publishers, 1983) and an excellent article by Jake Maynard in the *Greenbrier Valley Quarterly*.

Samuel W. Starks (1865 or 1866 – 1908), fraternal leader. *Though they still exist, fraternal organizations such as the Knights of Pythias, which Samuel Starks led, were much more powerful entities in the past. He was the first Black state librarian in the country, and today his monument in Spring Hill Cemetery mirrors his stature.*

Today's young people (so called Gen X, born 1965-1980, and Millennials, born 1981-1995) are simply not joiners. That's not a criticism, but a statement of fact. Almost every type of organization, be it fraternal, religious, or special interest, does not have the numbers it had in the past. One theory is that, thankfully, we have had a couple of generations without wars big enough to send huge segments of the population to a shared, significant experience. Our Founding Fathers and Revolutionary War leaders were almost universally Masons (with the exception of Charles Carroll of Carrollton, Maryland, who was Catholic; the Vatican and Masons have a dispute that goes back away) and The Grand Army of the Republic (Union) and United Confederate Veterans were powerful in every way post-Civil War. World Wars I and II were similar, with American Legion and VFW halls in almost every small town.

For whatever reason, that began to fall apart after the Vietnam War. Those returning veterans did not join the VFW or Legion in the numbers seen before. And today, many fraternal and religious and civic organizations are, frankly, in deep trouble, many losing more members to the Great Beyond than gaining new, younger ones each year. Even traditional, mainline denominational churches are bleeding membership, with younger folks often choosing large, more charismatic nondenominational "worship centers."

Again, that's not a criticism. Younger folks are, in my observation, keenly adept at recognizing hypocrisy, and, when an organization doesn't live up to whatever tenets it professes, they will not waste their time with it.

But, a few generations ago, America was in full blush of fraternal influence. The late 1800s-early 1900s are known as the "Golden Age of Fraternalism." The Moose, the Elks, the Odd Fellows, the Modern Woodmen of the World, the Knights of Columbus, the Independent Order of Good Templars, and many others still exist with much smaller numbers, but their physical facilities all around the state have had to become lunch counters and public event venues in order to survive.

The organization not yet mentioned, the Knights of Pythias, was the focus of an African-American community leader and businessman born in Charleston just after the end of the Civil War, Samuel W. Starks. He was the son of Lewis and Mary Starks, and we find him in the 1870 census living in Charleston with his parents and sisters Sally and Margaret. Like many in the area at that time, Lewis worked in the brine industry, as a cooper, or barrel maker. Everyone in the family is listed in that census as "Mulatto" but Mary, who is "Black." She died in Charleston in 1913 of pneumonia, at the age of 68. The census indicates both Lewis and Mary were born in "Virginia, now West Virginia," but there is no sign of them that I can find in the 1860 census, so, most likely, they were born into bondage and had been free only a short time when Samuel was born. I have not found a record of Lewis's death, but Mary was widowed before 1900, when she was living with her son on Washington Street.

Samuel took advantage of the educational opportunities available to a young Black man in Charleston at that time, and also learned his father's trade of barrel making. But the railway, with its promise of faraway places, held more allure, and he became a janitor in the Kanawha and Michigan Railroad office. The line, in its heyday from the 1890s through the early 1920s, connected Charleston to the Great Lakes and eventually was absorbed by the New York Central system. His industriousness was noticed, and he was given the chance to learn the telegraph operator craft. He worked as an operator in Columbus, Ohio and earned enough to travel to the Bryant and Stratton Business College in Chicago (which still exists, and counts Henry Ford, R. J. Reynolds, Joseph E. Seagram, and John D. Rockefeller I as alumni) to study bookkeeping, intent on becoming a businessman.

And become a businessman he did, opening, at various times, a grocery, theater, and other businesses back home in Charleston. He was also the manager of the Advocate Publishing Company, which produced the region's premier Black newspaper. He fought for civil rights through participation in the state's Republican party, against such injustices as segregation on public transportation. He built an office building on the corner of Dickerson and Washington Streets in Charleston, and bought the Herald Building in Huntington.

But, it was the Knights of Pythias that brought the Charlestonian to national fame. He helped found Capitol City Lodge No. 1 in Charleston. Like just about everything else, fraternal organizations of the day were separate. There was a White Masonic lodge, and a Black Masonic lodge, and the Pythians were no different. Samuel served as the state's Black Pythians' grand chancellor for sixteen years, and was elected to the order's highest office, Supreme Chancellor, in 1890.

The Knights of Pythias was an early entry into the Golden Age, having been founded in 1864 as the first fraternal organization to receive a charter under an act of Congress. It was inspired by a play by Irish poet John Banim based on the Greek legend of Damon and Pythias, extolling the power of friendship and loyalty. William McKinley, Warren G. Harding, Franklin D. Roosevelt, Hubert Humphrey, Nelson Rockefeller, Louis Armstrong, William Jennings Bryan, and Supreme Court Justice Hugo Black were all Pythians. Under Samuel's leadership, the fraternal membership grew from 9,000 to almost 150,000. He founded the Pythian Mutual Investment Association to encourage members to pool their money to invest in Black-owned businesses.

That kind of influence doesn't go unnoticed by politicians, of course. Governor Albert B. White appointed Samuel to serve as state librarian in 1901, the first in the country. He served in that office until his death, which, unfortunately, was at only 42. He developed peritonitis, an inflammation of the thoracic lining, and died on the operating table on April 3, 1908. Thousands, both Black and White, attended his funeral, West Virginia Institute President J. McHenry Jones was the Master of Ceremonies, and Governor William Dawson also spoke.

There are lots of West Virginia notables resting in Charleston's Spring Hill cemetery, some with impressive monuments. But, topping them all is the 32-foot granite obelisk over the grave of Samuel Starks, erected by the Knights of Pythias in 1911.

To clear up a bit of confusion: In some sources, we see Samuel's wife's name as Lillian. This is probably because "Lillian Starks" is listed as the informant when Samuel died. Lillian, though, was living with Samuel's mother Mary in 1910, and listed as her daughter. The 1880 census shows Samuel's wife's name as Fanny, which is often a form of Frances. And, his birth is variously listed as March 1865 (just before Lee's surrender at Appomattox) or 1866.

Have I already mentioned that genealogy is sometimes confusing?

From the Dayton (Ohio) *Daily News*, August 30, 1901, a piece on Samuel's re-election as Supreme Chancellor:

SAMUEL STARKS RE-ELECTED SUPREME CHANCELLOR COLORED KNIGHTS

CHICAGO – The supreme lodge of colored Knights of Pythias resumed its sessions today. The election of officers was the order and will likely take up the entire day. Samuel W. Starks of West Virginia was re-elected supreme chancellor; J. M. Mitchell of Texas, supreme vice chancellor, and C. D. White of Ohio, supreme prelate.

It is down on the program to re-elect Major General Robert R. Jackson of Chicago. It is also almost a certainty that the name of court Calanthe will not be changed to the Pythian Sisters at this session, and that no action will be taken on the liquor question. Tonight there will be a banquet at the Stevens house. The next biennial convention will be held at St. Louis.

Note: the women's Pythian organization never became the Sisters. I presume the "liquor question" may have been in regard to the Prohibition movement, very different from any "liquor question" that may come up in my own fraternal organization, the Knights of Columbus.

The *Advocate*, on April 11, 1908, had a fitting tribute:

The news of the sudden death of Mr. Samuel W. Starks at Charleston, W. Va., came as an inexpressible shock to his friends in this city, where so many of his fellow-craftsmen reside. The sorrow is universal and the tributes to his memory have been spontaneous and sincere. Just on the prime of a vigorous and useful life, the universally-beloved chieftain of one of the race's most progressive fraternities, serving with distinction in the highest office held by a colored man in his state, and principal owner of a journal of national influence, the death of Mr. Starks comes as a distinct loss to the people of the entire nation, regardless of race, for his life of forty brief years has been largely spent in cementing the whites and blacks in closer bonds of political, civil, and industrial union. To the Knights of Pythias and the Masons, to the people of West Virginia, to newspaper fraternity and country at large, as well as to his bereaved family and immediate friends, we extend the deepest sympathy in this hour of mutual sorrow. Others will doubtless be called to the stations which Mr. Starks has filled so worthily and well, but none will fill them so completely as did Samuel W. Starks. He as a leader who led ever toward the heights.

Spring Hill Cemetery is the largest in the state. Folks often visit for the beautiful views, birdwatching, and walking paths. If you find yourself in the area, pay Samuel Starks's resting place a bit of respect. You can't miss it.

Taylor Strauder (18?? – ????), murderer, litigant, and former slave. *In the legal system, precedent lives past the facts of a case, no matter how grisly.*

We really don't know much about the man whose name is attached to one of the most important civil rights cases of the 1870s. I place him here in the Born section, though we really aren't sure where he was born, but only that he was living in Wheeling and was indicted and convicted of murder there in 1874. We do know he was born into slavery, because, Supreme Court Justice William Strong (1808 – 1895) described Taylor as "…a colored man and having been a slave…" who had "reason to believe {that} he could not have the full and equal benefit of all laws and proceedings in the State of West Virginia for the security of his person as is enjoyed by white citizens."

We know he was married, and his wife's name was Anna. And that Anna died by being bludgeoned to death on April 18, 1872, with two strikes from a hatchet handle to the left side of her head, those strikes being delivered by none other than her husband Taylor. Gruesome stuff. Taylor had accused Anna of committing adultery, an all-to-common source of marital conflicts that lead to murder. Anna's 9-year-old daughter, Fannie Green, witnessed the murder, but her stepfather Taylor warned her that, if she told anyone, he would kill her as well. Taylor went on the run, but was arrested in Pittsburgh a week later.

The Wheeling *Daily Intelligencer* had all the lurid details just a day after the murder, while Taylor was still being pursued. The piece is long, so I have condensed it here:

HORRIBLE MURDER.

A Colored Woman Tomahawked by Her Husband.

He Brains Her With a Hatchet.

The Murderer Escapes.

A terrible murder was committed at an early hour yesterday morning, in a house at the corner of Market alley and Forth Street, above Union. The house was occupied by a colored man, Taylor Strauder; Anna Strauder, his wife; and Fanny Green, her daughter by a former husband, a little girl nine years old. The testimony elicited and printed below shows the tragedy to have occurred in this way: Strauder and his wife had risen from bed. Mrs. Strauder was sitting in a rocking chair in her night clothes. Strauder was sitting partly dressed on a lounge behind her, and the little girl was yet in bed. Strauder asked his wife where his shoes were. She replied that they were where he had left them the previous night. Thereupon, without further ceremony, Strauder reached and picked up a hatchet lying on the floor and dealt his wife two blows with the poll (sic) of it, on eon the temple, crushing it in, and another behind the ear. She appears to have been killed instantly, at least to have died without a struggle, as she was still sitting in the chair when found. While the awful tragedy was in progress, the little girl became alarmed and tried to get out of bed. Strauder commanded her to lie still and make no noise, on pain of death. She obeyed and Strauder left the house, but she, not knowing but that he might return and execute his threat, did not stir from bed.

The murder was discovered by Mrs. Lucinda Thomas, a sister of Mrs. Strauder, who went to the house between six and seven o'clock. She found her sister sitting in the chair, her head hanging down covered with blood, quite dead, but the body still limp and warm. She ran at once to the house of Justice Gillespy and communicated what she had seen. Squire Gillespy went directly to the house and found the dead woman as stated, and the little girl still in bed and greatly frightened. He communicated with the police, and summoned the following citizens a jury to sit upon the remains: (note: a dozen men whose names are unimportant to the narrative today are mentioned here. "To sit upon the remains" sounds odd, but, in this case, it was essentially to investigate and guard the crime scene. For all they knew, the perp could pop back in at any moment. They took testimony and served the function of a coroner's inquiry in our system today. -DK)

At nine o'clock the jury met and took the testimony of Mrs. Thomas, the little girl, and of Dr. R. H. Cummins, who examined the body. The following is the substance of the evidence elicited:

Lucinda Thomas says about 7 o'clock AM I came to my sister's and found her sitting upon the chair with a cut on her head. I think she was dead then. There was blood on the floor and she was still bleeding. I ran out of the house and went as fast as I could to Squire Gillespy's house, and told him that Taylor Strauder had done killed my sister Annie over at the house. He (the Squire) told me to go tell Mr. Junkins, and I went after Mr. Junkins.... (I) have heard Taylor Strauder say that he would kill her; he beat her and threatened to kill her about six months ago, and she had him arrested for it, and he has continued to quarrel with her ever since that time. I wanted her to leave him, but she was afraid he would kill her if she did, and was afraid he would kill her if she lived with him, so she told me herself but I have heard him myself threaten to kill her; it was about six months ago, and before he was arrested then.

Fannie Green, a child of nine years, sworn, says the dead woman is my mother. My name is Fannie Green, my mother's name is Annie Strauder. Taylor Strauder killed my mother with a hatched. He struck her two times on the head with it. My mother was sitting on the rocking chair. Taylor Strauder was sitting on the lounge just back of her, and I was laying on the lounge....(T)he hatchet was lying on the hearth. It is always kept downstairs, and used for chopping wood; don't know how it came to be up there, mother did not scream nor halloo, nor neither did I, for as I was going to he told me to not do it, for if I made any noise or get out of bed, he would kill me too, and I did not scream, but was afraid, and laid down; he then went out.

...(A) warrant was formally issued for the apprehension of Strauder, though officers had been out after hi since seven o'clock. It was ascertained that he had taken the early train north at Bridgeport. The conductor was telegraphed to know where such a person got off, but no answer had been received at the hour of writing this. A Wheeling gentleman, a sewing machine agent, heard of him at two o'clock in the afternoon at a house some five miles up the river on the Ohio side. He had left there two hours before. There are other stories about the direction of his flight. He was seen in East Wheeling about seven o'clock in the morning. He was seen on the Island about half past four on his way to Bridgeport. The tool keeper says he did not cross the bridge. There was a rumor last evening that he had been arrested near Steubenville but it lacks confirmation....

...(T)aylor Strauder is a very light mulatto about 32 years of age; about 5 feet 10 inches in stature and stoutly built. He has rather a spare face with high cheek bones and wears a scattering beard on his chin. He is a carpenter by trade and has been working the past winter...

(A)nna Strauder was a daughter of Henry Schley, a barber in this city. She married one "Dr." Green, who used to drive the medicine wagon of McBride, the "King of Pain." Green divorced her, we believe. At least they were separated, and she married Strauder about a year ago. The lilt girl Fanny is her daughter by Green. It appears from the testimony of her sister that the relations between her and Strauder have not been agreeable...

It's hard to read that without almost crying for that little nine-year-old girl, and the terror she faced. I am afraid the story of an abusive husband, and a woman scared for her life if she leaves, and also if she doesn't, replays itself again and again, even today, even to the point of murder. And, that scene of a murderer being on the loose and being reported as seen all over town would be little different today, except we would read it on Facebook.

On April 25, 1872, the Wheeling *Daily Register* reported an arrest, but it turned out to be the wrong man:

NOT THE MAN

A negro was arrested in Pittsburgh on Tuesday, on suspicion of being Taylor Strauder, but was released, as he was not the man. By-the-by, would it have materially injured the Pittsburgh Commercial, which sheet published our description of Strauder, to have stated that they copied or rather stole their description of the man from our columns? If it wouldn't hurt their circulation or their reputation for enterprise, we would be pleased to have them be a little more particular.

Whoa! Pretty snarky, there, *Daily Register!* I mean, catching the guy should really be the main thing, right?

The April 27, 1872 issue of the *Pittsburgh Commercial* reported as follows when Strauder, the real one this time, was captured:

THE WHEELING MURDER -*Arrest of Taylor Strauder in this City*

Our readers are already aware of the murder of a colored woman in Wheeling by her husband, Taylor Strauder, and the subsequent escape of the guilty party. On last Sunday, two colored men called at the mayor's office and stated that a colored man had been employed by them on the previous Saturday as a carpenter. They had reasons to suspect that he might be the murderer in demand and asked for a description of him. The officers had no description of the man, nor did any appear in this city until published in the Commercial yesterday.

Still humble, I see, *Pittsburgh Commercial*! They finally found a description and apprehended Strauder at his job site:

...(O)fficer Scott approached him just as he was driving a nail with a hatchet and asked him to lend the tool for a moment to straighten a nail. This the man did, whereupon officer Long drew his revolver and ordered the man to descend from the scaffold on which he was working. This he did also and the officers then took possession of him and conveyed him safely to the central Station. He was locked up for future disposition. The man stoutly denied being Taylor Strauder, but after being locked up he was fully identified by some colored people who know him. Since the commission of the crime he has shorn off his mustache and whiskers and had his hair shortened. Later in the afternoon, in conversation with another colored man, he admitted having killed his wife but claimed that he was perfectly justified in the act. Today Strauder will be taken to Wheeling.

Perfectly justified in the act? Lord help us.

Taylor was indicted of murder in the first degree in Ohio County. But, his lawyers, George Davenport and Blackburn Dovener, objected, saying the facts alleged in the indictment did not rise to murder in the first degree, and that the grand jury returning the indictment had been specifically selected to include only White people. Dovener, by the way, had served in the 15th West Virginia Volunteer Infantry during the Civil War, and spent time as a riverboat captain on the Ohio before becoming a lawyer. He was quite successful, and spent a dozen years representing the state in Congress. He is buried in Arlington National Cemetery.

Since the fact that Taylor Strauder had killed his wife was little disputed, he pled not guilty by reason of insanity. The trial was relatively short, held May 8, 1873, and the jury returned a guilty verdict in just over an hour. Taylor was sentenced to hang.

Here's where the legal machinations began. Taylor's lawyers appealed the sentence on the grounds that the defendant had not accorded his right to a preliminary examination, a relatively new procedure for the state at that time, despite the fact that he had requested one. The West Virginia Supreme Court agreed, and set aside the verdict.

When Taylor was re-indicted, his lawyers moved to quash the new indictment on the grounds that West Virginia law precluded Black people from serving on petit juries.

Yes, you read that right. Specifically, the law stated, "All white male persons, who are twenty-one years of age and not over sixty, and who are citizens of this State, shall be liable to serve as jurors..." White males only. No Blacks. No women. Of course, today we readily see that as unconstitutional, but it was the law.

This time, the all-White jury took even less time to convict. The lawyers objected to the racial makeup of the jury, but the defendant was again sentenced to hang.

Seeing an important Constitutional issue, they appealed to the United States Supreme Court. In a controversial and, for the day, perhaps surprising split decision, the Court agreed with them, ruling that the exclusion of Blacks from juries based solely on their race violated the Equal Protection Clause of the 14th Amendment. The verdict and sentence of the second trial were set aside.

Before the Court had even issued its ruling, Wheeling Chief of Police Henry Conant swore out a new warrant for Taylor Strauder's arrest, just in case. He tried to re-arrest Strauder right there in the federal courtroom, but the judge wouldn't have it.

After additional hearings and proceedings and decisions back and forth between the state and federal courts, Taylor Strauder was released.

But, all those hearings and arguments and decisions took nine years. He walked free in 1881. Having worked in the legal system for twenty years, I know that's the great deception of television shows like *Law and Order*. An arrest is made, there's a couple of commercials, and the defendant is on trial. That's not how it works. The wheels turn slowly. But, the Supreme Court case of *Strauder v. West Virginia* was a landmark decision on racial discrimination and Constitutional rights. It established that denying African-Americans the right to serve on a jury also denied African-American defendants their rights under the Equal Protection Clause of the Constitution. It took many years before those same rights were applied to women, but the decision was, undoubtedly, one of the most important civil rights rulings up to that time, and still sets precedent today.

This important West Virginia story with national consequences is, like much of life, a mixture of good and evil. Taylor Strauder brutally murdered his wife and traumatized his young stepdaughter. Though he did spend almost a decade behind bars while the case was being litigated, he dodged the ultimate recompense for his heinous crime.

Sometimes something good does come out of something evil, it seems.

We lose track of Taylor after his release. His stepdaughter Fannie Green married George Buchanan in 1880, in Wheeling. I hope she found peace and happiness.

Leon Sullivan (1922 – 2001), minister and civil rights leader. *He had few advantages in youth, but overcame that in a big way.*

Among Mountaineers, we have so many stories of "inauspicious beginnings" among our sons and daughters who went on to make a difference in the world. Leon Sullivan was born on Washington Court, an unpaved alley off Bradford Street in Charleston.

Leon's parents divorced when he was three years old. His mother, Helen Terrell Sullivan Parsons, was born in 1906 in Staunton, Virginia. She died at St. Francis hospital in 1950, and worked as an elevator operator in the Security Building, also known as the Kanawha National Bank Building. She was the daughter of Thomas and Carrie Richardson Trueheart, and, most likely, the granddaughter of slaves. The Truehearts were plantation owners, and there are records going back to the 1700s of their slaves being known by their surname. Carrie later married Henry Parsons, a janitor at the old Virginian Theater. (705 Lee Street. It opened in 1912 and closed in 1983 with its final showing of the James Bond film *Octopussy*. There were big plans to refurbish it, but it sat for years and was demolished in 1991 then paved over as a parking lot. Common story, isn't it?)

Growing up in segregated Charleston, Leon developed his own form of civil (extremely civil as a matter of fact) resistance. As a young teen, when he was refused service at soda fountains and movie theaters and the library, he would be respectful, but he would return again. And again and again and again, once respectfully reciting the Preamble to the Constitution. Eventually, he simply wore them down and he was served.

A standout student at the segregated high school, he attended West Virginia State College on an athletic scholarship (he was 6' 5"), but lost it when he was injured during his junior year. World War II was going on, and he went to work at the Naval Ordnance Plant that later became the FMC facility. He worked night shift, allowing him to continue his studies during the day. He felt called to the ministry in his Baptist faith while in his late teens.

(Future) New York Congressman Adam Clayton Powell visited Charleston, saw Leon's potential, and encouraged him to come to New York and enter Union Theological Seminary. He became pastor of a number of influential churches, eventually taking over Zion Baptist Church in Philadelphia, which was a small congregation of a few hundred when he arrived. By the time he retired in 1988, it numbered more than 6,000 members.

Leon saw self-improvement and mutual community assistance as non-negotiable elements of the faith, and developed the first Black-owned shopping center in the country, Progress Plaza on Broad Street in Philadelphia. "Don't buy where you can't work," he said.

He became the first African-American on the board of a major U. S. corporation (General Motors) in 1971. He wrote what became known as the Sullivan Principles, seven goals for both corporate and individual business investment, particularly aimed at the Apartheid regime of South Africa. Leon married Grace Banks of Baltimore. He died of leukemia in Arizona.

Leon's legacy is substantial, and we close with The Sullivan Principles:

1. Non-segregation of the races in all eating, comfort, and work facilities.
2. Equal and fair employment practices for all employees.
3. Equal pay for all employees doing equal or comparable work for the same period of time.
4. Initiation of and development of training programs that will prepare, in substantial numbers, Blacks and other nonwhites for supervisory, administrative, clerical, and technical jobs.
5. Increasing the number of Blacks and other nonwhites in management and supervisory positions.
6. Improving the quality of life for Blacks and other nonwhites outside the work environment in such areas as housing, transportation, school, recreation, and health facilities.
7. Working to eliminate laws and customs that impede social, economic, and political justice. (added in 1984)

Major General Joseph E. Turner (1939 –   ), aviator. *The air exploits of another Mountaineer, Chuck Yeager, set this Charlestonian on a path of service.*

Movie newsreels used to be a thing. In 1947, when 8-year-old Joseph Turner went to the (then segregated, of course) theater in Charleston, he saw a newsreel about the first time a human exceeded the speed of sound, and that like him, the pilot happened to be from West Virginia. A couple of years later, the youngster saw the man, Chuck Yeager, himself in action, flying a jet so low over the Kanawha River that he went under the bridge instead of over it. Young Joseph knew his life's path would point upward, even then.

Joseph was born to Joseph and Annetta Ellis Turner. They were married in Fayette County. The elder Joseph had been born in North Carolina. Annetta was the daughter of Carter and Catherine Ellis. Young Joseph spent some time with his Ellis grandparents on a Fayette County farm after his parents split up. There, he became acquainted with a young man (a decade older than himself) from a neighboring farm named Charles Rogers, who later was awarded the Congressional Medal of Honor for his valor in Vietnam, and retired as a two-star general. (See his story in this section, as well)

Annetta Ellis Turner worked delivering mail at the State Capitol, and also cleaned houses for wealthy White families in South Hills. Joseph attended the segregated Boyd Elementary and Junior High Schools and graduated from Garnet High School. Entering West Virginia State College, he earned a degree in Mathematics and, upon graduating in 1961, was commissioned a Second Lieutenant in the U. S. Army Signal Corps and entered flight school

And, fly he did. He logged more than 2,000 flight hours during his two deployments in Vietnam. "My aircraft did get hit a few times...We didn't have anyone killed. But you could find the bullet holes in the airplane. The crew chief would find them and patch 'em," Joseph once told West Virginia Public Radio in an interview. After leaving active duty in 1970, he remained in the Reserves, while working as a civilian pilot for Delta Airlines first in Atlanta, and later flying jumbo passenger jets from California to Hawaii.

He steadily moved up the ranks in the Reserve, eventually being named to the active position of Vice Director of Information Systems for Command, Control, Communications, and Computers in the Pentagon. He retired at the rank of Major General, and is the holder of the Legion of Merit, Bronze Star (with Oak Leaf Cluster), Meritorious Service Medal, Army Achievement Medal, and Air Medal (ten Oak Leaf Clusters).

General Turner married Norma Sims, and, though they live in California, still visit family and friends in the Mountain State. He was inducted onto the West Virginia Aviation Wall of Valor in 2019.

Harriet Wilson Whitely (1855 - 1941) *and* **Lula Dodson (1847 - ?),** **among the last West Virginians who had been born into slavery.** *Many of our lives intersected those born before Freedom. It's good to remember that it wasn't all that long ago.*

One of my pet peeves (it's a long list, trust me) as a student of history is how often I see some version of "The Civil War was really over State's Rights, not over slavery. It was a Noble Lost Cause." Frankly, in my experience, this usually comes from neo-Confederate White Supremacy apologists who somehow believe their "Southern Heritage" begins and ends with hero worship emanating from five years of insurrection, when, in reality, it has many more years and a prouder history of Mound Builders, Powhatan, Francis Marion, Robert Smalls, and Dr. King.

There. I said it. For further reading, I suggest *The Myth of the Lost Cause: Why the South Fought the Civil War and Why the North Won* (Edward H. Bonekemper III, Regnery History, 2015), *Robert E. Lee and Me: A Southerner's Reckoning with the Myth of the Lost Cause* (Brigadier General {Ret.} Ty Seidule, St. Martin's Press, 2021), and, as primary source material, the "Articles of Secession," by whatever name each convention dubbed them, of every single state that formed the Confederacy. They specify, quite clearly, that maintaining the institution of slavery was one of the primary reasons for leaving the United States of America. Big surprise.

And yet, those five years of treason and insurrection to maintain human bondage are going to be the basis of my proud Southern Heritage, worthy of statues in front of every courthouse? Give me a break. Your true motivation is showing. The revisionist historian perpetrators of the Myth of the Noble Lost Cause began their work even before the shooting had stopped, when it was clear things weren't going well for the Confederacy. The United Daughters of the

Confederacy and the Sons of Confederate Veterans have been most proficient and successful perpetrators of propaganda for 150 years.

University of Virginia Professor Gary W. Gallagher wrote, in his *The Myth of the Lost Cause and Civil War History* (Indiana University Press, 2000), "The architects of the Lost Cause acted from various motives. They collectively sought to justify their own actions and allow themselves and other former Confederates to find something positive in all-encompassing failure. They also wanted to provide their children and future generations of white Southerners with a 'correct' narrative of the war." And, Mark LaSalle wrote in the *San Francisco Chronicle* (July 24, 2015), "They say that history is written by the victors, but the Civil War has been the rare exception. Perhaps the need for the country to stay together made it necessary for the North to sit silently and accept the South's conception of the conflict. In any case, for most of the past 150 years, the South's version of the war and Reconstruction has held sway in our schools, our literature, and since the dawn of feature films, our movies."

Likewise and closer to home, the myth that what became West Virginia "wasn't really a slave area" like the rest of Virginia, and that, somehow, those held in bondage west of the mountains were held in "kinder, gentler circumstances" than those elsewhere is just as prevalent, and just as ridiculous.

Our state's slaveholding history is long. The estate of Thomas, Lord Fairfax in Hampshire County included 150 slaves in 1748. The Washingtons and the Lees all owned property in what is now the Eastern Panhandle, and owned slaves. Who do you think built those stately, historic mansions still surviving in the area today? There were weekly slave auctions in both Wheeling and Charleston. While only a minority of our residents owned slaves (as was the case in all the other slave states, for that matter), those who did owned a considerably higher proportion of the land and wealth, and most often held public office. By 1850, it is estimated there were almost 21,000 enslaved people in what is now West Virginia, making up about 7% of the total population, with the greatest number of slaves being held in (in order from the highest) Jefferson, Kanawha, Berkeley, Greenbrier, Hampshire, Monroe, and Hardy Counties.

Many people think West Virginia entered the Union as a Free State in 1863, but that's not entirely true, and the actual date of freedom for those held in bondage may surprise you: February 3, 1865, just two months before Lee's surrender to Grant at Appomattox, when the legislature passed a bill ending slavery in anticipation of the passage of the 13th Amendment to the U. S. Constitution. You see, the West Virginia Statehood bill signed by President Lincoln specifically exempted the new state from immediate emancipation, but, rather, in what became known as The Willey Amendment, "The children of slaves born within the limits of this State after the fourth day of July, eighteen hundred and sixty-three, shall be free; and all slaves within this state who shall, at the time aforesaid, be under the age of ten years, shall be free when they arrive at the age of twenty-one years; and all slaves over ten and under twenty-one years shall be free when they arrive at the age of twenty-five years; and no slave shall be permitted to come into the State for permanent residence therein."

With the passage of the 15th Amendment to the U. S. Constitution, in 1869, Black male citizens were "guaranteed" the right to vote (Jim Crow soon took care of that), but another result was that former Confederates also regained their rights. Thus, by 1876, seven of the eight successful candidates for state offices, including that of Governor, were former Confederate soldiers. Former abolitionist and our first governor Francis Pierpont even lost his seat in the House of Delegates.

While this book is full of "firsts" for African-American West Virginians, by necessity, there are also "lasts." When it comes to the Civil War era, it is hard to be definitive because records were not kept at all, poorly kept, or lost. There are various claims to those being the "last" Civil War soldier on both sides, some of which are clearly suspicious. When pensions or accolades are involved, some old codgers were tempted to stretch the truth about their own participation in the War. I believe my own great-great grandfather, for example, who freely told listeners in the 1940s that he had been wounded in the War as well as present at Lee's surrender ("That's where we had to lay it down") was, to put it kindly, mistaken, and not old enough to have served at all.

Sylvester Magee of North Carolina claimed to have been born into slavery in 1841, and said he ran away and enlisted in the Union Army in 1863, taking part in the assault on Vicksburg. Inconveniently, there are no documents backing up his claim. He died in 1971, making him, if correct, an astounding 130 years old at the time.

No disrespect, but I'm dubious, Sylvester.

A more likely candidate is Peter Mills, who was born in Prince George County, Maryland just before the beginning of the War, in 1861. He eventually migrated to Baltimore and then to Washington DC, where he dug sewers and played baseball. He then settled in Pittsburgh and spent most of his life there, working as a plasterer and construction worker. Just before his 111th birthday, he was involved in what the *Pittsburgh Post-Gazette* referred to as a "pedestrian accident injury" and died in September 1972, after even Sylvester Magee.

Who was the last person born enslaved to have lived in West Virginia? I simply can't be sure. But, Harriet Wilson and Lula Dodson were most certainly among them.

We know much of what we know about Harriet Wilson from a column written by Ned Smith for a Fairmont newspaper in 1941. He claimed that Harriet was the last person living in Fairmont who had been born into slavery. I do not know "Hattie's" original owner, but she, her mother Rebecca, and sister Helen were sold on the Marion County courthouse steps in Fairmont to Hiram Haymond, a local farmer, merchant, and businessman, when Hattie was five years old. Haymond had served as a delegate to Virginia's Constitutional Convention after the Commonwealth seceded in 1861. He didn't live to see the Confederacy's defeat, though. In debt, he moved west the following year and died in 1863.

After the War ended, a school for African-American children was established in Fairmont, and Harriet was among its students in 1869. Her sister Helen married Alfred Meade, a hotel porter, just after the War ended. Harriet's death certificate states she was living at 1218 Field Street at the time of her death on April 26, 1941, was the widow of Richard Whitely, and succumbed to Angina Pectoris due to Old Age.

She was living with the family of Howard and Cora Wilson, presumed relatives. But, ten years earlier in 1930, she is living with sisters Nannie Clark and Mary Black, both White, and listed as a "Servant," at age 77. The relationship must have been a long one, since she was with the Clarks as early as 1900, after Richard's death. Today, she rests in Evergreen Cemetery.

Lula Dodson, from down closer to my part of the state, was not actually born in what is now West Virginia, but we will certainly claim her, and I don't think she would mind being included in this section. According to her death certificate, she was born on September 21, 1845, and died of natural causes.

From the *Bluefield Daily Telegraph*, March 6, 1949:

103 Year Old Woman Dies Here Friday

Mrs. Lula Dodson, a Bluefield colored woman who was born in slavery 103 years ago, died Friday at the home of her daughter, Mrs. Georgia Dandridge, of 228 Floyd Street. Born in Henry County, Virginia in 1845, Mrs. Dodson had been a slave until the age of seven, when she was surrendered. Her husband, Green Dodson, died 22 years ago at the age of 70.

Mrs. Dodson, the mother of 14 children, had been I good health nearly all her life and was active until her death.

She is survived by two sons, Shedrick and Robert, both of Northfork, three daughters, Mrs. Georgia Dandridge and Mrs. Huldie Dodson of Martinsville, and Mrs. Patty Benson of New York City. Also surviving are 35 grandchildren, 38 great grandchildren, and five great-great-grandchildren, as well as a large number of other relatives.

Funeral services will be held Tuesday afternoon at Martinsville and burial will be in the family cemetery. The body is now at the Sinkford Funeral Home. It will be sent to Martinsville tomorrow on train No. 4.

Not so very long ago, your obituary noted what train your casket was loaded onto for your last ride! We find Green and Lula living in Horse Pasture, Virginia in the 1900 census, renting a farm house. Children listed at that time included James, Lucy, Pattie, Obadiah, Frank, Georgia, Swanson, Dump, and Shedrick, ranging in ages from 17 down to less than a year. Ten years later, they owned their home there. While Green is listed as Black, Lula is listed as Mulatto, and neither can read or write. Sadly, Lula's daughter Georgia, in whose Bluefield home Lula died, was soon to follow her mother into eternity, dying just five months later of Hypertensive Cardiac Disorder on August 16, 1949. She had moved to Bluefield from Pageton in McDowell County, after the death of her husband John, in 1940. He was also originally from Henry County, Virginia.

William Harrison "Bill" Withers, Jr. (1938 - 2020), songwriter and singer. *From Slab Fork to the Rock and Roll Hall of Fame, Bill invited us to lean on him.*

William Harrison Withers, Jr. was *Born on The Fourth Of July*, as the song goes, in 1938, in Slab Fork, Raleigh County, the youngest of six children. Suffering from a stutter when young, he found it went away when he was singing, and used that to help him overcome stuttering altogether. (He also used the supposed speakers' ploy of imagining other people naked while he talked. I speak to groups for a living, and have to admit that has never worked for me.) He grew up in Beckley, and was only thirteen when his father died. William Sr., a coal miner, had been born in Appomattox County, Virginia, and is buried in the Slab Fork Cemetery # 2...meaning, in the unfortunate vernacular of the day, the "Colored Cemetery." Segregation left an indelible mark on young Bill, who remembered well that Emmett Till, who was close to his own age, was murdered in Mississippi in 1955.

Bill joined the Navy when he was eighteen and served for nine years; his postings included Guam. After his service, he worked as a milkman for a time, and then in an airplane factory while performing in clubs at night and shopping his songs around to producers. Even after *Ain't No Sunshine* hit the charts, he continued in his factory job for a while, just in case he was to be a one-hit-wonder.

He needn't have worried. *Ain't No Sunshine* won the 1971 Grammy for Best Rhythm and Blues Song, and Bill was nominated for Best New Artist. He was nominated for a total of seven Grammys during his career, with *Just the Two of Us* and *Lean on Me* also scoring wins. Stephen Stills played lead guitar on his first album, Bill wrote and produced songs for Gladys Knight and the Pips, and shared the stage in concerts with the likes of James Brown and B. B. King. He was briefly married to one of the hottest actresses at the time, Denise Nicholas of *Room 222* and, later, *In the Heat of the Night* fame.

There is no doubt Bill could still have been successfully recording and even touring into old age. Instead, we had not heard much from Bill in years when he died. He was one of a relatively small number of pop stars who walked away from the business, while still being very successful at it, simply because that's what he wanted to do. In an interview with Andy Greene of *Rolling Stone* in 2015 on the eve of the Grammy Awards (taking place almost within sight of Bill's Los Angeles home), Bill said, "These days I wouldn't know a pop chart from a Pop-Tart." Lamenting the turn pop music has taken, he added, "Now everything is about image. It's not poetry. This just isn't my time." But, Bill from Slab Fork could pretty much do as he pleased. Since he wrote his own songs and many of them are still popular, he received substantial royalties, and he has made wise real estate investments around Los Angeles. Good for you, Bill. He died of heart disease, and is buried amongst the famous at Forest Lawn Memorial Park in Hollywood.

Lewis Woodson (*1806 - 1878*), minister and abolitionist. *He may not have been a descendant of Jefferson, but he made freedom his life's work.*

When studying family history, the first thing one learns is that so much of what is "known," passed down through lore, either can't be substantiated through research, or can be outright disproven. Modern DNA techniques make that even more common, and it has happened in my own family. Long story short, despite my German surname, I am Irish and Scottish to the core. You see, back in the mid-1890s, on

Coal River, my great-grandmother used to disappear on her mule for days at a time, and…well, that's for a different book.

Lewis Woodson's family held that his father, Thomas, was the eldest child of Thomas Jefferson and enslaved Sally Hemings.

The issue still ruffles feathers amongst some Jefferson purists. No matter how strong the evidence (and, make no mistake, it is very strong), it is not possible to determine with 100% certainty that Jefferson fathered Sally's children. The Smithsonian Institution and the Thomas Jefferson Foundation, in a major joint exhibit at the National Museum of American History in 2012, stated, "The documentary and genetic evidence strongly support the conclusion that Jefferson was the father of Sally Hemings' children." In my mind, it's settled.

Now, Sally was, as perhaps most enslaved Americans even at that time, of mixed race, most likely the result of Thomas Jefferson's father-in-law, John Wayles, raping one of his slaves, Sally's mother Betty. Sally, thus Thomas's wife Martha's half-sister, was of light complexion, and her children even more so. In fact, the family of only one of her offspring, son Madison, chose to continue to identify with the Black community after attaining eventually freedom. Our subject, Lewis, was of similarly light complexion. But, records of Sally's offspring do not mention Lewis's father Thomas Woodson as being one of them. While not conclusive, DNA evidence does not indicate Jefferson was a Woodson ancestor.

I used the term "rape" when describing the John Wayles/Betty Hemings relationship above, because, of course, that's what it was. Betty was in no position to give or refuse to give consent, and the situation was no different when Sally became Thomas Jefferson's property. Jefferson admirers like to believe the relationship was a romantic love affair, despite his obvious public sentiment about race.

Lewis was born in Greenbrier County, to Thomas and Jemima Woodson, and he was the eldest of eleven children. The 1820 Greenbrier County, Virginia census shows Thomas Woodson living with a family totaling 10 "free people of color." Unfortunately, the census did not name individuals other than the head of household until

30 years later, but we can assume Lewis is among them. The family migrated to "free soil" Ohio (the Chillicothe area) not long after that census, and Lewis is found there as an adult with a wife (Caroline Robinson, who had also been born in what was then Virginia) and four children by 1830. Not long afterward, Lewis and Caroline moved to Pittsburgh. He supported his family as a barber while he studied and ministered, becoming ordained in the African Methodist Episcopal Church.

Chillicothe, at that time, had a relatively large and influential community of Free Blacks, and became an active stop on the Underground Railroad as escaped slaves made their way north to freedom. By any measure, the Woodsons were an extraordinary family. Three of Thomas and Jemima's sons; Lewis, Thomas Jr., and John, all became AME ministers, and helped establish the first AME congregation west of the Allegheny Mountains.

Lewis founded a school and was active in the Pennsylvania Anti-Slavery Society. He befriended another young abolitionist originally from what is now West Virginia, Martin Delany (see his biography earlier in this section). He pastored the Wylie Avenue AME Church, now re-named the Bethel AME Church, on Webster Avenue.

Perhaps for safety reasons, Lewis often wrote under the pen name "Augustine." His letters in *The Colored American*, one of the most influential Black newspapers of the day, led later historians to dub him "The Father of Black Nationalism." He was opposed to wholesale integration. He was also opposed to the idea, supported by many abolitionists both Black and White, that former slaves should be given a homeland in Africa, but, instead, advocated strong, separate institutions of all types for Blacks here in the United States, including churches, schools, and newspapers. He foresaw the day when freedom for the enslaved would come, perhaps suddenly, and believed that Free Blacks should prepare by developing those institutions to be ready to absorb them when that day came.

In a way, Lewis Woodson's philosophy could be summed up not as supporting "Separate but Equal," but rather "Separate but Superior."

He wrote (as "Augustine") the following in the July 28, 1838 issue of *Colored American:*

"When you asserted that the whole history of the past was in favor of "contact," as being the most powerful means of destroying antipathies, the history of our own country must have entirely escaped your memory. The very act which gave it political existence, was an act of separation. Is the DECLARATION OF INDEPENDENCE, therefore, a "weak and foolish" document, and were its framers "weak and foolish" men? Have you forgotten the history of the separation of the Friends, the Methodists, and even the Presbyterians? Of the utility of these several separations I do not now pretend to speak. My object in referring to them is, to show that other men than me, or old father Abraham, have been "weak and foolish" enough to resort to separation, and the formation of societies of their own, as a means of curing existing antipathies.

The principle which I have endeavored to maintain in my three preceding letters on separate settlements is this, that it is right, and in accordance with the mind of God, for men whose condition has been rendered unhappy in one place, to better it if they can, by removing to another; and that the manner, time, and place of such removal, should be exclusively matters of their own choice. And through what kind of glasses you were looking, Mr. Editor, when this simple principle appeared to you like "colonization magnified," I am at a loss to know. Those which I use are a plain pair of Parisian manufacture;–and when I look at it through them, it has no such appearance. Purchasing contiguous tracts of land from the Congress of our native country, and settling upon them, so as to have society, churches, and schools of our own, without being subject to the humiliation of begging them from others, looks very much like being exiled to the cheerless coast of Africa, don't it? Surely your readers will be able to distinguish the difference.

But I can assure you that in the West it [the issue of separate black settlements] is not merely a matter of theory; it has long since been reduced to practice. My father now resides, and has been for the last eight years residing in such a settlement, in

Jackson county, Ohio. The settlement is highly prosperous and happy. They have a church, day and Sabbath school of their own. The people of this settlement cut their own harvests, roll their own logs, and raise their own houses, just as well as though they had been assisted by white friends. They find just as ready and as high market for their grain and cattle, as their white neighbors. They take the newspapers and read many useful books, and are making as rapid advancement in intelligence and refinement as any people in the country generally do. And when they travel out of their settlement, no colored people, let them reside where or among whom they may, are more respected, or treated with greater deference than they are."

Lewis was one of the founders of still-thriving Wilberforce College in Ohio, America's first college owned-and-operated by African-Americans. His sister Sarah, who had attended Oberlin College, was its first female teacher. The school had to close for a time during the Civil War, but reopened before the War was over, being purchased by the AME Church.

Though a Greenbrier Countian, Lewis and his family became associated with Pittsburgh, and his descendants remain influential in the area even today. One of his grandsons, Howard Lewis, became an engineer who helped design Washington DC's Union Station, and his great-great-great grandson, Timothy K. Lewis, was appointed to the federal court by President George H. W. Bush in 1991, and later elevated to the Third Circuit Court of Appeals.

When Lewis died in January 1878, his obituary appeared not only in the Black newspapers of the day, but also in his hometown *Pittsburgh Daily Post*. This from the January 14, 1878 issue:

DEATH OF REV. LEWIS WOODSON

One of Our Oldest and Most Prominent Colored Citizens

Rev. Lewis Woodson, one of the oldest and most widely known colored citizens of this vicinity, died at his residence on Fourth Avenue, near the Eagle engine house, shortly after Saturday midnight. The deceased has served in the capacity of barber, school teacher, lecturer, correspondent, and clergyman, and was always wide awake to the interests of his race. He was born a slave in 1804, but before he was nineteen, his father purchased his freedom and moved to Southern Ohio. Here the young man by private studies fitted himself for a school teacher. Soon afterwards he took a circuit as a Methodist preacher. In 1831, he came to Pittsburgh and opened the first schools in which tuition was offered to the colored youth in this city. The calling was not very lucrative, however, and in 1835 he abandoned the book and birch for the brush and razor and opened a barber shop on the site now occupied by the Seventh Avenue Hotel and afterwards he carried on the business under the St. Charles hotel. In 1863, he again went to preaching and since that time has been pastor of nearly a score of colored churches, among them the Wylie Avenue African M. E. church. He aided in the erection of the old Wesley church. He was an active and zealous "stockholder of the underground railroad," and took in, sheltered and aided to escape many a fugitive slave.

The deceased had a family of ten children, most of whom are living and all married but one. He leaves also forty-five living grandchildren and three great-grandchildren. His relatives are among our most orderly, industrious, and prosperous colored citizens. Today crape is suspended in honor of his memory in five different barber shops, carried on by his sons and daughters' husbands. The funeral will take place tomorrow afternoon. The services will be conducted at the Wylie Avenue colored church.

Note: this article states Lewis was born into slavery, but some sources disagree. We do know that, by 1820, his family was listed as "Free people of color," but I have not found them in the 1810 census, so whether or not they were free at the time of Lewis's birth (presumed to be 1806), I cannot say for certain.

There were notices of his death in newspapers around the country. Interestingly, I can't find any in the archives for his native West Virginia. He certainly wasn't the last Mountaineer to end up living in Pittsburgh, and there will be more in the future. In the big sweep of history, he just might be the most influential, though.

2 LIVED

Edward "Ed" Kitchen Austin (1909 – ?), coal miner and family man; Viola Carter Austin (1921 - ?), mother and caregiver. *Those who quietly work to raise a family are our unsung heroes. His and his wife's quiver was pretty darned full.*

There are a couple of iconic photos that keep cropping up for those of us who research West Virginia history. One was taken in April 1974, and is in the National Archives. It is a color photo of a slight, humble-looking man standing in front of what appears to be an old coal company house, with a couple of youngsters on the porch. He's smoking a pipe. The caption reads, "Retired Coal Miner Ed Austin with Some of His 20 Children in Fireco, West Virginia, near Beckley. The 64-year-old Worked in the Mines From 1925 to 1956. He Receives Black Lung Payments and a United Mine Workers Pension." Search "Ed Austin Fireco WV" and I am sure it will come up for you.

My father worked for almost twenty-five years in the mines in Jonben, next door to Fireco, and knew Ed through the UMWA local. According to their marriage license, Edward Austin and Viola Carter were wed in Fireco on February 18, 1939, by Rev. R. C. Brawn. Ed was born in Monroe County, Alabama, the son of Kato and Ritta Ann Austin, and Viola in Jonben. (The first name of Ed's mother shifts in documents due to poor handwriting, everything from Ritter to Betty to Ruth) Viola was the daughter of George and Anna Carter. Ed's birth year was given at the time as 1909, but is recorded as 1911 in some documents. There was a bit of an age difference, with Viola having been born in 1921. The 1940 census shows "Eddie," 29, and Viola, 21, Austin living in the Shady Spring District of Raleigh County, which would have included Fireco then. They had no children at the time.

Boy, would that change, when (in no particular order, Maurine (died 2016, lived in Germantown, MD), Kenneth, Edward Jr. (died 2016, lived in Streator, IL) Orlando, Michael, Danny, Marian, Frederick, Lenora, Annette, Brenda, Barbara, Lucille, and Aaron came along. Sadly, as was so common at the time, six additional children died in infancy. Growing up in the adjoining school district, I remember the Austins being good high school athletes, some served in the military, and at least one became a minister.

Now, an obituary from the *Raleigh Register*, January 7, 1971, presents us with a bit of a mystery. It lists the death of Rev. Edward Austin:

Final rites for the Rev. Edward Austin, 86, of Fireco, will be conducted at 2:30 p.m. Saturday in the Ritchie and Johnson Funeral Parlor Chapel, with the Rev. J. H. Wright in charge. Burial will follow in Greenwood Memorial Park. He died at 10:30 p.m. Monday in a local hospital following a long illness. Born April 16, 1884 in Selma, Ala., he was the son of the late Kato and Florence Austin.

A retired miner and member of the M. W. Prince Hall Grand Masonic Lodge No. 108, Hazard, Ky., he made his home with his nephew, Edward Austin.

So, Ed's older uncle lived with them, but also listed his father as Kato Austin, but with a different mother's name? Or was this actually Ed's father, living with yet another Ed who was a nephew? Names and records and stories are sometimes hard to sort out, as any historian or genealogist knows.

It is sometimes so difficult tracing African-American genealogy that, when you see a documented lead, it's almost too good not to follow. Apparently, Ed's father Kato also came to West Virginia. He and Ritta were married in 1898, and Cato (spelled with a C" in these earlier records) were married in 1898. He was born in Mississippi, and she in Alabama. They were living in Alabama in 1910, with sons James, two, and baby Edward. He was a Jr., because we first find him living with his parents Cato, 36, and Florence, 35, Austin in Alabama in the 1880 census. Cato Sr. was born in Mississippi, and Florence, listed as Mulatto, was born in Alabama, but her parents were born on North Carolina.

Now, that puts Cato Sr. and Florence having been born in 1844 and 1845. Ten years earlier, in the 1870 census, Cato Sr., 24, is still in Mississippi, a farm laborer in the household of Peter and Susan Collins, Black "Farm Renters" in Hinds, Mississippi. Backward from there, of course, is where history changes. There is no sign of Cato, nor of Peter Collins, in the 1860 census, meaning that, most likely, they were someone's property, still only counting as three-fifths of a human being according to the United States Constitution, and unworthy of being named in the count.

But, thankfully, we know much about the Austin's story, thanks to a piece in the September 9, 1969 edition of the *Raleigh Register*, by Dan Hodel, accompanying a photo of Ed and Viola. It gives us not only a look at their lives, but the lives of Viola's parents:

Fireco Family Is Courageous In The Face Of Many Hardships

There was a time when passenger trains served Fireco, traveling to Mullens and Beckley.

There was a time when miners worked for $2.40 per day…when looking down at Fireco at night meant something…and when the unions entered the mines. The home of Mr. and Mrs. Edward Austin contains memories like these, and others that go much farther back.

Among others, Mrs. Austin cares for are possibly Raleigh County's oldest set of twins – her mother and uncle, Annie Carter and George Burgess, who were born on Christmas Day in 1881. They were born and reared in Ridgewood, Va., coming to Raleigh County just after World War I. Burgess was a coal miner until 1951, last working for the Sterling Smokeless Coal Co.

The Austin household presently numbers 15. Mrs. Austin must care for the elderly twins; Austin's uncle, the Rev. Edward Austin; Mrs. Austin's sister who is deaf and dumb, and the eight of her 14 children who are still at home. The task has never been easy. Austin tells of the Depression, when "you could work a whole week loading coal and get but one or two dollars script taken at the store." Men would sit up at night playing cards, just waiting for the "shifter" to come by and let them know if they could work the next day.

In the mid-thirties, when John L. Lewis got the right to organize workers, both Burgess and Austin joined the United Mine Workers of America. Wages were up to $5.40 per day within two years, something to talk about then. Strikes, in which the union had to truck food into Fireco, were to follow.

But Austin's memories of Raleigh County history go back farther than that. In the 1920s, the Virginian Railway served Fireco with passenger service into both Mullens and, at one point, Beckley. Burgess came to Fireco before the railroad, when there were only three houses and farming was the only occupation. There were no trees in Fireco then; today there are no farms.

The white house with blue trim which serves the Austin family today sits just above the siding where the Virginian used to rest at night. The Austins have lived in their present home "up on the hill" for 23 years. Mrs. Austin was born and reared in Fireco. She has 14 children and 10 grandchildren. The burden of caring for 15 persons, four partially disabled and none eligible for employment, takes a good deal of her daily time.

Edward Austin was born on Nov. 9, 1909 in Selma, Ala. He came to Fireco in 1925 and was a coal miner for the age of 16 until 1956. Both he and Burgess receive miners' pensions which make up the major part of the family's income.

Both men have been through many of the hardships that were, and still are to some extent, "the miner's lot." Earning $2.40 a day, then joining the union, the men saw the beginning of a change which has yet to be completed. Four strikes, one of six weeks' duration, have been recorded by Fireco miners.

During one wildcat strike, John L. Lewis was fined an extremely large amount ty the courts and the miners in Fireco chipped in $50 per man to help out the union. No doubt that money, sorely needed after a strike, was a painful loss to many families.

Austin apparently suffers from silicosis, a disease that saps his strength and threatens his health. Yet "company" doctors have other names for the disease and he is yet to draw compensation for his illness.

It's been years since Fireco had a doctor, and today when illness sets in you "rice out to the hospital (Beckley Appalachian Regional Hospital) just as hard as you can go." With medical expenses rising and their need a daily reality for the Austins, the Mountaineer Family Health Plan has apparently been a blessing for them. Austin is also vice president of the Fireco Community Action Association. Their work was instrumental in obtaining running water for their homes just recently. Fireco had gone a period of 20 years without a water supply and 40 years without water in the homes.

Austin keeps busy, helping to paint the local church and maintaining a garden. When he gets a chance, he goes fishing. Mrs. Austin also has a garden, but little spare time. She cans most of the things they grow to keep the family above water. Incidentally, it's a family policy to stay out of one another's garden.

The family income consists of miners' pensions, Social Security, and welfare. They are barely adequate. Welfare, for example, pays $19 per month to Mrs. Carter and to Mrs. Austin's sister, Della. This is supposed to pay for food, leaving out rent, medical care, clothing, and a good deal of "the American Dream." But the Austins are undaunted by the hardships they have faced. Their children who are grown up have left the area in search of better opportunities. The Austins took advantage of every opportunity that came their way, and certainly they have worked as hard as anyone else. But the American Dream never quite applied to everyone, and that not our fault, is it?

Were it not for those photos in the National Archives, I have to admit that I would not have thought about the Austins for this book, having not really heard anything about the family since my adolescence. But, I am glad they are part of it, because their quiet life of raising a family and caring for others is an example of what is best in us, and their family history quite a story, bridging the gap between pre-Civil War cotton fields and the West Virginia coal mines.

Constantine Clinton Barnett (1869 - 1935), physician and educator. *When "separate but equal" usually wasn't, he brought healthcare and nursing education to Huntington.*

The Mediterranean-style brick building at 1201 7th Avenue in Huntington, the last time I saw it, anyhow, was in decline, despite having been placed on the National Register of Historic Places in 2009.

It had been owned by the Trustees of the International Hod Carriers' Building and Common Laborer's Union from 1947 through 2007. It began life as a frame house, but was modified and grew through additions in 1912, 1918, 1925, and perhaps more times as well. Why was more space needed? Because the building was transformed from a residence to a hospital in 1912, and concurrently a nursing school, in 1918, under the direction of Dr. Constantine Clinton Barnett.

Dr. Barnett was born in Buckingham County, Virginia just four years after the end of the Civil War. His father, Nelson Barnett, had been born into slavery, but became a prominent Baptist minister, so C. C.'s circumstances may have been somewhat better than many others around him. His mother, also born into slavery, was the former Bettie Woodson. The family relocated to Huntington when C. C. was just a toddler, and Huntington was really not yet much of a town. As is still common today, other extended family members often migrate after one group has "made it" in a certain area, and this happened with the Barnetts, which is how C. C.'s younger cousin Carter G. Woodson, the founder of Black History Month, eventually followed his elder brother and ended up in Huntington as well.

C. C. attended school in Huntington and Ironton, and then attended the University of Michigan at Ann Arbor before transferring to Howard University School of Medicine, where he graduated in 1899. To support himself through school, he had what we would now call side-gigs, including barbering and working in a hotel. He taught in Kentucky briefly, and then returned home to practice medicine in 1901.

The fast-growing railroad town was the recipient of many immigrants, and had no real shortage of doctors or hospitals...for White folks. But, in the age of strict segregation, Black patients were treated by White doctors and, if hospitalization was needed, either denied access altogether, or cared for in segregated wards, where the same "separate but equal" disparity was all too often apparent. Since the few Black doctors did not have admitting privileges in the hospitals, there was little choice. After several years of private practice, C. C. saw the need for a separate facility, and the Barnett Hospital opened in 1912. It eventually grew to 50 beds, 10 doctors, 8 nurses, 2 operating rooms, and an x-ray department, and became nationally recognized for its efficient administration and positive outcomes.

C. C.'s first wife, Katie, died in 1909. He married his second wife, Clara, a trained nurse, in 1912. As the hospital prospered, they saw both a need and an opportunity, and opened a concurrent nursing school at the facility, at the time the only higher education option open to African-Americans in the city. The school eventually won accreditation by the National Medical Association, something rare for Black institutions of the day. He later pushed for the formation of Lakin State Hospital for the treatment of mental illness in the African-American community, and served as its director for a time. It was the very first facility specifically established for the treatment of Black mental patients in the country.

Even with all the success and recognition, the Barnett Hospital could not withstand the Great Depression. Having mortgaged the building to stay afloat, C. C. lost ownership of it to the bank. The City continued to operate it as a hospital until 1939, when it closed for good. The last I heard, the building had been bought from the Union by someone with a keen sense of history, with intentions of preservation. I hope she can succeed.

The *Hinton Daily News* reported on February 27, 1935:

DR. BARNETT CONTINUES ILL – Dr. C. C. Barnett of Huntington continues to be seriously ill in the hospital in Huntington. Dr. Barnett is the former superintendent of the State hospital at Lakin, and a very little hope is held for his recovery.

He did recover somewhat, but not for long. He died on December 29, 1935 of hypertension and heart disease. When the new Frederick Douglass High School building was constructed on 10th Avenue in the 1920s, the original facility, built in 1891 on 8th Avenue and 16th Street (now Hal Greer Boulevard), became an elementary school and was renamed Barnett Elementary, in C. C.'s honor. The building was demolished in 1994. If I am not mistaken, AutoZone Auto Parts now occupies the space.

John Warren Davis (1888 – 1980), educator and civil rights leader.
He brought national attention to West Virginia's largest HBC.

History is too often thought of as distant, but it certainly is not. As this is being written, I am not quite old enough to draw Social Security, yet had many conversations as a lad with my great-grandmother, whose father was a soldier in the Civil War. Also as this is being written, there are still children of parents born into slavery living here in America. An example is Mr. Daniel Smith, age 89, who is a Korean War veteran and lives in Washington. His father, Abram, was born on a plantation in Massies Mill, Virginia, and Daniel is a result of Abram's later-in-life marriage to a younger woman. So, not distant at all, especially when you think about the different times one life can span. John W. Davis (definitely not to be confused with West Virginia's only presidential nominee) is an example, having been actively involved with civil rights pioneers Booker T. Washington and W. E. B. Du Bois, but also consulted during the Jimmy Carter administration.

John was born in Milledgeville, Georgia, the son of Robert Marion and Katie Mann Davis. Robert was a merchant. His mother was classified as "Mulatto," her father being a White minister and her mother Black. It was in his maternal grandmother's home that he was primarily raised, after his parents moved to Savannah with their other children. He was an exceptional student, and, at age 15, enrolled in Atlanta Baptist College, which eventually became Morehouse. He was a defensive end on the football team, earned an honors degree in Education, and did what would today be called "Work/Study" as the personal servant of the college's first Black president, John Hope. His college roommate was Mordecai Wyatt Johnson, who later became president of Howard University. After being promoted to the business office, John earned enough to attend graduate school at the University of Chicago, earning a Ph. D in chemistry and physics before returning to his alma mater to teach. While at Morehouse, he became friends with both Booker T. Washington and W. E. B. Du Bois, eventually siding more with the latter's philosophy.

John married Bessie Rucker in 1916. She was the daughter of Henry Allan Rucker, who had been born into slavery but became a long-term head of revenue collection in Georgia during Reconstruction, a position that made him a powerful force in the state's Republican Party, and one of the country's most influential Black politicians. Bessie died in Charleston at the age of 40. Her death certificate lists liver cancer as the cause. John remarried in 1932, to Ethel Elizabeth McGhee, the dean of women at Spelman College in Atlanta.

In 1919, John was enticed to the Mountain State, by being offered the presidency of what was then called the West Virginia Collegiate Institute, in Institute. Today, of course, named West Virginia State University, it was one of the original nineteen land-grant colleges established by the Morrill Act of 1890. (See more on the interesting history of the school, first called the West Virginia Colored Institute and built on the grounds of a slave-holding plantation, in the section on mathematician/scientist Katherine Johnson). His close friend Carter T. Woodson served as the Academic Dean, while also working on his groundbreaking *Journal of Negro History*.

Things were not good at the school when John arrived. Its buildings were not in good repair, and its academic program not particularly respected. With Woodson's help, Davis wasted no time in improving the institution. Though known as a strict taskmaster, he called in assistance and advice from his considerable circle of influential associates, and the school's reputation began to change, so much so that it became the country's first African-American college to be accredited by the North Central Association of Colleges and Schools, in 1927.

John remained as the school's president through 1953, seeing enrollment increase almost a hundred fold during that time. And, by then, the greatest change to American education was on the horizon: integration, which he supported, knowing the "separate but equal" paradigm of the past was anything but. In 1946, he said, "Negro education postulates doctrines of minimization of personality, social and economic mediocrity, and second class citizenship. The remaining task for it is to die. The aim of all segregated institutions should be to work themselves out of a job." Remember, this was almost a decade before *Brown v. Board of Education of Topeka*.

So intent was his belief that he began enrolling White students in the late 1940s, even when it was technically illegal to do so. With its central location between Charleston's Morris Harvey and Huntington's Marshall, the school was a great choice for servicemen and women returning from World War II with GI Bill education benefits. By the early 1960s, a majority of the school's students were White.

Among the many accomplishments John brought to the school was an innovative extension service. He was able to secure government funding from the Works Progress Administration and the State to establish Camp Washington-Carver in Fayette County, as an African-American 4-H camp and education center.

Now, for some of you, the mention of Camp Carver brings back some of the same memories it does for me, I bet. The Dixie Cups. The Platters. Chubby Checker. The Coasters. The Shirelles. Freddie Cannon. Lou Christie. And, my personal all-time favorites, The Drifters. DOO WOP SATURDAY NIGHT. The annual outdoor oldies concert ran for 18 years, until the bigger name oldies acts began fading away, and, with them, the attendance.

Remember when the park personnel began checking your coolers as you walked in to stake out your spot in front of the stage? No, it didn't work with me, either, but that's another story, right? Good times.

John's national reputation grew along with the college's. He was first appointed to a Presidential Advisory Committee by Herbert Hoover in 1931, and served every subsequent president in some capacity for the rest of his life. Harry Truman appointed him as Director of the Technical Cooperation Administration program in Liberia, and John Kennedy made him a consultant to the Peace Corps in 1961. Throughout his career, he was active in the National Urban League and the NAACP, serving the latter on its Legal Defense and Educational Fund at the specific invitation of Thurgood Marshall.
After retiring, John and Ethel moved to New Jersey. He suffered a heart attack at home and died at age 92. His obituary from the *Washington Post:*

Dr. John Warren Davis, 92, a retired college president and former government official who was a consultant to The NAACP in New York, died Saturday at his home in Englewood, N.J., after a heart attack.

Dr. Davis was president of West Virginia State College in Institute, W.Va., from 1919 to 1953. He was director of the Technical Cooperation Administration, Point IV, program in Liberia from 1952 to 1954.

He had been affiliated with the NAACP's Legal Defense and Education Fund in New York City since 1955. Over the years he administered scholarship programs for black undergraduate and law students. He had been a consultant since 1972.

Dr. Davis was a native of Milledgeville, Ga., and was a 1911 graduate of Morehouse College. He did graduate work at the University of Chicago and was awarded honorary doctorates by West Virginia State College and Harvard and Howard universities.

He was a member of the National Science Board of the National Science Foundation from 1950 to 1956 and had been a consultant to the old U.S. Information Agency on minority hiring.

Survivors include his wife, Ethel McGhee Davis, of Englewood; two daughters, Dorothy D. McDaniel of Memphis, Tenn., and Caroline D. Gleiter of Falls Church; two grandchildren, and three great-grandchildren.

The family suggests that expressions of sympathy be in the form of contributions to the NAACP Legal Defense and Education Fund in New York City or to West Virginia State College in Institute.

Elizabeth Simpson Drewry (1893 - 1979), teacher and legislator.
Possibly a victim of election shenanigans early in her career, she made up for it as a tireless and effective leader.

Elizabeth Simpson Drewry represents another "first" for African-Americans in the Mountain State, as the first Black woman elected to the West Virginia Legislature. Note *elected to.* Minnie Buckingham

Harper, also written about in these pages, was the first Black woman in the West Virginia Legislature, or any other legislature in the United States of America, for that matter. But, she was appointed to fill the seat after her husband's death, and was never elected. Elizabeth got there solely on her own.

During the coal boom, McDowell County was an incredibly diverse place. There were large Italian and Hungarian and other European immigrant populations, and a sizable Black community in most towns, with many families coming up from the south, particularly Alabama, North Carolina, and Virginia, to work the mines or provide services to the burgeoning coal camps. Elizabeth's was one of these. Her father, H. Grant Simpson, was a barber, and her mother, Katherine Douglass Simpson, a homemaker. They were originally from Pittsylvania County, Virginia, and Elizabeth's biography states she was born there. The 1910 census for Elkhorn shows us the family of Grant Simpson, 40, barber, born in Virginia, and Kate Simpson, 38, also born in Virginia. Both are listed as "Mulatto" and still have several children at home.

Elizabeth became a mother herself at a very young age, only 14 according to her biography on file with the West Virginia Department of Arts, Culture, and History. She married William H. Drewry, a professor at Bluefield Institute (later Bluefield State College) The paper trail is a bit confusing, as is often the case. The 1930 census shows Elizabeth, age 38, as married, but the Head of Household, with daughter Lucile Drury, 23; sister Alphonso Hunnicutt, 30; niece Anna Hunnicutt, 5; and boarder Malinda Cobbs, 70. William died in Chicago in 1951.

Elizabeth attended school in Ohio, and then graduated from Bluefield Institute in 1934 with a degree in Elementary Education. She taught in the Black coal camp schools in the county, and was active in Delta Sigma Theta, the National Association of Colored Women, the Red Cross, NAACP, and many other community improvement organizations.

Her political involvement, and particularly her party affiliation, followed a familiar pattern. She was, at first, active in the Republican

Party. Since the Civil War, most African-American politicians had been Republicans, the Party of Lincoln. But, with the Great Depression and the New Deal, many supported FDR and the programs that bolstered things like labor union membership, workplace safety rules, Social Security, and other programs. The shift in affiliation that began with FDR continued over the next half century, and was greatly accelerated by the time Richard Nixon's "southern strategy" to bring southern White voters opposed to civil rights legislation into the GOP. Today, look at the electoral college map after a presidential election, and the makeup of state legislatures in the south, and it looks like the shift has been pretty much complete. The term "solid south" once meant solidly Democratic, but now means just the opposite.

There are "green shoots," though, as seen in Virginia and Georgia in 2020. But, that, too, is another story.

Elizabeth's first political activity was as a Republican poll worker in 1921. In 1936, she changed her party affiliation and eventually became a member of the McDowell County Democratic Executive Committee after serving on the Northfork Town Council. She first ran for a seat in the House of Delegates in 1946, and again in 1948, but was not successful.

Remember I used the term *shenanigans* above? Here's what happened: By 1948, McDowell County was solidly Democratic, and had five House of Delegates seats. The race was really decided in the primary, since the five Democratic nominees were all but assured to be elected in November. The number of votes separating Elizabeth and rich White guy coal operator Harry Pauley of Iaeger for that final slot on the general election ticket was very small. In the initial vote count, Elizabeth was pronounced the winner. But, Pauley (did I mention he was a rich White guy coal operator?) protested and demanded a recount, which disclosed 64 disputed ballots.

Care to guess how many of the 64 disputed ballots were declared for Pauley? Yeah, all 64, giving him a 32 vote victory over Elizabeth. Pauley went on to become Speaker of the House in the early 1960s.

Elizabeth's defeat was only temporary. In 1950, she won the fifth spot on the Democratic ticket, and received nearly 18,000 votes in the general election, going on to serve 13 years in the House.

As could be expected from her profession and community service work, she became an advocate for education, labor rights, civil rights, and women's rights. One of her landmark successes is a little hard to believe looking backward from today: She introduced legislation to allow women to serve on juries.

She introduced that bill in 1955. Only four years before I was born, women could not serve on juries in our state. We were the last in the country to "allow" that basic civil right to women.

Mountaineers may always be free, but our politics have not always been smart.

In declining health, Elizabeth retired from her long legislative tenure in 1964.

Now, for some more shenanigans: Apparently, in 1951, someone tried to bribe Elizabeth to vote the coal operator's way on a mine safety bill. This from the *Hinton Leader*, March 1, 1951:

School Supervisor Said to Have Tried to Bribe Delegate

House Investigating Alleged Crime in Connection With Bill

CHARLESTON – Mrs. Elizabeth Drewry, D., McDowell, yesterday identified state Negro school supervisor, I. J. K. Wells, as the man who offered her a $1,000 bribe in connection with the hotly-debated :fire boss" issue.
Mrs. Drewry, testifying before a House investigating committee, said Wells approached her before the Feb. 16 session and told her he would give her the money if she voted to keep the bill out of committee.

She said she refused the offer and has not seen the man since, but was positive in her convictions. Wells did not appear before the committee and it was reported that he was out of the state.

Howard Thompson, assistant Sergeant At Arms, reported that Wells was en-route to Charleston from a national Education Association meeting in Atlantic City. Thompson said he got the information from the man's wife when he tried to serve a summons on Wells Thursday.

Mrs. Drewry, a school teacher at North Fork and the only Negro in the legislature, told the investigation she was approached the same morning on the street by a white man with the same offer. She said she would be unable to recognize the ma if she saw him again.

W. L. Mills, another McDowell delegate, testified that he was offered $5,000 to be split between him and Del. Jerry Stidham, D. Logan, if they saw to it that the bill got out of the mines committee with a favorable report.

Stidham is chairman and Mills co-chairman of the mines committee. Mills said the matter was dropped after Mrs. Drewry told of her attempted bribe before the House. The two delegates appeared before the special five-man committee appointed Monday to investigate bribery charges and "any other undue pressure" exerted against any House member.

-clutches pearls- Gasp! Such a thing in West Virginia politics! Can you imagine?

Toward the end of her career, during a particularly contentious session in 1963, Elizabeth was quoted in the *Raleigh Register* talking about the legislative debate: "This is the worst I've ever seen. Why, I believe they'll have plain old fist fights right here on the floor of the House!" (February 1, 1963)

I think, even then, my money would have been on you, Elizabeth.

Memphis Tennessee Carter Garrison (1890 - 1988), educator and activist. *She spent a lifetime doing the hard, everyday footwork of fostering equality in the Mountain State.*

One of my former bosses used to say, "There are show horses, and work horses. I would rather have work horses." Now, I am not okay with comparing people to livestock of any kind, and I mentioned that at the time. True, there are people who like the limelight and recognition for what they do, and they are necessary to inspire others. But there are also people who quietly but tirelessly do the job without regard for recognition, and I find them even more inspiring, mission-focused and task-driven, in the language of my former career as a federal bureaucrat. Memphis Tennessee Garrison was one of the latter, living a long and productive life bettering our state.

Memphis was born near Roanoke, but her father moved the family to McDowell County for work in the coal mines when Memphis was a child. Her parents, Wesley and Cassie Hairston Carter, had both been born into slavery. I haven't located a death certificate for Wesley, but Cassie died in Gary in November 1941, and was living with Memphis, by then long (since 1918) married to William M. "Melvin" Garrison, at the time, and her status was "Widowed." Melvin was a coal mine electrician, and he and Memphis did not have children.

She attended the segregated school available to her, and then went on to earn a BA with honors at Bluefield State College. She taught in the McDowell County public schools until her retirement, completed advanced studies at The Ohio State University, became the first female president of the West Virginia Teacher's Association, and was active in the NAACP, pushing West Virginia to pass an anti-lynching law and involving the Black community in the Easter Seals campaign. She also became a mediator and welfare worker for the coal company (a subsidiary of U. S. Steel at the time), helping settle racial disputes and bringing nutrition and recreational programs to the area.

That activism didn't come without a cost in those days, though, and she was suspended from teaching for a year for engaging in political activity. After retirement, she moved to Huntington in 1952 and continued her community work the rest of her life. Her modest house at 1702 10TH Avenue is now owned by the Carter G. Woodson Memorial Foundation and has been placed on the National Register of Historic Places, and the African-American Civil Rights Historic Preservation Fund granted almost $150,000 toward its restoration in 2020. Memphis is buried in Forest Lawn Memorial Gardens, in Huntington, mission-focused and task-driven to the end.

This memorial is from the Huntington *Herald-Dispatch*:

HUNTINGTON -- She sent textbooks to Africa, shed light on the desegregation movement and worked with children others considered a lost cause. The list of accomplishments by Memphis Tennessee Garrison is so long it's hard to imagine that anyone could forget her. But many people still don't know who she was, according to Lynda Ann Ewen, a retired Marshall University professor who co-edited "Memphis Tennessee Garrison: The Remarkable Story of a Black Appalachian Woman. "Garrison passed away in 1988, but not before she made her mark on Huntington, on West Virginia and on the country," Ewen said. "Garrison is probably the most important woman in West Virginia history. She represented West Virginia in the very early part of the civil rights movement in this country. She held national offices in the NAACP. She was sent to organize chapters across the country," she said.

Garrison's research with children with developmental problems went on to be used by Columbia University. She was also the first female president of the West Virginia State Teachers Association and became vice president of the American Teachers Association. "She had many opportunities to leave the region, but never would. She claimed she was a West Virginian heart and soul," Ewen said. During the Depression and long before breakfast programs, Ewen said Garrison brought meals to schools for the kids. "Any one single thing she did, we probably have other people who did those kinds of things. What's remarkable is the long series of things she did and the number of firsts she was involved in," Ewen said. Newatha Myers, president of the Carter G. Woodson Foundation, said Garrison was one of her mentors. "She was a great lady," she said. Myers recalled Garrison teaching her how to do the NAACP's Christmas Seal drive, right down to mailing the actual envelopes. Rather than start a family of her own, Myers said Garrison chose to dedicate herself to the civil rights movement." That was her life, fighting for freedom and justice," Myers said. The Woodson Foundation owns the Huntington properties formerly owned by Garrison, and is currently working to clean up her former home at 1701 10th Ave. Myers hopes the home will become a museum for Garrison artifacts so the young "will remember their past and get involved in the future." Phil Carter, a social work professor at MU, said Garrison should be among the first recognized on "walls of fame" or monuments in Cabell County. "She is and was an icon among the leaders of the NAACP, nationally, internationally and locally," he said. He said Garrison was a known and trusted leader who formed partnerships with many interest groups. She took her skills from McDowell County, where she grew up, to Huntington, where she lived for more than 30 years. He said Garrison also advised students in the local Student Nonviolence Coordination Committee, which led the desegregation movement in the 1960s in Huntington. "She was an inspirational person," he said.

Leon P. Miller (1899 - 1980), lawyer and judge. *McDowell County is the home of several political "firsts" for African-American Mountaineers, but Judge Miller offered a twist.*

We have talked about the political realignment that slowly brought the bulk of Black Mountaineers from the Party of Lincoln to the Party of Franklin D. Roosevelt, John F. Kennedy, Lyndon B. Johnson, and Barack H. Obama. That realignment had largely taken place by 1968, but West Virginia's first Black elected judge, Leon P. Miller, definitely put his own stamp on McDowell County politics. Not only was he a Black Republican, but he won election as a write-in candidate, something notoriously difficult in the state.

Born in Tennessee and having grown up in Roanoke, Miller was a graduate of A & T College and the University of Pennsylvania College of Law. He first practiced in Williamson beginning in 1922, then moved to Welch two years later to form a partnership with Harry J. Capehart and Arthur Froe, back when most Black Mountaineers were still members of the GOP. He must have been counted amongst the "party faithful, because President Eisenhower appointed him as United States Attorney for the Virgin Islands, a post he held from 1954 through 1962. With that substantial portfolio, he was appointed to temporarily fill the McDowell judgeship when the incumbent, Judge I. R. Morgan, died in office before the May, 1968 primary. Neither party, though, had a candidate file for the primary in time to be placed on the ballot, so there were none on the general election ballot. Write-ins ruled the day.

Well, write-ins and stickers.

Stickers? Ah, the joys of West Virginia politics. You see, if you want to be "written in," you didn't have to be actually, um, *written*. A voter could simply attach a gummed sticker with the desired candidate's name on it onto the paper ballot, and voila! A write-in vote!

Of course, with modern voting machines, that's no longer an issue. The practice gained some notoriety in 1976, when long-time Congressman Ken Hechler, a native New Yorker who had been on President Harry Truman's staff, had marched with Dr. King from Selma to Montgomery, and worked tirelessly for Black Lung legislation, decided to run for governor instead of reelection to the House of Representatives, where he held the record for not missing a vote. Losing badly in the primary, he ran a write-in campaign in his old southern coalfield district, against the nominee, newcomer Nick J. Rahall, a young protégé of Senator Robert Byrd. His stickers were everywhere, distributed by faithful supporters. I remember seeing them floating along the side of the road, on the sidewalk, in the schoolyard, just about anywhere one choose to look in the days leading up to the November general election. It was not to be, but he closed his elected career by serving multiple terms as West Virginia Secretary of State.

As folks went to the polls in McDowell County during the 1968 general election, poll workers offered them stickers with sitting temporary Judge Miller's name, and, when the counting was done, McDowell had its first Republican elected to a county-wide office since the 1930s.

From the *Welch Daily News*, November 13, 1968

Miller Elected Criminal Judge

McDowell County, West Virginia's most southern area, today held the probable distinction of giving the state its first Negro judge.

An official canvass of the general election vote was completed here Tuesday afternoon, revealing that Welch Attorney Leon P. Miller has been elected Judge of the McDowell Criminal Court by a write-in vote. He is 69.

Tallies showed that Miller received a total of 1,317 write-ins and 1,197 "sticker votes." He easily nosed out Beediah Hassan, Welch native and now practicing law in Charleston, who was given a total of 666 votes, 484, of them write-ins and 182 "sticker votes." A surprising 74 write in votes were counted for T. J. Scott of Welch.

Miller, who has been serving as special judge of the court since last April, will qualify for office and will be sworn in as soon as the McDowell County Court certifies him as the victor. He has been named to the Bench by the McDowell County Bar each term of court since the death of Judge L. R. Morgan.

Although Morgan died before the May primary neither party entered a candidate on the ballot for the November 5 general election. But a write-in campaign for Miller and Hassan was quietly organized and on election day gummed stickers for both men were passed out to voters.

The new jurist is also the first Republican elected to a major office in this county since the early 30s.

Local observers today pointed out that the write-in vote was a personal tribute to the new jurist who overcame strong party ties in overwhelmingly Democratic McDowell County.

A native of Knoxville, Tenn., Judge Miller was born April 27, 1899 and was reared in Roanoke, Va. He attended school there before enrolling in A and T College at Greensboro, N. C.

The jurist received his law degree from the University of Pennsylvania Law School in 1922 and practiced at Williamson for two years before coming to Welch in 1924.

He and the late Harry J. Capehart, Sr., were partners in a successful law firm for many years. In 1954, President Dwight D. Eisenhower appointed Miller as United States Attorney for the Virgin Islands. He held that post until 1962 when he returned to Welch to resume the practice of law.

During the Republican administrations of the late 20s, Judge Miller served as an assistant prosecuting attorney for the county from 1928 to 1932. He was married to the former Miss Mildred Foster of Greensboro, N. C. They reside on Court Street.

Judge and Mrs. Miller are parents of three daughters, all of whom have distinguished themselves in public service. Mrs. Artrelle Wheatley of Caracas, Venezuela is a former worker for the Ford Foundation.

At the request of the government she gave up the post when her husband became head of the peace corps in Caracas.

Mrs. Jane Miller Johnson is presently employed by the Presbyterian Hospital of New York as a psychiatric social worker. The third daughter is Mrs. Lydia Patricia Miller Adams, of the Virgin Islands, a physical therapist in charge of the Island's crippled children's division.

The Millers also have five grandchildren.

When Judge Miller retired from the position after four years, he made *Jet* magazine's Words of the Week column, in the January 11, 1973 issue. He was quoted as saying, "When I see a young man who has stolen something on a lark when he was half drunk, I can't help thinking that there are men in Charleston who have stolen millions and are walking around free." I can't disagree with that, Yerhonor.

Leon Miller is buried at Restlawn Memorial Gardens in Bluefield.

Dr. Mildred Mitchell-Bateman (1922 - 2012), physician, mental health advocate, and administrator. *She helped move mental health treatment into the twenty-first century.*

The formerly-named Huntington State Hospital is the second oldest in the state, created by the legislature in 1897, and originally called the State Home for Incurables, not exactly a title meant to exude optimism. By the 1950s, it had a census of nearly 1,800 patients, including developmentally disabled and geriatric cases. Over time, more enlightened treatment paradigms reduced "warehousing" patients, and today the institution is a 90-bed facility closely associated with Marshall Medical School. Since 1999, it is no longer Huntington State Hospital, but, instead, Mildred Mitchell-Bateman Hospital, named after the first African-American woman to head an agency in West Virginia state government. Mildred was appointed Director of the Department of Mental Health in 1962, and served in that office for fifteen years.

Mildred was born in Brunswick, Georgia. Her father Suder was an influential minister, who had been born in South Carolina. Her mother Ella was a nurse and native Georgian. Like so many others after World War II, the family eventually made their way north, where Suder became pastor of the First African Presbyterian Church, on 18th and Christian Streets, in Philadelphia, one of the city's largest Black congregations. He was, at the time of his death, the only Black representative on the Presbyterian Church USA Board of Foreign Missions.

Rev. Mitchell's story is quite interesting in its own right. I found this in a book titled *History of the American Negro – South Carolina Edition*, edited and apparently self-published by Arthur Bunyan Caldwell in 1919:

The Presbyterian Church has always insisted on an educated ministry, so one finds at the head of the Presbyterian work in the State, even among the Colored people, college men, equipped not only for the religious, but for the educational leadership of their people. Frequently, indeed, their ministers are also teachers, sometimes in parochial school, sometimes in the public school, sometimes combining the two. Thus the forces making for intelligence are closely correlated with the forces making for character.

Among the capable young men of the race devoting themselves to this line of endeavor must be mentioned Rev. Suder Quilerford Mitchell, pastor of the Presbyterian Church and Principal of the graded school at the historic old college town of Due West.

He is a native of Mayesville, in Sumter County, where he was born October 9th, 1889. His parents were Benjamin and Charlotte (Prince) Mitchell. At an early age the earnestness of the elder Mitchell and his pastor, Rev. I. D. Davis, D. D., became a helpful influence and later developed into a dominant factor in the life of this young man. As a boy, young Mitchell attended Good Will Academy, where he made a good, clean record as a student. Later he matriculated at Biddle University, wining his Bachelor's degree in 1911. Of the twenty-five who graduated at that time, he stood third. He spent the next year at Biddle, specializing in Philosophy and Languages. This was followed by the Theological Course in the same institution, leading to the S. T. B. degree in 1915. While in Biddle, he spent his vacations largely in the Pullman service, which took him to every part of the country and gave him that breadth of vision and range of personal experience which comes from travel alone. So apart from the money thus earned, what he learned during his vacations supplemented hat he got from his books during the school term. He began active work in 1912, while engaged on his theological course.

While in college he was President of the Athletic Association, President of the Y. M. C. A, advanced to the office of Commandant in the Military Department, which then existed; a member of the University Quintet. While connected with the Quintet, he attended and sang before five General Assemblies of the Presbyterian Church in the U. S. A. He trains his own choir now and does most of his playing. Next after the Bible, his favorite reading is Biography.

In 1915, he was called to work at Due West, where both Church and school have prospered under his administration. At least fifty members have been added to the Church and a new school building is in contemplation.

Though young in years, Rev. Mitchell comes to his work well equipped and is a "workman who needeth not be ashamed of his workmanship." He regards a liberal education supplemented by industrial development as, perhaps, the most pressing need of his people. Rev. Mitchell has taken no active part in politics, but is a member of both the Masons and the Pythians. He owns property in York County.

"…even among the Colored people…" Hard to read, I know, but that's the way it was written. Suder was the son of Ben and Charlotte Mitchell, both born around 1850, and both, most likely, into slavery, since I cannot find evidence otherwise in the census. What a journey this family made in three generations.

Mildred attended Barger-Scotia College and Johnson C. Smith University in North Carolina, and then on to medical school at The Women's Medical College of Pennsylvania, graduating in 1946. That institution, on Arch Street in Philadelphia (a stroll down which takes one past Ben Franklin's grave and Betsy Ross's house), was the second medical institution in the world established specifically to educate female MDs, and is now part of the Drexel University College of Medicine. The young doctor came to the Mountain State for an internship at Lakin State Hospital near Pt. Pleasant. Lakin State, opened in 1926, was originally named the "Lakin State Hospital for the Colored Insane," and was, at the time, one of only two psychiatric institutions in the country entirely run by African-Americans serving an all-Black population. After her internship, she spent three years at the Meringer School of Psychiatry in Topeka, Kansas, but returned to Lakin State as the clinical director, eventually being named its superintendent, in 1958. She married therapist William L. Bateman in 1947.

When the state's Department of Mental Health director Charles Zeller died while in office during 1962, then-Governor Wally Barron named her acting director, and then director, the first Black woman to lead a state agency. During her fifteen-year tenure, she advocated placing patients closer to their homes, recognizing the importance of family and community contact. She became the first Black woman to serve as vice-president of the American Psychiatric Association, and served on President Carter's Commission on Mental Health. When the Department of Mental Health was merged with the Department of Health during the 1977 state government reorganization, Mildred resigned and became the head of the Psychiatry Department at the newly-opened Marshall Medical School.

Her obituary, from the *Leaf-Chronicle*, Clarksville, Tennessee, published on January 28, 2012:

Mental health pioneer Mitchell-Bateman Dies

Dr. Mildred Mitchell-Bateman, a mental health pioneer in West Virginia and the namesake of a state-run psychiatric hospital, has died. She was 89.

Family members tell media outlets that Mitchell-Bateman died Wednesday evening a Charleston Area Medical Center's General hospital. Her daughter, Donna Taylor of Charleston, said she had recently developed pneumonia.

"She was amazing," Taylor said. "She and my dad instilled in me the importance of education and how it can improve your lifestyle and impact those around you."
In 1962, Mitchell-Bateman became the first black woman to head a state agency when she was named director of the former state Department of Mental Health. She held that position for 15 years, until then-Gov. Jay Rockefeller merged the agency into the larger Department of Health.

Mitchell-Bateman resigned as director and became chair of the Psychiatry Department of Marshall University's medical school.

Mildred Mitchell-Bateman Hospital in Huntington was named for her in 1999. According to the hospital's website, Mitchell-Bateman was an advocate of community health centers and placing mentally ill patients in facilities near their homes. She also developed a program aimed at giving hope to patients who had been considered untreatable.

Daughter Danielle Shanklin of North Lauderdale, Fla., said her mother fought for equality and justice.

"She was sent here, I believe, as a guardian of people,: she said.

Born in Brunswick, Ga., Mitchell-Gateman was the daughter of a minister and a registered nurse. At 12, she helped Red Cross volunteers after a tornado ripped through her hometown. She decided then, in an era when even her own mother wondered if it was possible, to become a doctor.

She studied at colleges in North Carolina and Pennsylvania. While interning in Philadelphia, she landed a job in West Virginia as a staff physician at Lakin State Hospital, then a hospital for black mentally ill patients.

She married therapist William L. Bateman, then left Lakin to practice medicine privately and study psychiatry. She later returned to Lakin and eventually became its superintendent. There, she helped improve salaries and limited the employees' work week to 40 hours.

Mitchell-Bateman changed the way patients were housed, integrating those with low social skills with the larger population. She also gave patients training for jobs at the hospital and paid them hourly wages, replacing the chips they had been given to redeem at the hospital canteen.

She was a pioneer, indeed.

Major General James W. Monroe (1940 -), soldier and the U. S. Army's 28ᵗʰ Chief of Ordnance. A young ROTC student at West Virginia State College met his wife and began an outstanding military career in the Mountain State.

West Virginians have always been at the forefront of America's military. While General Monroe was born a Tar Heel, his path to success was set upon in Institute. His father was a farmer and sometimes electrician in Scotland County, North Carolina. He came to West Virginia State College, now West Virginia State University, for the ROTC program, but also played basketball, the saxophone, and joined Omega Psi Phi.

James began his career at Fort Knox, Kentucky, and was later a platoon leader for two armored cavalry platoons with the 9ᵗʰ Cavalry in Germany. His leadership abilities were evident, and he was selected to attend the U. S. Army Command and General Staff College at Fort Leavenworth. After a series of increasingly important posts, he was promoted to Brigadier General in 1991, and selected as the 28ᵗʰ Chief of Ordnance and commanding General of the U. S. Army Ordnance Center and School in Aberdeen, Maryland in 1994.

Now, Chief of Ordnance is quite the thing for the entire U. S. Army. Ordnance is what they do, all over the world. The office was established by the Continental Congress, and the first Chief, Benjamin Flower, was appointed in January 1775. James was the second African-American to hold the post. Brigadier General Johnnie E. Wilson, a native of Baton Rouge, Louisiana, served from 1990 – 1992.

While at West Virginia State, James met his future wife, Charlyne Williams, a Georgian. Her father Charles was an agent for the Afro-American Insurance Company, and her mother Ella, a teacher. The family relocated to Atlantic City, New Jersey, where she was a cheerleader. At State, she majored in Elementary Education, played the cello, and joined Alpha Kappa Alpha. The couple married in 1963. James's career as a soldier took them to ten states and two foreign countries during their marriage. Sadly, Charlyne succumbed to cancer in 2017, in Pompano Beach, Florida.

The Monroe's two children were Donya, who works in the financial sector in Las Vegas, and Bryan, a Pulitzer-Prize-winning journalist and university professor. Bryan once headed the National Association of Black Journalists, was a CNNPolitics.com editor, Editorial Director for *Jet* and *Ebony*, and headed the *Biloxi Sun Herald's* coverage of Hurricane Katrina, for which the Pulitzer was awarded. He died of a heart attack at his home in Bethesda, Maryland, at only fifty-five years of age, in January 2021.

Now, it's trendy these days to find a way to work a recipe into books as they are written, no matter the genre. As examples, I offer *Like Water for Chocolate*, by Laura Esquivel, the *Corinna Chapman* books by Kerry Greenwood, *A Trifle Dead* and *Drowned Vanilla* by Livia Day, and, my all-time favorite, *Fried Green Tomatoes at the Whistle Stop Café*, by Fannie Flagg. Thanks to the Davenport, Iowa *Quad-City Times* (March 3, 2004), I can offer you a recipe from Major General and Mrs. James W. Monroe, that they originally submitted for Our Lady of Victory Church's fundraising cookbook:

Keep Them Guessing Dip

1 (8-ounce) jar pineapple preserves
1 (8-ounce) jar apple jelly
1 (5-ounce) jar horseradish
¼ tablespoon course ground peppercorns
1 (8-ounce) package cream cheese
1 box of crackers

Mix together first four ingredients. Store refrigerated in an airtight container. (May be kept for six months in refrigerator.) Serve mixture over block of cream cheese with crackers. This is an excellent dip to have on hand for any occasion. Let guests try to guess how it is made. This dip is always a big hit!

We say it so much it may sound rote, but it's sincere: thank you for your service, General Monroe.

Thomas Gillis "T. Gillis" Nutter (1876 - 1959), legislator, lawyer, and businessman. *He was admitted to the American Bar Association when it "officially" did not accept African-Americans.*

Before the fall of "separate but equal" with the *Brown v. Board of Education* decision in 1954, there were many cases of cutting off one's nose to spite one's face, as the saying goes, from state and local governments, including here in the Mountain State. The case of the city swimming pool in Montgomery was an example. The city had a pool. One pool. It barred Blacks from swimming it, which was legal to do at the time. But, since *Plessy v. Ferguson* in 1896 and thanks to T. Gillis Nutter, governmental entities couldn't as easily get away with "separate" meaning "non-existent." In 1948, Nutter sued Montgomery in federal court, and won. If the city provided a swimming pool and barred Black swimmers, it would have to provide one for them as well.

How did Montgomery respond? They closed the pool, rather than open it to African-Americans. No pool for Whites, so they didn't have to provide a "separate but equal" pool for Blacks. Simple solution.

Of course, many cities and public parks across the country had swimming pools, and Nutter's victory set precedent for similar suits by the NAACP across the country. Some pools integrated, while others followed Montgomery's nose-spite-face strategy. Six years later, as a consequence to *Brown*, some counties took the same track with their entire school system. The Constitution says we have to integrate our schools? Well, you know what the Constitution doesn't say? That we have to provide public education at all. So, we'll just stop. Governor J. Lindsay Almond of Virginia, for example, closed all public schools in Charlottesville, Norfolk, and Warren Counties rather than integrate. Prince Edward County also closed all its public schools, but offered to provide tuition grants "for all students, regardless of race" to attend private schools.

Of course, as the government well knew, there were no private schools that accepted Blacks in Prince Edward County. Up through 1963, just before I started my own public schooling in the southern West Virginia coalfields, Black students either left the county to attend school or received no education in Prince Edward. It took yet another Supreme Court case, *Griffin v. County School Board of Prince Edward County* (1964) to remedy that situation.

T. Gillis Nutter was born in Princess Anne County, Maryland, to William and Emma Henry Nutter. William was the son of Caleb and Virginia Nutter, and Emma the daughter of Peter and Julia Henry. He was the eldest of two sons and two daughters, and he attended the segregated schools available to him on Maryland's rural eastern shore. He attended Howard University in Washington D. C., graduating with a law degree in 1899. His brother Isaac later did the same, and went on to found a successful criminal defense practice in Atlantic City, New Jersey.

T. Gillis, though, was called back home shortly after graduation, because his father died and the family had to be supported. He took a position as a school principal in Fairmount. After the family situation stabilized, he moved to Indiana to be admitted to the Bar, since Maryland forbade Blacks from doing so.

I am not quite sure why he decided Charleston, West Virginia was the land where his future lay, but he relocated and worked for several already-existing law firms over the next several years. Eventually, his widowed mother moved in with him, and he owned his own home at 304 Elizabeth Street. He helped organize and became an officer of the Mutual Savings and Loan Company, the only Black-owned bank in the state at that time, and worked for the state Auditor's Office.

In 1918, T. Gillis Nutter ran for the House of Delegates, and won over his White Democratic opponent in a district that was only about ten-percent Black. He was re-elected in 1920, during a time when the Ku Klux Klan was resurgent and there were very few Black officeholders between Wheeling and Miami.

Politics were beginning to realign, and this caused a rift between T. Gillis and his brother Isaac. In New Jersey, Isaac saw the beginning of a progressive agenda taking hold in the Democratic Party, despite the fact that it's conceivable that most KKK members at that time were probably Democrats. In the 1928 election, the brothers split, with T.

Gillis remaining loyal to the Republican Party and its nominee Herbert Hoover, while Isaac supported progressive Catholic Al Smith.

Who would think family members could ever fall out over politics?

T. Gillis married Sarah "Sadie" Meriwether from Washington DC, who, along with West Virginian Lavinia Norman, was one of the twenty founders of Alpha Kappa Alpha Sorority at Howard University in 1906. She helped found a chapter at West Virginia State in 1922, and was the first Black member of the West Virginia Society for Crippled Children. She died in 1950.

The Nutters were active in the NAACP and the First Baptist Church in Charleston. T. Gillis was also a member of the Knights of Pythias and Elks. He died on June 23, 1959, at St. Francis Hospital in Charleston, of heart disease and pneumonia.

Bud Peterson (1892 – 1949), *last American prisoner to be executed by hanging; and* **Matilene Dean (1925 - ?),** *convicted murderer. Their cases, though separate, affected how history would record their sentences.*

As I write this as a West Virginian transplanted to the beach in South Carolina in semi-sort-of-retirement, the Palmetto State just passed a law allowing for electrocution and a firing squad being acceptable means of execution, because those lethal injection drugs are just so darned hard to come by. As of right now, capital punishment is still illegal in the Mountain State, but the "Pro-Life, Family Values" gang that want to reinstate it so badly may well have their day. It seems to be going in that direction.

When we think of execution by hanging, we may envision cowboy movies, and certainly an antiquated practice. But, West Virginia was the last state in the Union to still have the gallows as its official execution method. The last hanging took place at Moundsville in 1949, to be replaced by electrocution in 1951. To date, nine convicted prisoners have been electrocuted, the most recent in 1959. Before that, 103 had been hung after we became a separate state in 1863. The official witnesses to the first two electrocutions included a young state delegate named Robert C. Byrd. When Raleigh County native Hulett C. Smith became governor, he supported and signed the bill abolishing the death penalty.

Bud Peterson of Logan County was the last to face the gallows. Things moved much more quickly in those days. He was sentenced on January 14, 1949, and executed just one month and eleven days later.

Bud had been part of the great migration of African-Americans into the West Virginia coalfields. Information is scant, but his death certificate states he was born in Georgia, and his only listed relative was Mrs. Annabelle McCoy, his sister. "Male, 53, Colored, Miner. Executed." is about all we get from that source. Criminal court documents say he came to West Virginia from Alabama.

So, what can we find in the census? It presents a typical story of frustration. The 1940 Census for next door Mingo County gives us the only possible candidate for being our subject that I can find. It lists, in the transcription, "Bad" Peterson and Lucile; it gives their ages as 75 and 73 (making him too old to be 'our' Bud), his birthplace Georgia and hers Mississippi. But, looking at the actual census sheet, it's plain this is yet another case of inaccurate transcription. There are question marks in the "age" box, and faint numbers penciled in to the side. The transcriptionist picked up the question marks as the number 7, adding a faint 5 to Bud's, and 3 to Lucile's. Another clue: living in Williamson at the same time is Annabelle McCoy, a lodger working as a cook, born in Alabama (remember Bud's death certificate). I am pretty sure that's them, and the exact year of Bud's birth, like so many of that era, is undetermined.

All that gives you an idea of what detective work goes into family history research, if you aren't already familiar with it. But, thankfully, in this case, that sloppy transcription is cleared up by looking back another ten years. The 1930 census clearly shows Bud, 28 and born in Georgia, and Lucile, 26 and born in Mississippi, living in Logan County. Moving from mine to mine across the Logan/Mingo/McDowell boarders during that era was common, and Bud's birth year was definitely a moving target.

On June 29, 1947, Bud argued with Bessie Annie Manns Wright, supposedly over poker money. Bessie was 40, the daughter of Monroe and Annie Thomas Manns, and, according to her death certificate, divorced from her husband George. They had been married in 1937, in Amhurstdale. The cause of her death was "gunshot wound in head and right arm."

There are few particulars of the crime near the time it occurred in the local newspapers to which I have access, but, in this case, that doesn't matter. Because the initial conviction was appealed, the West Virginia Supreme Court did us the service of giving us the full story, in great detail, via *State v. Peterson*, Opinion No. 10027, decided December 7, 1948. Peterson's lawyers, W. F. and O. D. Damron, argued that the Logan County Circuit Court had committed an error by admitting the testimony of the murdered woman's son, George Wright Jr., only seven years old at the time he was sworn in and put on the stand. The state was represented by future governor William C. Marland. The Supreme Court ruled the child's testimony admissible, there were multiple other witnesses to more circumstantial evidence, and thus Bud's fate was sealed.

From *State v. Peterson:*

"The defendant, Bud Peterson, charged with the murder of Bessie Wright on June 29, 1947, was convicted in the Circuit Court of Logan County of murder of the first degree without recommendation, and sentenced to be hanged. To this judgment of sentence, he prosecutes this writ of error.

Defendant came to the State of West Virginia from the State of Alabama in 1920. From 1925 until the time of his arrest for the alleged homicide, he had been continuously employed as a coal miner in Logan County, and when arrested he was living in the town of Riley, in Logan County, located approximately fifteen miles from the City of Logan. A bonus having been paid to the miners on June 28, 1947, Peterson, as well as other miners in Logan County, did not work.

At the trial, in order to controvert the State's position that defendant shot and killed decedent, defendant set up an alibi as his sole defense. It therefore becomes necessary to review the evidence in this case, bearing on the question of defendant's whereabouts at the time and place of the homicide.

According to the State's evidence, defendant was in the vicinity of the town of Riley from about two o'clock in the afternoon of June 28, 1947, until the time he was arrested about two o'clock in the morning of the following day. About midnight of June 28, he came to the home of William McCreery, whose home adjoins the house in which decedent, Bessie Wright, resided, and in which she met her death, and tried to borrow five dollars for the purpose of entering a poker game. Upon his request being refused, he stated that he would go to the Wright home and get the money "or raise sand." Defendant then left the McCreery home, and was seen by McCreery and his wife to proceed across the lot between the two houses and then go up on decedent's porch. According to McCreery, who is corroborated in substantial detail by his wife, defendant "hollered and knocked on the door". Receiving no answer, he yelled that if decedent did not open the door, "he would take an axe and knock the damn thing down." But still receiving no response, he tore the screen off the window, raised the window, and went into the house.

McCreery said that he was able to see defendant because there was a light over a sign between the two houses, and defendant evidently had turned on a light in decedent's kitchen, so that the witness "could see in there." Mrs. McCreery testified that, by a light on decedent's porch, she could see defendant on the porch trying to push in the door leading into the house, and that he went to the window, pried off the screen, opened the window, and entered the house. Both witnesses testified that shortly thereafter they heard a shot, and after a short interval two more shots. In a short time deceased's two sons, George Wright, Jr., age seven, and Bowzer Wright, age five, came running across the lot to the McCreery house and informed the McCreery's that their mother had been shot. Thereupon, McCreery went to the decedent's home, where he found decedent's body lying on the floor of the upstairs bedroom. He then went to a nearby house, where decedent's estranged husband was living, and told him what had happened. The sheriff and an ambulance were called, the ambulance arriving about an hour later. At the trial, George, the older of the two boys, testified that he "saw" the defendant fire the shots which killed his mother.

Also according to the State's evidence, defendant was seen in a car driven by one Isaac Martin, and shortly thereafter, while defendant was walking along the road, he was arrested by a deputy sheriff, taken to the room in which decedent's body was lying, and then to jail.

One Dennis Bradford testified that he was an occupant of the Martin car at the time defendant was also an occupant, and shortly after defendant left the car, he found a gun, which he kept for some time until, upon request of the State Police, he turned it over to them.

According to all of the State's witnesses, the shooting occurred sometime between 12:30 and 1:00 o'clock in the morning of June 29, 1947. The McCreerys testified that defendant came to their house about midnight. Luther Creasey, who lived in a house next door to the McCreerys on the side opposite from that of the house occupied by Bessie Wright, testified that he heard three shots shortly before defendant was arrested; and he fixed the time of the shooting at exactly 12:45 a. m., at which time he set his watch by the radio. Richard Herald, deputy sheriff, testified that between 12:30 and 1:00 o'clock in the morning of June 29, he received a call concerning the shooting in the office of a justice of the peace at Man, and that he drove directly to the Wright house, arriving there before the ambulance.

On the other hand State's witness, Isaac Martin, testified that he, together with State's witness, Dennis Bradford, picked up defendant between 11:30 and midnight on June 28 — not later than a little after midnight; that with Bradford sitting in the front seat and defendant in the back seat, they drove to Riley, where the ambulance and other cars were seen in the vicinity of the Wright house; and that defendant remained in the Martin car until after they left the scene of the homicide. Shortly after leaving the vicinity of the Wright house, defendant left the car at Martin's request. Witness then drove the car a short distance farther along the road with Bradford still sitting in the front seat. Then turning back toward the place where defendant had alighted, he saw defendant standing at the side of the road under arrest.

In general the testimony of defendant and State witnesses, Bradford and Martin, bearing on the question of defendant's whereabouts from the time he entered the car until his arrest coincides in substantial detail, but according to the State's evidence, it took more than an hour for the ambulance to get to the scene of the shooting, and, according to defendant's evidence, Martin picked up defendant around midnight on June 28, and arrived at the scene of the shooting after the arrival of the ambulance. So there is a clear conflict in the evidence as to defendant's whereabouts at the time of the homicide. As Martin testified that immediately after the defendant entered Martin's car at Martin's home at Braeholm, a distance which he estimated between one-half and three-quarters of a mile from Riley, he proceeded directly to Riley, which he said required between fifteen and twenty-five minutes, and the fact that he arrived at the Wright home after the ambulance strongly indicates that he and Bradford did not encounter defendant until about an hour after midnight on June

29, in which event there would be almost an hour of defendant's time not accounted for, and the jury would have the right to believe that Martin and Bradford were mistaken as to the time they met defendant and that, in fact, defendant was taken into the Martin car after the homicide was committed. So we think that the evidence is such as to justify the jury in disbelieving defendant's alibi, as it evidently did.

During the course of the trial, George Wright, Jr., age seven, was given the oath regularly administered to adult witnesses, and, without any preliminary or other examination on the part of the trial court, was examined by the prosecuting attorney on the question of his competency as a witness, and then subjected to direct examination by the prosecuting attorney. Finally, he was cross-examined on behalf of the defendant by the latter's attorneys. On direct examination the witness testified that he and his brother were at home on the night their mother was killed; that after they had gone to bed in the room occupied by their mother, someone was heard coming up the stairs; that he saw the defendant turn on the light in the bedroom; that defendant had a gun in his hand, which witness testified he had seen before; that defendant asked decedent to give him some money, threatening that if she did not he would shoot her; and that after decedent told defendant she did not have any money, defendant fired one shot at decedent, and thereupon the children went under the bed; and that then one more shot was fired, causing decedent, who was standing up, to fall to the floor. When, according to George's testimony, the children heard defendant go out the screen door, they came from under the bed, looked at their mother who was lying on the floor, tried to talk to her, but eliciting no response, they went to the McCreery home.

Immediately before and at the conclusion of the preliminary examination conducted by the prosecuting attorney, bearing on the competency of the infant witness, George Wright, Jr., defendant's counsel objected to the witness testifying and the court, upon overruling the objection made at the close of the preliminary examination, ruled that the witness was competent to testify, and, without objection on defendant's part or motion that the jury be instructed to disregard the remark, stated in the presence of the jury: "This seems to be a very bright boy for his age. Son, when they ask you questions you just tell the truth."

After a careful consideration of the evidence in this case, we are of opinion that it is sufficient for the jury to have found, as it did, that the defendant, Bud Peterson, is guilty of the willful, deliberate, premeditated and unlawful killing of the decedent, Bessie Wright; and further we are of the opinion that it was for the jury to find that the defendant, Bud Peterson, did not establish by a preponderance of the evidence defendant's defense of an alibi, and there being substantial evidence tending to prove the actual presence of the accused at the place where, and at the time when, the crime was committed, the conviction should stand, unless other alleged errors appear in the record."

There were about a dozen official witnesses and press members who witnessed Bud's hanging. According to the Associated Press, just before the trap doors of the gallows dropped open, he said to the witnesses that he had been treated well at the prison. He then added, "Look what sin has brought me. You folks should stay on this side with Jesus."

Bud's family (presumably his sister) chose not to claim his body, so he is buried with a small metal marker at the Moundsville prison cemetery, known as White Gate. It shows only his name and the years of his birth and death.

Ironically, (or not surprisingly?) the first convicted prisoner the State of West Virginia hanged after it took over the grim duty from the counties in 1899 was also a Black man, Shep Caldwell, from McDowell County.

So, since the law had changed, did they tear down the gallows after Bud's execution? Not so fast. Even though the law moving the state's death business into the age of electricity had been signed, there was one more execution pending that had been sentenced under the old law, and thus to be carried out by on the gallows even though the electric chair was in place. And, but for intervention by the West Virginia Supreme Court siding, this time, with the accused, that execution would not only have been West Virginia's and the country's last legal hanging, it would had been the state's only execution of a woman. Yes, a young Black woman.

Matilene Dean, also of Logan County, was convicted of murdering Mack Nixon, aka "Shamrock," in the early hours of November 8, 1948 on Buffalo Creek. She was found guilty and condemned to die by hanging, recognized as the last to do so. A headline in the Hinton *Daily News,* March 23, 1949, read:

STATE GALLOWS TO CLAIM LAST VICTIM MAY 20 -Logan Woman Will Be Last Of 87 To Be Hanged.

Moundsville — When Matilene Dean hangs next May 20, she will be helping close out the death penalty system used by West Virginia for half a century. Under a new law passed by the last legislature and signed by the governor, the state will exact its capital punishment via the electric chair. Its application covers only those condemned after enactment of the change. Since the Logan county negress was sentenced prior to that, the noose will be used in a farewell turn to take her life for murder.

Again, the most complete recounting of the evidence comes to us through the background narrative from the Supreme Court. So, for all you *True Crime* fans, here's the blow-by-blow:

From State v. Dean, Opinion No. 10167, decided April 4, 1950:

"Matilene Dean was indicted in and tried before the Circuit Court of Logan County, and convicted of murder of the first degree without recommendation. To the judgment of the circuit court based upon a jury verdict, sentencing her to be hanged at the state penitentiary at Moundsville, defendant prosecutes this writ of error.

The defendant, a negro woman twenty-three years of age, and a native of Logan County, residing at the village of Stowe, early on the morning of November 8, 1948, shot and killed Mack Nixon, commonly known as "Shamrock," and sometimes referred to by that name in this opinion. Until about a year prior to the homicide she resided with her mother in the village of Shamrock in Logan County. Thereafter and until she was arrested she resided with and worked as housekeeper for one Sam Richardson, a widower, for fifteen dollars a week at the Richardson home in the village of Stowe, located on Buffalo Creek, approximately fifteen miles from the City of Logan.

On November 7, 1948, defendant left the village of Shamrock by bus late in the afternoon and arrived at Logan a short time later. Again boarding a bus at Logan about 7:30 on the same evening, she arrived at Stowe after dark about 8:55 that night. Upon alighting from the bus at or near the village of Stowe, she saw a man on the highway acting "strangely," which prompted her to stop at the home of Richard Coleman, who lived a short distance from the Richardson home. She asked Coleman to turn on his light so she could see her way to the Richardson house.

While talking with Coleman, the decedent Nixon, approached her through the darkness and called "Matilene," whereupon defendant identified herself and inquired if the person was "Shamrock." Nixon, who had a flashlight informed defendant that he was going to the Richardson house, and the two then proceeded there, where they found Richardson in his work clothes preparing to go to work. Decedent offered Richardson a drink of whiskey, which was declined. Then defendant in the presence of Nixon asked Richardson how much money he would draw the following Saturday, and took from her purse a statement which purported to show the money due, along with eighteen dollars in United States currency. When Richardson was ready to go to work, defendant and Nixon accompanied him to a place called the "grill" located near the highway between Stowe and the village of Lundale, where Richardson got on the bus for the purpose of going to his working place.

After Richardson got on the bus, defendant left decedent and began walking toward the village of Lundale, assigning in the record as her reason for not returning to the Richardson home with decedent that she was "afraid to go back, he was acting so funny." At Lundale she went to the home of Marie Redley (sometimes spelled "Ridley" in the record), a friend. About five minutes later Shamrock followed her into the Redley house and "started talking loud." Defendant says when she asked decedent to be quiet, he began to "curse and go on," and that she walked out of the house and left him there. Marie Redley, although summoned, did not appear to testify.

Defendant then went to the nearby home of Tom Hall, and upon knocking she was admitted by Hall, who at the time of the trial was dead. As defendant walked into the Hall home, she was followed by decedent who was "cursing and going on." Defendant testified that when she asked Shamrock "What do you mean cursing me, you make people think I am something to you," he "slapped me and my nose bled." Defendant says that decedent then called Hall a vile and insulting name and said, "Do you want to take that up?" Hall then got a .22 caliber rifle from the closet. Defendant left the two during the argument which ensued, and "didn't stop." Proceeding to her home, she locked the doors, sat down and wrote two letters. Then examining to see that the doors were locked, especially the kitchen door, she went to bed and fell asleep.

Defendant testified that she next saw decedent in her bedroom, standing over her bed, holding a shot gun; and that when she asked, "Sam, is that you?", decedent replied, "Shut up, G — damn you, shut up, I will blow your G — damned brains out." Defendant then said, "If I have anything you want, just take it," and got out of bed, opened her wardrobe, and, according to her testimony, found her pocketbook was missing. Defendant asked decedent for her pocketbook, and he said he did not have it. Then she accused decedent of breaking into her house, which he denied, saying "your house was already open." Defendant called over to Mrs. Leeper, her closest neighbor, who lived in a house thirty-five or forty feet away from the Richardson house, told her what had happened, and asked her and her husband, William Leeper, to come over as "This man came over here and broke in my house"; but Mrs. Leeper's only response was, according to defendant, "What man, can't you get him out?" After a "good argument" with decedent, defendant says she went over and knocked on the Leeper's door, but the Leepers refused to help her.

Thereafter defendant ran down to the Coleman house, and tried to get Coleman to take her to the state police, but was told he did not have enough gasoline. She then borrowed two nickels from Mrs. Coleman so that she could call the "States," evidently meaning the state police. Next she proceeded to a neighboring house, occupied by a Mr. Myers. There she tried unsuccessfully to call the state police, but the telephone was out of order. Meanwhile the decedent was standing "up there cursing." Going to another nearby house, occupied by Pete Zanders, she told Zanders what had happened, but Zanders, having been informed by defendant that decedent had taken Richardson's shot gun, refused to go to the Richardson house, but drove defendant to Lundale to the residence of one William Mosley, a constable of Triadelphia District, Logan County, and asked the constable to arrest decedent. Mosley told defendant he would "Be right on down." Upon having been driven by Zanders to the vicinity of the Richardson home, defendant went to the Leeper home, stayed four or five minutes, and then went into the Richardson house, but found no one there.

Shortly thereafter defendant went again to the Coleman house, and told Mrs. Coleman that Richardson's money, gun and whiskey were missing. From the Coleman house, defendant proceeded in the direction of Lundale to the home of a Mrs. Moore. She gave Mrs. Moore the two nickels Mrs. Coleman had given her, and tried again to call the state police from that place, but received no response. She then proceeded to the nearby home of Annie Arthur, where decedent roomed and told Annie Arthur that "Shamrock broke into my house," and asked her, "Did he bring a gun?", to which the Arthur woman, replied, "No, sir"; but that decedent had been in and out of the house all night. Defendant found decedent at the Arthur home in bed, and asked him to accompany her home. She says she made this request "so when the laws come he would be there and catch him with my money." When defendant and Nixon arrived at the Richardson home, she asked decedent to let her have the gun, and said that decedent could have the money. Nixon replied that he did not have the money, and upon searching for the gun (a 12 gauge shot gun), found it lying by the couch in the living room.

At this point we note that the events above narrated are uncontradicted, and are substantially corroborated in this record.

According to defendant, she took the shot gun and went out of the door leading to the porch, and then down to the bottom of the ten steps leading therefrom; that decedent followed her through the door with the .22 rifle in his hands, saying, "you son of a bitch, you bitch, you got the gun, haven't you, damn it, you accused me this morning, so I will kill you now"; that decedent pointed it at defendant and defendant said, "I just pulled this little long thing [evidently meaning the trigger of the shot gun] and the thing went off." Decedent fell, and the rifle, she says, fell on the porch beside him.

It seems that Leeper, hearing the shot, came over and met the defendant at the gate.

Constable Mosley testified that when he arrived at the Richardson house shortly after the shooting, in response to defendant's call for assistance, he found two guns in the house, a single barrel 12 gauge shot gun, and a .22 caliber rifle; that the shot gun was standing a little to the left of the door, leading from the porch into the house as one enters it, about four feet from where decedent was lying. He identified the shot gun as one lying on the counsel table, and in answer to the inquiry whether there was "anything about the stock that would cause you to remember it, if you saw it?", he replied, "Up on top there, taped up." Mosley says that he left the rifle in the house, but took the shot gun and left it at the office of deputy sheriff Clyde Staley, and, without objection, he said that the sheriff brought the shot gun over to the court house.

Clyde Staley, a deputy sheriff of Logan County, testified that he found an empty shot gun shell lying on the upper side of the house between the Leeper and Richardson houses; and when asked where the empty shell was, the witness testified that it is "here in this shot gun. I picked it up and put it in." This witness testified that Mosley put this gun in the office of the justice of the peace at Man, and that "They turned it over to me, and I put the shell in the gun." In answer to further inquiry this witness testified again that the shell in the gun was the one which he found in the Richardson yard, and that it had been in witness' possession locked up ever since that day. Whereupon counsel for defendant objected to the introduction of the empty shell on the ground that the witness does not know "whether that shell was fired on that occasion or not." This objection was overruled, and the empty shell was admitted into evidence, to which ruling counsel excepted. After further inquiry of this witness, counsel stated that "We renew our objection to the introduction of the empty shell on the ground that it does not correspond with the one introduced by the State," which motion was overruled, and defendant by counsel excepted.

Leeper on direct examination testified that he saw Matilene "Richardson" place "the shot gun in the left hand corner of the porch;" and on rebuttal that she carried the shot gun up the steps "and she took it in and set it down on the right hand corner of the grate." This witness testified that after the shot was fired, he saw defendant break out the empty shell; that the shot gun was then placed or was thrown on the ground; but, as witness went up the steps to where decedent was lying, "she took it in and sat it on the left hand corner of the grate," and then came out on the porch past decedent's body and went down the steps.

Shortly after the shooting defendant was driven by a man whose given name was "Roosevelt," to the Mosley house for the purpose of surrendering. Arriving at the Mosley house, she learned from Mrs. Mosley that her husband had gone to Stowe in response to her previous call. On returning home, she found the constable there, and he promptly arrested her, put her in his car, and took her to the city jail at Man.

William Leeper testified in contradiction to defendant's version of the shooting. He testified that he heard defendant and decedent quarreling "Back and through" the Richardson house over the lost money; that when he first heard them talking, he went to the foot of the bed, pulled back the side of the window shade at or near the foot of the bed; that he saw decedent coming around the corner of the house at the back thereof; that before he got to the window he heard decedent say, "Give you your money, Matilene, I don't have your money"; and that as decedent was running away from her, he said, "Matilene, what did you bring me down here for, get me up out of bed to kill me?", to which she replied, "Yes," and he ran away from her. The witness then testified that defendant walked slowly while decedent ran; that decedent turned around on the porch, facing defendant as if to walk down the steps, and said, "Matilene, you are not going to shoot me, are you?", and then the fatal shot was fired.

Mrs. Leeper testified that when defendant came to her home the second time (evidently after she had returned from her first trip to the Mosley home), decedent picked the shot gun up, and left her with nothing but three shells, which defendant then had in her possession, one of which she dropped on the floor of the Leeper house; that on that occasion defendant said, "If Bill Mosley was too long, if Bill Mosley didn't come in five or six minutes, she was going up and get him, if she had to fool him back down, if she didn't kill him."

Channie Coleman testified that when decedent came to her house the first time that she told her that "Shamrock had broken into her house and stole some whiskey and money out of her wardrobe, twelve dollars out of her pocketbook, and Sam's shot gun," and when she woke up he was standing over her with a shot gun, and he left her with two shells; that she then asked the Colemans to take her to the state police, but witness' husband told her he did not have any gasoline. According to Mrs. Coleman, defendant walked the floor for a little while, and then said "I just don't know what to do, he has Sam's shot gun"; that "Sam loved that shot gun better than he does me. Shamrock hates me. I know what I will do, I will go up there and get him and tell him I am scared to come home; and ask him to come with me, and kill him before he gets there."; and that she said she was going to the state police, and she then asked the witness for a dime so she could call the state police from Mrs. Moore's house. She next returned to the Coleman house about ten minutes before five in the morning, telling the witness that she had killed the decedent; and that he was lying on the front porch dead, and stated that she was going to give herself up. That after Richard Coleman told her that he did not have gasoline enough to take her, and to get "Roosevelt" to take her up, defendant left.

The foregoing testimony of William Leeper, Mrs. Leeper, and Channie Coleman to the effect that defendant threatened in their presence to lure decedent to the Richardson house, and then kill him, is denied categorically by this defendant.

We have narrated the events portrayed in this record in detail, because the initial question presented to us in this most important case, which involves the life of a young woman, is whether there is sufficient evidence in the record from which the jury could have found, beyond a reasonable doubt that defendant was guilty of premeditated, deliberate and malicious homicide. From some aspects of the record, it seems that defendant had been greatly harassed by the decedent, but from another view of the record, it would seem that she prevailed upon defendant to return from the place of his residence, where he was in bed, and go to the Richardson home, for the purpose of killing him."

So, whether Matilene was to follow Bud Peterson up the steps to have a noose placed around her neck and become the country's final execution by hanging hinged not on the fact that she shot and killed Shamrock, but on the difference between premeditation and a situation in which there could have been an element of self-defense, or at least fear and "passion of the moment." There was also a legal technicality: a juror, one Clifford Burns, had been asked during voir dire whether or not he "was biased in favor of or prejudiced against the members of the Negro race?" and answered in the negative.

The next paragraph is disturbing.

But, on the night after Matilene was found guilty, Burns was overheard in a Peach Creek poolroom saying, "If it was left up to me I would hang all them goddamned niggers." When questioned about whether that sentiment was appropriate for someone who had just been part of the legal proceeding in the form of the question, "You mean to tell me you want to see that woman put to death because she is a nigger," Burns answered, "Yes, ma'am."

The verdict was set aside, and Matilene was awarded a new trial. The state could then easily pursue a conviction that could garner a life sentence. There wasn't nearly as much press coverage after the noose was no longer an option, so the particulars of the new case aren't as readily available. Regardless, the gallows at Moundsville was (yes, it's singular) finally torn down, and the sagas of both Bud Peterson and Matilene Dean are sad ones. I came to know many uplifting and inspiring stories researching this work, but these are not among them.

By my count, 47 of the 155 legal executions in West Virginia since 1863 were of Black convicts, more than 30%. Oh, and don't forget at least 28 illegal lynchings of Black Mountaineers since 1882. According to the latest available census information, the Black population of the state is 3.6%, by the way. Almost 42% of death row inmates across the country today are Black, while the overall Black population is just 13.4%. The national Academy of Sciences study in 2014 found that approximately 4% of death row inmates are innocent.

To me, all that just doesn't add up.

Byrd Prillerman (1859 - 1929), educator. *The accomplishments of those born into slavery and rising to the top of their professions are to be honored, even more so when those professions helped lift up others. A tragic fire at his namesake school in 1962 helped speed integration "on the Gulf."*

I am a Raleigh County native, and always thought of it as generally divided into three parts: the eastern agricultural section from which I hail, the north/northwest Coal River area, and "The Gulf," the latter encompassing the small town of Sophia and rich coalfields in areas south, bordering Wyoming County. Just inside the county line is Amigo, West Virginia, now practically a ghost town at the confluence of the Guyandotte River and Winding Gulf, a stream that runs only about sixteen miles for its entire course through the former coal towns of Stotesbury, Tams, Ury, and Helen, all of which were thriving communities in their day. The Amigo post office was established in 1915, and closed in 2011. With a population of 123 people and a median age of 62.1 (compared to the US median of 37.4), one would be quite an optimist to see a great future for the community on the immediate horizon.

Something about Amigo's demographic that differs from the past: according to the most recent census data available, those 123 souls living there today are all White. That certainly wasn't the case when Byrd Prillerman High School (which actually included grades 1-12) opened there in 1927. It burned in 1962.

The school still has an active alumni association, and regular reunions. Randy Radford, who was an elementary student there at the time of the fire, later had a distinguished career with the Department of Defense, managing security operations at the Pentagon. In a 2014 *Beckley Register-Herald* interview, he noted how something tragic became a trigger for progress. "Initially, the burning of the school was very traumatic. It was a mixed blessing, though, because I was with children in the neighborhood whom I played with, and at the time, I didn't understand why we went to different schools." In other words, the school's burning pushed Raleigh County into integrating its students before it would have otherwise.

In 2001, a marker was placed near the site of the school, a project spearheaded by 1935 graduate Parthenia Ruth Fountain Edmonds, who went on to graduate from West Virginia State College in 1939. It reads:

"Byrd Prillerman High School was established here in 1927 for the Afro-American students in this coal mining area. Named in honor of a former slave who was an eminent state educator and President of West Virginia State College. The two story frame building, first used as a white elementary school, was remodeled and added onto. The Byrd Prillerman school became a stone and brick building that had 14 rooms and a Gymnasium for the students in the first to twelfth grades. The first graduating class in 1931 had four members. The building was destroyed by fire on Jan 12, 1962. The 204 students and 10 teachers were transferred to the other integrated schools including Mark Twain, Sophia and Stoco High Schools, all consolidated into Independence High School later. The nearby football practice field full of tree stumps, provided an ideal setting as the players said they learned how to dodge the stumps. This continued in the games and lead to several state championships. From 786 graduates during its 31 years of existence, many followed in the footsteps of Byrd Prillerman."

That's part of Byrd Prillerman's legacy. Now let's look at the man. He was born into bondage in October 1859, in Shady Grove, Franklin County, Virginia, the property of one Jacob Prillerman (1778 – 1858), a War of 1812 veteran, from which the family gets its name. Jacob's grandfather Jacob was a veteran of the Revolution, who immigrated to Virginia from Switzerland in 1747, changing the original name spelling from "Brullmann." Byrd's father, Franklin Prillerman died in 1872, and his mother Charlotte died in 1881. Franklin was a skilled blacksmith, and was sent by his owner to ply the trade (for the owner's profit, of course) in the busy salt processing fields of the Kanawha Valley. Byrd's mother Charlotte was Jacob Prillerman's daughter, Jacob having raped Charlotte's mother, also his property. Yet again, that's the word I use, because that what it was.

After emancipation, the family remained in Virginia for a couple of years, and then Franklin brought his family, including 9-year-old Byrd, back to the Kanawha Valley on foot, renting a house near Sissonville. When Byrd had the opportunity to attend a "Colored School" in Charleston run by Henry Clay Payne, he jumped at the chance and the course of his life was set. He was soon teaching in Sissonville, and then attended Knoxville College, where he graduated with a B. S. degree in 1889, and returned to Charleston to resume his career as a teacher.

While there were a number of "Colored Schools" throughout the state, there were very few opportunities for Blacks to pursue college education. In fact, at that time, there was exactly one Black college in the state, Storer College in Harpers Ferry. Together with Rev. C. H. Payne, he lobbied the state government to create the West Virginia Colored Institute, which opened its doors in 1892, with Prillerman as head of the English department. He became president of the school in 1909, and oversaw its elevation to accredited college in 1915. He retired in 1919, but continued service with the West Virginia Sunday School Association.

Byrd married Mattie Eugenia Brown in 1893, and they had six children (two died young), some of whom also had careers in education. Mattie died at Charleston General Hospital in 1921, of appendicitis. Disappointingly, her death certificate lists only "Don't know" in the birthplace/parents section. Byrd died in St. Francis Hospital in 1929, possibly of prostate cancer.

From the *Charleston Daily Mail*, April 26, 1929:

Byrd Prillerman, Educator, Is Dead

Founder of West Virginia State College Succumbs at Hospital Here

Dr. Byrd Prillerman, 69, one of West Virginia's most prominent Negro educators, and former president of West Virginia Collegiate institute, now West Virginia State college, died shortly after 11 o'clock Thursday night at the St. Francis hospital following an operation.

Dr. Prillerman was one of the most widely known and best educated Negro teachers in the state. He received a bachelor of science degree from Knoxville college in 1889; master of arts degree at Westminster, New Wilmington, Pa., in 1894, and a degree in literature from Selma university in 1916.

He first started teaching in Poca district, this county, on November 10, 1879. He succeeded in obtaining a first grade teachers' certificate. To improve his literary qualifications, he entered Knoxville college September 3, 1883, from which place he was later graduated.

Returning to Charleston, he was employed as a teacher in the public schools here and was made assistant principal. Realizing that there was need for higher education for Negroes in West Virginia, he took up the matter with Governor A. B. Fleming in 1890 and obtained the establishment of the West Virginia Colored Institute in 1891. Dr. Prillerman was employed as first assistant to the principal in 1892. The West Virginia Collegiate Institute, which Mr. Prillerman headed for 10 years as president, was founded by a federal statute of 1862, which required that equal educational facilities for Negro children. It did not become established as a State school for Negroes until March 17, 1891, in pursuance of an act passed by the legislature of 1890 providing separate schools for Negroes.

Elected School Head

J. Edwin Campbell, of Ohio, was the first principal of the institute in 1891, and Prillerman was made assistant principal. He served in this capacity until 1909 when he was chosen a president. On August 31, 1919, Prillerman was made assistant principal. He served in this capacity until 1909 when he was chosen a president. On August 31, 1919, Prillerman voluntarily retired as president of the school, on account of his age and he became president emeritus. He was succeeded by John W. Davis, of Washington, who still holds the position as president.

Immediately after his retirement as active had of the school, Prillerman became interested in Sunday School work among the Negroes and was engaged by the International Council of Religious Education to work in West Virginia. He worked through the West Virginia Council of Religious Education, with headquarters at Charleston. In this capacity he traveled about the state organizing and standardizing Sunday schools for the children of his race. He was busy up to the time he was stricken with illness about a week ago.

The West Virginia Teachers association for Negro teachers was organized largely through his efforts in 1896. He served as president of this association for nine years. Previous to this, Dr. Prillerman became an active member of the National Education association and was a member in that organization at the time of his death.

In 1915, Dr. Prillerman succeeded in having the name of West Virginia Colored Institute changed to West Virginia Collegiate Institute. In May, 1919, he graduated the first Negro students to receive a degree in West Virginia.

Entertained Educators

Under his administration, he brought to the college some of the most distinguished educators in the nation. They included J. W. E. Bowen, D. D., Ph.D., Atlanta, Ga.; Rev. M. W. Clair, Washington, D. C.; Professor W. E. B. Dubois, Ph.D., editor of "Crisis", New York; Miss Nannie H. Burroughs, A. M., president of the national training school, Washington; Prof. Kelley Miller, A. M., dean of Howard university, Washington; Prof. George D. Hayes, Ph.D., Fish university; Joe Mitchell Chapple, editor of National magazine; P. P. Claxton, former United States commissioner of education, and the late Dr. Booker T. Washington.

In 1893, Dr. Prillerman married Miss Mattie E. Brown, a native of this state and a graduate of Wayland seminary. He is survived by two sons and two daughters, Delbert McCullough, the oldest son; graduated from Michigan Agricultural college in 1917, and served in France during the war. He is now a professor in chemistry at the West Virginia state college. The younger son, Henry Laurence, graduated from the institute in 1917, later served in the army, and is now teaching in this state. Ednora Hae , the oldest daughter, graduated from the academic course of the institute in 1919. The other daughter is Miss Myrtle Prillerman, of Institute.

Dr. Prillerman, who owned valuable real estate, used as one of his favorite themes: "A well painted two-story house owned by a Negro is sharper than a two-edged sword."

Dr. Prillerman's body is at the Harden and Harden mortuary. Funeral arrangements have not been completed.

Those early Black educators who were born into slavery and overcame all the obstacles of the day in order to develop quality opportunities for those coming behind them were truly heroes.

Dr. Ira De Augustine Reid (1901 - 1968), educator and sociologist.
His time in the Mountain State was short, but his national influence impactful.

Dr. Reid grew up in relatively comfortable circumstances, the son of a distinguished Baptist minister, Daniel Augustine Reid. He was born in Clifton Forge, Virginia, but grew up in Harrisburg, and later the Germantown section of Philadelphia, Pennsylvania. The public schools he attended there were integrated, something that would not have been the case during that time had the family stayed in Virginia.

Connections are important, and the bright young man was personally recruited to attend Morehouse College in Atlanta by its president, John Hope. He received a BA from Morehouse in 1922, then a MA in Social Economics from the University of Pittsburgh in 1925, and, ultimately, a Ph.D. in Sociology from Columbia University in 1939, at a time when there were few Black students there.

Tucked in between segments of his own higher education, Ira did a couple of stints teaching high school to get some real-life experience and, presumably, pay a few bills. The first of these was being the director of the Texas Collage High School in Tyler. He did work at the University of Chicago during the summer of 1923, and then spent the next academic year teaching social sciences at Frederick Douglass High School in Huntington, West Virginia. Selected as a National Urban League Fellow at the end of the term, he then moved on to Pitt for the next segment of his own education.

Dr. Reid's most influential legacy is in having produced some of the first broad sociological studies of African-Americans in the United States. He worked on the National Interracial Conference's landmark *The Negro in American Civilization: A Study of Negro Life and Race Relations in the Light of Social Research* (1930). He became the Director of Research for the National Urban League, and continued to apply strict sociological methods to studying distinct communities of African-Americans.

Naturally, Ira and his work came to the attention of America's most celebrated sociologist (of any race), W. E. B. Du Bois (1868 – 1963), one of the founders of the NAACP and author of *The Souls of Black*

Folk. In 1937, Du Bois described Reid as "the best-trained young Negro in sociology today." The two worked closely together until 1944, when Du Bois was "forced to retire" or be fired as the Chairman of the Sociology Department at Atlanta University. Reid took his place, and remained there for several years, until becoming restless and accepting a number of visiting professorships around the country.

Abandoning his Baptist roots, Dr. Reid and his wife became members of the Society of Friends, or Quakers. Like so many social activists, he came under the scrutiny of McCarthyism in the 1950s, and the State Department suspended his passport from 1952 through 1954, when he successfully challenged the action. During the 1960s, he traveled extensively, serving as a visiting professor in both Nigeria and Japan…both of which are a long way from the old Frederick Douglass High School in Huntington.

Dorothy Johnson Vaughn (1910 – 2008), mathematician and Congressional Gold Medal recipient. *Another Mountaineer Hidden Figure eventually got the recognition she deserved.*

Along with the graceful Katherine Johnson, a second NASA "Human computer" was a true Mountaineer, though born in Missouri. Dorothy was only seven years old when her family relocated from Kansas City to Morgantown. The 1920 census shows us the family of Leonard H. (54) and Susie (Susan) (54) Johnson living on Beechurst Avenue. Leonard, born in Mississippi, was a waiter at a boarding house. Susie was Leonard's second wife, and had been born in Missouri. Our subject Dorothy is ten years old. Her mother, Anna Anderson Johnson, had died in 1912. Also present in the home was boarder Owana Peeler, 6, and mother-in-law Emily Vaughn, 97. Emily died of pneumonia later that same year. Her death certificate lists her father, Cato Vaughn, as having been born in Kentucky. Cato was a common slave name, and it's likely all Dorothy's grandparents were born into slavery.

That's an interesting combination, with more than 90 years separating the house's residents. Young Owana was related in some fashion, because, on her death certificate, Susan's maiden name is listed as Peeler, her father not given, and her mother Emily Vaughn. By 1930, Owana is listed as the couple's adopted daughter. Now, I have looked at many old death certificates in my day, and Susan's, of August 3, 1931, is the most puzzling I have ever seen in the Medical Certificate of Death section. Signed by Dr. M. H. Brown, the blanks are all empty except the following: Principal cause of death: DON'T KNOW. I attended the deceased: DIED SUDDENLY. Was there an autopsy? NO. That's it. No conjecture, no observation, no "possible" cause. For a woman only 65 years old, that seems like someone wasn't trying very hard. Leonard died of a "stricture of the urethra" in 1938.

Dorothy attended segregated Beechurst High School and graduated as class valedictorian in 1925. She was awarded a scholarship from the West Virginia A.M.E. Sunday School Convention, and attended Wilberforce University in Ohio, which had been founded by Greenbrier County native Lewis Woodson. She joined Alpha Kappa Alpha and graduated cum laud in mathematics. She did graduate work at Howard University and taught mathematics in segregated schools in Farmville, Virginia. She married Howard Seymour Vaughan Jr. (1910 – 1955) and the couple eventually moved to Newport News, Virginia, where Howard's family were well-to-do. They eventually had six children.

Dorothy began working at Langley Research Center during World War II. By 1949, she had become head of what was known as the West Area Computing Unit, a segregated group of "Human computers" later made famous by Margot Lee Shetterly's book and the later film *Hidden Figures*. West Virginian Katherine Johnson was initially assigned to Vaughn's group, but then was transferred to Langley's Flight Mechanics Division.

One of the most notable things about Dorothy's career was how she embraced and facilitated the very thing that made Human computers obsolete. When electronic computing was introduced in 1961, she became an expert computer programmer, teaching others how to tame the new beasts. Her work was especially essential to the Scout Launch Vehicle Program, which helped the United States catch up to and eventually surpass the Soviet Union in the area of communication and observation satellites. She again worked with Katherine Johnson on John Glenn's launch into orbit.

Dorothy was a humble and devout woman, taking the bus to work and donating time to church work. But, on screen, she was portrayed by Academy Award winner Octavia Spencer in *Hidden Figures*, and she was posthumously awarded a Congressional Gold Medal in 2019. She has a moon crater and a satellite officially named after her. On the years of segregation and separation from White colleagues even while doing such important work, she simply said she changed what she could, and endured what she couldn't. When you think about the change she saw in one lifetime, albeit a long one, it's awe-inspiring.

Her obituary from the Cooke Brothers Funeral Home site:

HAMPTON - Mrs. Dorothy J. Vaughan, 98, died on Monday, Nov. 10, 2008, at Sentara Careplex in Hampton. She was born on Sept. 20, 1910, in Kansas City, Mo., to Leonard H. and Annie A. Johnson. In 1917, the family moved to Morgantown, W.Va. She graduated from Beechurst H.S. in 1925 and received a B.S. degree in 1929 from Wilberforce University In Zenia, Ohio. She became a member of Zeta Chapter of Alpha Kappa Alpha Sorority in 1926.

In 1943, she moved to Newport News and was employed as a mathematician at Langley Field for NACA (National Advisory Committee for Aeronautics), which was the forerunner of today's NASA space program. She was among the first group of Blacks to be employed as mathematicians. They were placed in a segregated section and were responsible for doing the mathematical computations for the engineers conducting aeronautical experiments. Using slide rulers, calculators, and film readings, they provided the engineers with the data needed to conduct various performance testing, such as the variables effecting drag and lift of the aircraft. These experiments were conducted in the wind tunnels at Langley.

Prior to moving to Newport News, she was a teacher at Robert R. Moton H.S., in Farmville, Va., and a member of Beulah AME Church. In 1993, she was honored as a 50 year member of St. Paul AME Church of Newport News. She actively participated in the Music department, Dora Brown Missionary Society and the Bread distribution program until her illness. Also she was a member of the Silver Bells at the Phillis Wheatley Y.W.C.A.

She was preceded in death by her husband, Howard S. Vaughan Jr..

She is survived by her children, Ann V. Hammond (Rudy), Maida Kathryn Cobbins (George), Leonard S. Vaughan (Mary), and Kenneth H. Vaughan; grandchildren, Dr. Maurice G. Cary, Kimberly Israel, Maida Robinson, Minister Kenneth H. Vaughan Jr., Dr. L. Stephen Vaughan, Dr. Tracie Vaughan-Veney, Michele V. Webb, Heather V. Batten, Melissa Vaughan and Bradley Smith; 14 great-grandchildren; sister-in-law, Emma Vaughan; daughters-in-law, Priscilla (Pat) and Audrey C. Vaughan; a niece, Janet Vaughan; nephew, De'Jon Lee.

A special thanks to Doctors Phillip Dennis, and David Gore.

Viewing will be held from noon to 7 p.m. Thursday, Nov. 13, at Cooke Bros. Funeral Chapel, 1601-27th St. NN, VA. 23607. A funeral service will be held at noon Friday, Nov. 14, at St. Paul AME Church. Interment will follow at Hampton Memorial Gardens.

Booker Taliaferro Washington (1856 – 1915). *One of the most influential Americans of his day, his determination was rooted in his Malden youth.*

The Civil War figures so prominently in our history. It brought about our separation from Virginia, and almost all of the people written about in these pages were, in some way, influenced by the conflict. It wasn't really all that long ago, in the sweep of history. At this writing, the Veterans Administration is still paying at least one Civil War pension, to the unmarried daughter of a soldier who began the war as a Confederate, but ended it fighting for the Union. Granted, he was 84 years old when said daughter was conceived, but it's just not that distant. I am a late Baby Boomer, and knew at least one daughter of a Civil War soldier very well when I was a lad. She was my great-grandmother.

The practice of human bondage, legal and institutionalized, just a few generations back is even harder to process. We do not know definitively when the last American born into slavery died (records were even poorer for them than for Civil War veterans, but it was at least into the 1960s-70s, so my life, and those of many readers, likely overlapped with at least a few of those born a slave. One such claimant we have already mentioned was Sylvester Magee of Mississippi, who died in 1971, at the "claimed" age of 130.

That was, by the way, after he sued his wife for divorce, in 1969. The spark was just gone, I guess.

Booker was born on the James Burroughs tobacco plantation in Franklin County, Virginia. His birth year is an estimate; he didn't know it for certain. His father was said to have been a white man living on a neighboring plantation. With the advent of widespread DNA testing, perhaps someday we will know his identity. After emancipation, Booker's mother Jane brought her son to Malden to join her husband, Ferguson Washington, also born a slave. Ferguson had escaped during the war, and Malden was the site of thriving salt works, tapping the sea water from ancient oceans trapped underneath layers of rock for millions of years and boiling it down to get salt. Ferguson died in Malden on November 14, 1924. Booker took Ferguson's surname when he first attended school. He didn't know until later that his mother had given him the surname Taliaferro, so Booker added it as a middle name later. He worked in the salt works and in the coal mines, earning money to later attend the Hampton Institute in Hampton, Virginia, and the Wayland Seminary in Washington, D.C. He so impressed the professors at Hampton that they recommended him as the director of a new teachers' college in Tuskegee, Alabama.

The Tuskegee Institute as it was later called (now Tuskegee University) was literally built by its students, right down to making the bricks. Booker was a zealot for self-sufficiency and learning useful trades. His autobiography *Up from Slavery* (1901) became a bestseller, and he was invited to the White House to dinner with President Theodore Roosevelt, the very first African-American to receive such an invitation. Roosevelt took political heat for the act, particularly from southern politicians, in words we now find revolting.

Booker never forgot his roots. His first wife, Fannie Smith, was from Malden; she died after their first child was born. He returned to West

Virginia many times, particularly to West Virginia State College in Institute, where he gave the first commencement address.

In *Up from Slavery*, Booker wrote,

Finally we reached our destination, a little town called Malden, which is about five miles from Charleston, the present capital of the state. At that time, salt-mining was the great industry in that part of West Virginia, and the little town of Malden was right in the midst of the salt furnaces. My step father had already secured a job at a salt furnace, and he had also secured a little cabin for us to live in. Out new house was no better than the one we had left on the old plantation in Virginia. In fact, in one respect it was worse. Notwithstanding the poor condition of our plantation cabin, we were at all times sure of pure air. Our new home was in the midst of a cluster of cabins crowded closely together, and as there were no sanitary regulations, the filth about the cabins was often intolerable. Drinking, gambling, quarrels, fights, and shockingly immoral practices were frequent.

Such was Malden just after the Civil War, and no, that last line wasn't only applicable when the state legislature was in session. *Up from Slavery* is available to read for free online. I recommend it for everyone, but especially Mountaineers. Two quotes from Booker T. Washington have stuck with me since I first read his books as a teenager:

If you want to lift yourself up, lift up someone else, and *I will permit no man to narrow and degrade my soul by making me hate him.* They are just as true today.

Dr. Carter G. Woodson (1875 - 1950), educator and sociologist.
As an historian and author, Woodson gave the world Black History Month, and much more.

West Virginians have done our fair share of creating lasting celebrations. Thank Ann Jarvis for Mother's Day, Marian Herndon McQuade for National Grandparents Day, and Dr. Carter G. Woodson for Black History Month. The son of slaves who worked in the West Virginia coal mines to finance his pursuit of education, he was truly the Father of Black History

The Woodson's family saga in some ways follows that of Booker T. Washington a decade earlier. Carter's father, James Henry Woodson, was a farmer and carpenter. Both he and his wife Anne Eliza Riddle Woodson were illiterate. They lived in Buckingham County, Virginia. The 1880 census shows five-year-old Carter, incorrectly transcribed Charlie, with his parents and five siblings ranging in age from two to twelve. Carter was named for his grandfather Carter Woodson, born in Fluvanna County, and was the property of John W. Toney, who had family connections to a nearby landowner named William Woodson. This elder Carter's wife Sydney was the property of James Harris in Buckingham County before Emancipation. With no available public education, our Carter was essentially self-taught the basics. Along with his older brother Robert (who later found work as a plasterer and is buried in Highland Cemetery, Huntington), he came to West Virginia to work in the coal mines, but also hoping to further his education at Douglass High School in Huntington, from which he graduated in 1897. In 1900, we find him living in a boarding house in Nuttall, a Fayette County coal camp, run by William and Sallie Shorts, and teaching school. He was shortly thereafter called back to Huntington to become principal of Douglass, while also earning his BA in Literature from Berea College.

The Woodson brothers found success in West Virginia, so, as is often the case, more of the family followed. Father James Woodson died in 1903 and is buried in Huntington's Spring Hill Cemetery. Anne Woodson died in Huntington in 1916. Carter's younger sister Bessie Woodson Yancey (1882 – 1958) also became an educator, teaching in West Virginia coal camps, and a poet. From her book *Echoes from the Hills:*

If you live in West Virginia,
Come with me and pause a while.
See her wealth and power rising,
See her plains and valleys smile!
Give to eastern states their culture,
Give to northern states their fame,
Give to southern states their virtues
Which no other states may claim.
But in words of deathless glory

Far and wide where all may see
Write the name of West Virginia,
Champion of Liberty!

Beautiful. Most of Carter's siblings made their lives in West Virginia and are also buried in Huntington.

I have always believed that travel is an integral part of education, and Carter's world expanded drastically from 1903 through 1907, when he worked as a school supervisor in the Philippines, which the United States had only recently acquired as a result of the Spanish-American War. From the farm in Virginia and the coal camp in West Virginia to tropical Asia was, no doubt, quite a leap for the young man. Upon his return, he attended the University of Chicago, where he became a member of Omega Psi Phi, and then went on to Harvard, where he completed his Ph.D. in history during 1912, just the second African-American (after W. E. B. Du Bois) to earn a doctorate.

Even with that accomplishment, he was, at first, unable to find a college teaching position due to racism. He taught in the segregated public schools in Washington DC, and that's where we find him in the 1910 census, living as a boarder in the home of Robert and Rebecca Murdock on Eleventh Street. He eventually joined the faculty of Howard University, and became Dean of the College of Arts and Sciences. In 1920, he was enticed back to West Virginia by his friend John W. Davis (the Black college president, not the White Clarksburg politician. See his story earlier in this section), and became Academic Dean at West Virginia Collegiate Institute, now West Virginia State University, in Institute, from 1920 through 1922.

After returning to Washington, Carter devoted much of the rest of his life to research and writing. His proposal that African-American history is worthy as a separate and distinct discipline met resistance, even among some other Black academics. But his idea of Negro History Week, as it was initially dubbed, gained popularity almost immediately after he proposed it, and was first celebrated in 1926. He chose the second week of February, since it held the birthdays of both Frederick Douglass and Abraham Lincoln. The celebration eventually expanded, and Black History Month has been proclaimed by every president since Gerald Ford.

Just like with every single thing in our society today, it seems, controversy continues. Each year, we see "Oh. So why isn't there a WHITE History Month?" and similar stuff. And even Morgan Freeman, one of my favorite actors, isn't a fan of the concept, saying, "I don't want a Black History Month. Black history is American history," the same argument Carter G. Woodson faced from many of his fellow academics in the 1920s.

Big fan here, Morgan, but I have to disagree. On this, I am on the side of the poor son of freed slave parents who came to West Virginia and went down in history.

Carter G. Woodson died of a heart attack in his Washington DC home at the age of 74. He never married, admitting that he was married to his work.

Now, as with many of our subjects, I found a contemporary death notice on Dr. Woodson. This is from the *Alabama Tribune*, April 14, 1950. Note it also mentions the passing of Dr. Charles R. Drew, the pioneer blood transfusion researcher who developed the modern blood bank.

The National Association for the Advancement of Colored People this week mourned the loss of two distinguished Americans and Spingarn medalists, Dr. Charles R. Drew and Dr. Carter G. Woodson. In a wire to Mrs. Drew, expressing the Association's condolences, Acting NAACP Secretary Roy Wilkins referred to Dr. Drew as "One of the nation's outstanding scientists, and individual with a deep understanding for bettering human relationships." Mr. Wilkins said that the world looked to Dr. Drew, winner of the 29th Spingarn Medal for his outstanding work in blood plasma research, "for a future of continued achievement and contribution to mankind."

Of Dr. Woodson, teacher and historian who was awarded the 12th Spingarn Medal for his years of "devoted service in collecting and publishing the records of the Negro in America," Mr. Wilkins said: "His contributions will remain an everlasting monument to a truly great American. Dr. Woodson pioneered in telling the true story of the Negro in the American scene.

While reading that Deep South newspaper page, something else caught my eye. This article ran right beside it:

Whites, Negroes Foiled in Steps for Mixed Dance

(St. Louis) - Nine colored youths and four white persons, calling themselves the Committee for Fair Play, showed up to join a square-dance class at Sherman Park Community Center last Wednesday night, but the class failed to open.... Miss Waxman (a participant) told Miss Dorothy Zimmerman, the center's director, that the mixed group had come for instruction in dancing. She wanted to know when the class was going to get started. Miss Zimmerman replied that the class was too far advanced for the new group. She also said its members preferred to have its classes without colored persons.

Dr. Woodson's parents were born into bondage, and the newspaper shows, at the time of his death, much had been accomplished but there was still far to go. Much as today.

3 DIED

John Hardy (18?? – 1894), folk song subject. *Was he desperate, or brave? Big, or little? It depends on who is singing. But, he was real.*

When one thinks of folk ballads originating in West Virginia, John Henry, about whom we write below in this chapter, immediately comes to mind, as well as, perhaps, William "Billy" Richardson, the subject of the tune *Billy Richardson's Last Ride*. But, amongst true folk tune and early country music experts, John Hardy figures just as large, and, like Richardson but unlike Henry, his existence is unquestionable.

Visiting McDowell County today, it's almost hard to imagine what it was like during the expansion of the coalfields. The most recent data I can find sets the population at 17,620, with a median household income of $22,154, putting 32.6% of Free State of McDowell citizens below the national poverty line. The median value of owner-occupied housing units is $35,000, compared to the West Virginia average of $119,600 and the national average of $217,500.

How does that compare to the past? The 1950 census showed 98,887 people living in McDowell County. Think about that.

One of the biggest statistical differences between today's McDowell and that of a hundred years ago is in the percentage of foreign-born population. The county was once a center of ethnic diversity, with large communities of Italian and other eastern European immigrants. Today, slightly less than 1% of the county population hails from abroad.

Like other areas of the coalfields, many of those coming to timber the forests and build the railroads and mine the coal were Black. Today, only 8% of the county's population self-report as being so, compared to 13.4% nationally. During the post-World War II period, when mechanization allowed coal to be mined with far fewer human hands, many McDowell Countians of all backgrounds left for jobs elsewhere. But, still today, McDowell more than doubles the overall West Virginia Black population figure of only 4.8% (2019 pre-census estimate). Ranking lower are only Alaska, North Dakota, Hawaii, New Mexico, South Dakota, Oregon, Maine, New Hampshire, Wyoming, Vermont, Utah, Montana, and Idaho.

One of those early Black immigrants into the area was John Hardy, a railroad worker. We don't know exactly from where he came or how long he had been there. As any genealogist knows, most of the 1890 United States census is unavailable, having been destroyed in a fire, so finding him a few years before his death isn't possible, and I can find no likely candidates in southern West Virginia already present for the 1880 census. So, it's reasonable to assume that John was one of those workers more recently arrived.

The early work camps were filled with rowdy boarding houses for the male workers, different from the orderly coal camp communities with single-family dwellings that many of us can remember. John was evidently a gambler, and the volatile combination of alcohol and a payday craps game let to a row with a man named Thomas Drews (who also isn't found anywhere in the 1880 West Virginia census) at the Shawnee Coal Company camp in Eckman, near Keystone. Worst came to worst over the grand sum of twenty-five cents, and John Hardy killed Drews. Up to that point, the story was, sadly, one that has been repeated for centuries.

What happened next is a mixture of documented fact and legend that may, indeed, also have factual elements. First, what is on paper: Hardy was tried and evidently found guilty, but the only court document surviving is the execution order: "*State of West Virginia vs. John Hardy* – Felony- To wit, This day came again the State by her attorney and the prisoner who stands convicted of murder in the first degree. The prisoner saying nothing why such sentence should not be passed, it is therefore considered by the Court that the prisoner, John Hardy, is guilty, and that the said John Hardy be hanged by the neck until dead on Friday the 19th day of January 1894." Hangings were literally the biggest spectator events of the day, and more than 3,000 people were said to show up in Welch to see John off.

That's all we have as far as an official record, but the oral tradition is richer, thanks to Alan Lomax (1915 – 2002), one of history's most important ethnomusicologists. Born in Texas, he became the director of the Archive of American Folk Song at the Library of Congress. He traveled the country recording songs and interviews both here and, after World War II, even in Europe, finding the seeds of so many American folk songs traveled in the pockets of immigrants to our shores. He was instrumental in ushering in the American folk music revival, aiding the careers of Pete Seeger, Burl Ives, Woody Guthrie, and others. But, hanging around with folk singers during the McCarthy era had consequences, and his career suffered for a time by his being branded a leftist sympathizer.

He left us a shelf full of written works and a truckload of films and audio recordings, and they are a treasure. His interviews while researching the song tell that a lynch mob formed outside the McDowell County jail, intent on breaking Hardy out and hanging him. But, the sheriff did his duty and protected Hardy until he could be duly tried. While awaiting execution, Hardy had a conversion experience and the sheriff allowed a local preacher to baptize him in the river before walking up to the gallows. Hardy is said to have composed the song himself in jail, even confessing his sins and singing it on the scaffold before the trap door opened, admonishing all young men to avoid the evils of drink, liquor, and bad company.

But, what song did he write, and sing? There is where things get murky. There are, apparently, dozens of versions. Some begin with John Hardy being a desperate little man, others with him being a brave little man, while contemporary accounts describe the real John as a pretty big guy. And, instead of a rowdy single male, the song references both a wife and daughters. The next census, taken in 1900, show a few African-Americans living in McDowell County with the surname Hardy, but none that really fit as being John's widow or children.

Ah…the real John. It gets murkier still, because some versions of the ballad seemed to combine the stories of John Hardy and John Henry. The two incidents took place three counties and a quarter century apart, but what is that to a balladeer? As early as 1919, West Virginia folklorist John Harrington Cox tried to tease them apart in an article in *The Journal of American Folklore*.

In any event, the version most known today was recorded by the country music pioneering Carter Family in 1930. Later notes from the music publisher call John Hardy "A genuine folk ballad which Maybelle had known all of her life." Taking nothing away from the Carters, but their version was not even the first time the song had been recorded. The earliest on record was Eva Davis's rendition for Columbia Records in 1924, and several others followed throughout the 1920s before the Carters recorded it.

Since then, though, the Carter version has prevailed…and prevailed it has, having been recorded by practically everyone who is anyone in the world of folk music, plus some artists not known as folksy, or even country, at all. Sure, it's been recorded by Bobby Bare, Roy Clark, Flatt & Scruggs, Burl Ives, The Kingston Trio, Lead Belly, Bill Monroe, The Osborne Brothers, Jerry Reed, Don Reno, and Pete Seeger, but also by Manfred Mann, The Twilights, Bob Dylan and The Grateful Dead.

How's that for a song with broad appeal?

It's the Carter Family version with which we will close out discussion of John Hardy, an African-American laborer who came to help open southern West Virginia to the rest of the world, did an evil thing, paid with his life, but ultimately, if the legend is to be believed, found redemption:

John Hardy, he was a desperate lilt man,
He carried two guns every day.
He shot a man on the West Virginia line,
And you ought to seen John Hardy getting away.

John Hardy, he got to the Keystone Bridge,
He thought that he would be free.
And up stepped a man and took him by his arm,
Says, "Johnny, walk with me."

He sent for his poppy, and his mommy too,
To come and go his bail.
But money won't go a murdering case.
They locked John Hardy back in jail.

John Hardy, he had a pretty little girl,
That dress that she wore was blue.
As she came skipping through the old jail hall,
Saying, "Poppy, I've been true to you."

John Hardy, he had another little girl,
That dress that she wore was red.
She followed John Hardy to his hanging ground,
Saying, "Poppy, I would rather be dead."

I been to the east and I been to the west,
I been this wide world around.
I been to the river and I been baptized,
And now I'm on my hanging ground.

John Hardy walked out on his scaffold high,
With his loving little wife by his side.
And the last words she heard poor John-O say,
"I'll meet you in that sweet bye-and-bye."

John Henry (18?? – 18??), steel drivin' man. *Lord, lord. Of course he's real. How could a West Virginian think otherwise?*

It's a beautiful drive down to the Summers County community of Talcott, situated on the Big Bend of the Greenbrier River. Once known as Rollinsburg, it now bears the name of the civil engineer with the Chesapeake and Ohio Railway who was in charge of building the Big Bend Tunnel in the 1870s.

There is little to which to compare the great change brought to southern West Virginia by the completion of the C&O from the protected harbor at Hampton Roads, Virginia, through Richmond, and on to the Ohio River. The closest that comes to mind is a once sleepy and barely-populated sand plain in Nevada called Las Vegas pre-and post-Hoover Dam, but even that doesn't come close. Various private and public partnerships worked on the massive project, with the Virginia Central inching westward from the coast, until the Civil War intervened. At the end of the War, the Virginia Central had only five miles of useable track, and $40 in its bank account.

When hostilities ended (well, mostly), the Virginia Central owners tried to get investment from Great Britain (which had been sympathetic to the Confederacy), but failed to do so. Their only recourse was to turn to the Yankees in New York City, and, that meant Collis P. Huntington of the Central Pacific, who, about to complete the Transcontinental Railroad in the west, was open to new ventures, sure to be profitable, bringing vast lumber and coal reserves to a nation trying to rebuild with a backbone of steel rail and locomotives and bridges. Like he had done in the west, Huntington began working on both ends, to meet somewhere in the middle. By 1869, the line had reached White Sulphur Springs, so the fashionable set could have the porters offload their trunks filed with ball gowns and evening dress while taking the waters at the Greenbrier. Stagecoach connections were available from White Sulphur Springs to Charleston, where one could board a steamboat and, through various connections, eventually end up in Cincinnati or even New Orleans. A new city was constructed as the western terminus, one of the few in West Virginia laid out in neatly intersecting streets and avenues, and, of course, named after the boss.

The race was on to complete the hardest part, between Huntington and While Sulphur Springs, right through some of the most mountainous territory in the east. Vast numbers of workers were needed, beginning an influx of economic immigrants into southern West Virginia that would continue through the 1920s. Workers of all backgrounds came, but many of the skilled masons were Italian, while the unskilled workers were Irish and African-American. The two ends met at Hawks Nest, Fayette County, on January 28, 1873. In today's dollars, the westward expansion had cost around half a billion dollars, opening coalfields that have yielded untold trillions in wealth since.

Part of that route required tunneling through Big Bend Mountain. Work began in February 1870, and the workers broke through to the other side of the mountain on May 31, 1872. The rock is mainly a compact shale that weathers when exposed to air, making roof falls a hazard. The top was supported by timbers during construction, but the permanent lining is brick, laid in an arch style like that still supporting Roman viaducts that have been standing for more than two millennia. So, while the first train passed through the tunnel in 1872, masonry work continued for years, but the tunnel saw regular use beginning in 1873.

Without modern equipment capable of actually boring through rock, tunnels were dug by using black powder to blast away small sections of the mountain. Workers then loaded the rubble into mule carts to be taken outside and dumped, while the next blast was prepared. This was done, of course, with no dust masks, no hearing protection, and no health benefits or compensation or life insurance if the blast was a little too big, or if some of the top fell before it could be timbered, or so many other perils.

Now, John Henry enters the scene as a driller. That doesn't mean holding a big machine to drill out rock, as we would still see in primitive mining operations in some parts of the world even today. In order for the gunpowder charge to be effective, it had to be compressed into a small hole back into the rock. The hole was made by a "shaker" holding a steel bar, or drill, onto the rock and someone else, dubbed the steel-driver, hitting the end of the bar with a sledge hammer. With each strike, the shaker "rock and rolled" the drill, reaming out chunks of rock and dust that would otherwise absorb the next blow.

Shakers holding those rods really hoped their steel-drivers had good aim, would be my guess.

In the 1870's though, things were changing. A new device, powered by the same force that sent the Iron Horse along the tracks, came on the scene, tentatively at first. The steam-powered drill did not effectively "rock and roll" its drill, so rock dust softened its impact. But, it's relentless drilling motion could make up for that defect. And, it didn't have to be paid to continue what it was doing.

According to legend, John Henry took great pride in being one of the best steel drivers in the business, and, in the steam drill, foresaw the day when machines would replace people trying to make a living, so he set out to prove himself better than the machine. He persuaded the boss to arrange a man-against-machine competition. John would beat the impersonal hunk of machinery, or die trying. In the end, John, with a ten-pound (or possibly twelve, even!) hammer in each hand, drilled a fourteen-foot hole in the rock, while the steam drill could only drill nine. He won. He beat the machine. And then he laid down his hammer and died of exhaustion.

Or, so the song goes. But what about the evidence? What was meant to be the definitive detective work on the song and legend was produced by Guy B. Johnson in his *John Henry: Tracking Down a Negro Legend,* in 1929. Johnson was a sociologist and social anthropologist at the University of North Carolina for more than forty years. In 1927, Johnson visited Summers County in search of the truth. He interviewed many locals, some of whom said they actually remembered John Henry. One, Neil Miller (a son of Andrew Jackson Miller), said he worked on the tunnel as a teenager and saw John Henry daily. The contest, he assured, was real. "I saw John Henry drive steel in Big Bend Tunnel. He used to sing, always singing some old song when he was driving steel. He was a black, rawboned man, 30 years old, 6 feet high, and weighed 200 pounds. He and Phil Henderson, another big Negro, were pals, and said that they were from North Carolina. Phil Henderson turned the steel for John Henry when he had the contest with the steam drill at the east end of the tunnel...John won. He wouldn't rest enough, and he overdid. He took sick and died soon after that." So, John's death may not have been immediate.

Ever the researcher, Johnson contacted the Chief Engineer of the C&O, and was told no steam drills worked on the tunnel. When pressed for documentation, though, the engineer replied he had none, since "all such papers have been destroyed by fire." How convenient. But, steam drills were coming into pretty common use, most often alongside traditional drilling, during that period. In fact, the *Richmond Dispatch* noted in January 1871 that steam drills were being used in construction of the Lewis Tunnel to the east, between Talcott and Millboro, Virginia.

The imposing 8-foot statue of John Henry, commissioned by the Hilldale-Talcott Ruritan Club from sculptor Charles Cooper and unveiled in 1972, weighs almost three tons, and is a masterpiece. It originally right beside the road on top of the mountain, but has since been moved down to the tunnels, where a park has been developed. As a teenager in the mid-1970s, some friends and I camped almost on that very spot once, putting pennies on the track to be run over by the train as it went through the adjoining, newer tunnel still in use. I probably still have one somewhere. That night, we walked into the old tunnel, with water dripping down through the bricks, and were convinced we heard a hammer and steel. (I know. You're thinking there may have been alcohol involved, aren't you? Neither confirming nor denying, I will only note, after a bit of research, that the Heublein Company produced a premixed cocktail it branded Brass Monkey in the 1970s through the 1990s that could, in sufficient quantity, make one ponder whether or not life is really worth the bother.) We were by no means the only ones. Even early on, when masons were still finishing up the brick laying some years later, the "haunted" stories began, and have never stopped.

Moving the statue to nearer the site of the event and constructing a park with more space was a good thing to do, but, like so many stories in this book, there is an element of sad history to it. You see, that magnificent statue was, almost from its creation, a target. Bullet holes. Pic-ax gashes. Pulled from its pedestal and dragged. Did the same ever happen with the marble statue of feudist and Confederate veteran Devil Anse Hatfield in Logan County, that has been standing for almost a hundred years? I would hope not, but my point is probably pretty obvious.

And, speaking of the Lewis Tunnel: Some researchers have concluded that John Henry existed, but somewhere other than West Virginia. Historian Scott Reynolds Nelson of the University of Georgia asserts he has found records of a 19-year-old African-American man who was a convict in a Virginia penitentiary, and was leased out for tunnel work, a common practice of the day, not much better than slavery. Nelson hypothesizes that the actual contest took place there. Still others, such as John Garst also at the University of Georgia, speculate that John, born a slave, worked and won and died in the Coosa Mountain Tunnel near Dunnavant, Alabama. I will comment no further on those *spurious* theories, being the polite Mountaineer I am.

Ah, the song. Like most folk ballads, there are almost as many versions as there are singers. The first time I see the song mentioned in print is in the *Journal of American Folklore*, by Louise Rand Bascom, in 1909, which is not really all that long after the actual drilling stopped, in the scheme of things. She said she found it being sung in the mountains of western North Carolina. Just three years later, researcher E. C. Perrow collected a more complete version in eastern Kentucky. One of the first printed versions we would recognize as nearly complete was published as a "broadside" sometime between 1900 and 1920 under the name W. T. Blankenship (certainly a surname found in southern West Virginia), but there is no evidence that is any more than a commercial name used on a music sheet turned out by Tin Pan Alley. In other words, we don't know who wrote this most common version, and we all have our favorite singer of it. Mine, by the way, is Johnny Cash. Everybody, now!

When John Henry was a little tiny baby
Sitting on his mama's knee,
He picked up a hammer and a little piece of steel
Saying, "Hammer's going to be the death of me, Lord, Lord,
  Hammer's going to be the death of me."

John Henry was a man just six feet high,
Nearly two feet and a half across his breast.
He'd hammer with a nine-pound hammer all day

And never get tired and want to rest, Lord, Lord,
*   And never get tired and want to rest.*

John Henry went up on the mountain
And he looked one eye straight up its side.
The mountain was so tall and John Henry was so small,
He laid down his hammer and he cried, "Lord, Lord,"
*   He laid down his hammer and he cried.*

John Henry said to his captain,
"Captain, you go to town,
Bring me back a twelve-pound hammer, please,
And I'll beat that steam drill down, Lord, Lord,
*   I'll beat that steam drill down."*

The captain said to John Henry,
"I believe this mountain's sinking in."
But John Henry said, "Captain, just you stand aside--
It's nothing but my hammer catching wind, Lord, Lord,
*   It's nothing but my hammer catching wind."*

John Henry said to his shaker,
"Shaker, boy, you better start to pray,
'Cause if my twelve-pound hammer miss that little piece of steel,
Tomorrow'll be your burying day, Lord, Lord,
*   Tomorrow'll be your burying day."*

John Henry said to his captain,
"A man is nothing but a man,
But before I let your steam drill beat me down,
I'd die with a hammer in my hand, Lord, Lord,
*   I'd die with a hammer in my hand."*

The man that invented the steam drill,
He figured he was mighty high and fine,
But John Henry sunk the steel down fourteen feet
While the steam drill only made nine, Lord, Lord,
*   The steam drill only made nine.*

John Henry hammered on the right-hand side.
Steam drill kept driving on the left.
John Henry beat that steam drill down.
But he hammered his poor heart to death, Lord, Lord,
  He hammered his poor heart to death.

Well, they carried John Henry down the tunnel
And they laid his body in the sand.
Now every woman riding on a C and O train
Says, "There lies my steel-driving man, Lord, Lord,
   There lies my steel-driving man."

Walter Johnson (1888 – 1912), lynching victim. *Unimaginable brutality and complicity by the authorities were commonplace, not that long ago.*

Prepare to be sickened. While these entries were not written in the order presented, this is one of the last pieces I wrote for this book, knowing it would be both unpleasant to research, but necessary.

I will give you more than the usual amount of directly-quoted local newspaper accounts, to show the full impact of how events like this were depicted in the press, and seen by the public, in the day. What struck me, in addition to the animal brutality, the complicity of the authorities, and the second-page seeming normality of mob rule, was that all these events happened within the lifetime of my grandparents, and I am not an old man.

On September 12, 1912, a 14-year-old (or 15, depending on the account) girl in Bluefield, Neta Virginia White, raised the alarm from the window of her parent's home on Carolina Avenue, where she was alone. She said a Black man had come to the door, saying her father, Gordon White, a foreman in the rail yard, had sent him to get a measuring line. When she turned to go to the basement to get the tool, the man grabbed her from behind and stuffed a handkerchief in her mouth to stop her from screaming. The assailant released Neta and ran when the family dog came to the rescue. Neta fainted, and yelled for help through the window when she came to.

In seemingly no time, a crowd of 150+ men began scouring the area for the assailant, and continued into the night. Walter Johnson, a young railroad worker, was arrested. When asked to identify Johnson, both young Neta and her father failed to identify him. The police then stripped Johnson and dressed him in clothes similar to those Neta had described her assailant as wearing. "That's the man!" she said when she saw him again, and Gordon agreed.

Where is it we have heard something like this before? I know it was somewhere…oh, now I remember. A measuring line, instead of a chifforobe. Neta instead of Mayella. Walter instead of Tom Robinson.

Knowing the potential danger, the sheriff sent Johnson out of town, possibly at Lashmeet, in the custody of a deputy. The angry, drunken White mob showed up at the jail with blood lust, and stormed it, intent on lynching Johnson. Not being able to find him after ransacking the facility, they even blew up the jail's vault, thinking Johnson could be hidden inside. Johnson's whereabouts having been leaked, the mob went to the railyard and asked for a special train to take them there. Being denied didn't stop them. They knew how to run an engine, so they simply took one, along with two box cars. The mob easily extracted Johnson from his supposed protector and brought him back to Princeton, where they were barely, and only temporarily, persuaded to turn him back over to the sheriff.

The mob continued to grow. The sheriff deputized several men to help "protect" the prisoner…from the mob itself. Shortly after these men took their post, the mob again stormed the jail and easily took Johnson from his cell, led by Gordon White. They put a chain around his neck, marched him a short distance down the street while he was being clubbed and stoned, hung him from a telegraph pole, and riddled his body with bullets.

As I mentioned, reading the contemporary news stories, while sickening, gives us better insight to the times than a modern statement of the facts. First, from the Hinton *Daily News*, September 5, 1912:

NEGRO ARRESTED at BLUEFIELD and MOB FORMS to LYNCH HIM – OFFICERS SUCCEED IN GETTING HIM AWAY

A telephone message from Princeton at three o'clock this afternoon states that the negro was arrested in Bluefield, at five o'clock last evening and brought to Princeton in an automobile, by the officers. Soon after about 150 men from Bluefield came to Princeton and searched the jail, but the negro had been slipped out and could not be found. A general search was made for the negro by the Bluefield men and a number of railroad men from Princeton joined in the search, which was kept up nearly all night.

This morning it was said that the negro was at Rock and the railroad men asked the railroad officials of the Virginian for a special train to go to that place. Being denied, they took an engine and two box cars and left Princeton about nine o'clock for Rock. No word has been received since that time and it is not known what happened.

The supposition is in Princeton that the negro will be taken to Welch or Huntington for safe keeping, but as the deputy sheriffs have him in charge, no one seems to know their plans and it is possible that they are not far from Princeton at the present time. The mob at the jail created intense excitement and much disorder followed. The girl identified the negro at Bluefield before he was brought to the Princeton Jail.

These two "dispatches" were attached to the news story:

Princeton: Walter Johnson, colored, was arrested last night on a charge of making an assault on Nita White, a white girl, aged fourteen years. Another negro was arrested, but his name could not be learned. The negroes were placed in the county jail here, but later slipped out by the officers.

Bluefield, Sept. 5: Riot and disorder held full sway at Princeton last night where a mob of one thousand armed men are hunting for Walter Johnson, a negro charged with assaulting a young white girl here this morning. Earlier reports that the negro had been taken from the officers and lynched proved to be incorrect, but the frenzied mob is hunting the entire neighborhood of Princeton where the officers have the man in hiding.

The mob forced the jailor to let them in the jail, and not finding Johnson, wreaked their vengeance on the interior of the building. Seeing a large combination safe, they blew it open thinking the negro might be hid in it.

According to reports received here, the mob has consumed large quantities of liquor, and fired shots in all directions about the streets of Princeton. One negro was caught by the enraged men on the street at Princeton and severely beaten.

Everything here is quiet, though feeling is intense and all negroes are keeping in their homes.

The following day, from the Hinton *Independent-Herald*:

NEGRO LYNCHED AT PRINCETON

Walter Johnson paid awful penalty for assault on white girl – EXCITING NIGHT

Walter Johnson, a negro, accused of assaulting, or attempting to assault a 15-year-old girl, at Bluefield on Wednesday was hanged to a telegraph pole and then riddled with bullets, by an infuriated and drink-mad mob of over 3,000 persons, at Princeton, county seat of Mercer County

The lynching occurred last night at 9:50 o'clock, the mob rushing the jail where Johnson was confined and taking him out. He was marched down the street to a telegraph pole, where he was strung up. The mob then opened fire with guns and revolvers on the twitching body, filling it with bullets.

The tragedy was sudden and unexpected. A few minutes previous the crowd had listened to speeches from Judge Maynard of the criminal court, Rev. T. S. Hamilton, and other leading citizens, urging them to wait until this morning when a special term of court would be convened to try the negro and let justice work speedily and effectively. Special officers were then sworn in to guard the prisoner during the night.

The crowd was the more easily persuaded to this course by the announcement that identification of the prisoner was not complete and that the governor had telegraphed urging that justice take the place of "lynch law."

The father of the girl at this moment, however, appeared and gained the sheriff's permission to go into the jail and identify the prisoner if possible as his daughter's assailant.

"That's the man," declared White, the girl's father, pointing to Johnson. The mob outside heard this identification and, under an impulse of unreasoning fury they stormed the jail.

The sheriff was powerless to protect his prisoner, who was rushed out to his doom by the ob.
It is said that drinking was indulged in by the actors in the lynching.

Johnson was captured by a posse with four other negroes and the girl identified him, in a way, as the man. A deputy took him to the county jail at Princeton. Hearing that a mob was marching from Bluefield last night to lynch the negro, the deputy took his prisoner to his home at Lashmeet.

The mob went to the deputy's house and took the prisoner forcibly back to the jail at Princeton. They were in doubt about only one thing – when to lynch him, night or morning.

And this "dispatch" attached:

(Bluefield) Bluefield was stirred yesterday as never before in the city's history and all day long, especially last night, the excitement became intense and the streets were full of men drawn up in little knots earnestly talking of the desperate and fiendish, but fortunately unsuccessful, attempt made to assault a sixteen-year-old girl by a negro yesterday morning.

It seems that between 7 and 8 o'clock yesterday morning Miss Neta White, who was alone at her parents' home No. 126 Carolina Avenue, heard a knock at the door and went to see who was there. When she opened it a negro was standing between the wire or screen door and the door that she opened. He told Miss White hi had been sent by her father, Gordon White, a construction foreman on the yards, to get his tape line. The young lady turned to go to the basement for the line, and the negro grabbed her, after she had taken but one step towards the top of the stairway and clapped a large bandana handkerchief over her face and attempted to stifle her cries by forcing it in her mouth. The girl screamed and a pet dog which was in the basement tried to get into the upper part of the house, and it is thought this frightened the negro and he ran. The girl fainted and was possibly unconscious for some minutes and when she came to found herself in the parlor to the left of the hall and, crawling to the window called to the neighbors and the alarm was quickly given. The neighbors found her lying in the floor, prostrated by fright and excitement.

Dr. Scott was summoned and after thorough examination gave out a statement that while the young lady was suffering shock and extreme nervousness she was otherwise uninjured, her fiendish assailant having failed to accomplish his hellish purpose.

Excitement. Hellish purpose. The *Clarksburg Telegram* was even more descriptive of the brutality:

ANGRY MOB STRINGS BLACK MAN BY NECK
In the Presence of Sheriff, Judge, Ministers and Armed Guards

Bluefield, W. Va. — Pleading for mercy, followed by thousands right into the presence of the county criminal judge, sheriff and scores of armed guards, Walter Johnson, negro assailant of Nita White, was hanged to a telegraph pole and riddled with bullets at Princeton last night.

Judge Maynard and a minister addressed the crowd, but oratory only fed the mob's fury. The negro was beaten with clubs, rocks, and other missiles en route to the place of death.

A chain was placed around his neck and he was hoisted to a pole and thousands of angry men fired deadly shots into his body. Men then paraded around the body shooting wildly in the air. The mob then searched the city for other negroes to similarly deal with them.
The body was taken down today and buried by the father of Johnson, who was present and saw the entire proceedings. The negro was severely injured before being lynched. The mob threatened anyone who moved the body from the pole. The crowd at the lynching is estimated at 5,000. Utter quiet followed.

The mob arrived at Princeton with the prisoner in charge last night. Judge J. Frank Maynard addressed the crowd and asked them to refrain. The Rev. Mr. Hamilton pleaded for the negro and others attempted to speak, but the mob shut him off.

The mob at first agreed to hold off last night to allow the girl to go to Princeton last night to see if she could again identify him, if she made certain of it the mob was then to string him up.

However, another mob went from Bluefield in a few minutes Crowds kept leaving and it was realized they would take him into their own hands.

But, the following day:

WRONG MAN LYNCHED
Bluefield – Serious doubt is expressed whether the mob lynched the right man at Princeton for an assault committed on a small girl. Officers say they are positive Walter Johnson was not guilty of the crime for which he paid the death penalty, and are making an investigation.

A subsequent investigation revealed Johnson had an easily verifiable alibi for where he was at the time of the attempted assault, and it was nowhere near Carolina Avenue. The investigation conclusively established Johnson's innocence. Yes, arrests were made when the governor became concerned about bad publicity, but no one, even Gordon White, ever faced a prison sentence for the young, innocent man's brutal murder.

That governor, William E. Glasscock, a Republican from Morgantown, was the same governor who declared martial law in the coalfields three times during his four-year term of office to prevent unionization. He issued a statement to the NAACP that declared, "I am as much opposed to lynching as your association can possibly be and during my term of office have prevented four lynchings, on one occasion appearing myself in person with a company of militia and personally directing the movements of troops. I am sure that if I had been informed a few hours earlier of the seriousness of the situation I could have prevented this disgrace to the State."

Glasscock. I'll say no more.

From the *Chicago Day Book*:

Gov. Glasscock has asked the Mercer County authorities to call a special term of court to investigate the lynching of Walter Johnson, a negro. Johnson was accused of attacking Nita White, the 16-year-old daughter of a railroad man. It is now certain he was innocent. The Mercer County mob, which lynched Johnson by mistake, is trying to correct the error today. It is looking for the real criminal, with intention to lynch him also. An investigation will be conducted by Criminal Judge J. Frank Maynard and Assistant Prosecutor Ross, both of whom risked their lives to save Johnson from the mob.

Gordon White was eventually charged with Walter Johnson's murder.

Also from the *Day Book*:

Gordon White, railroad foreman and father of Nita White, was held to the grand jury on a charge of murder in the first degree today. Released on $10,000 bail. White charged Walter Johnson, a negro, with assaulting and mistreating his daughter. A mob gathered and lynched Johnson. Later Nita said that Johnson was not the negro who attacked her, and Gov. Glasscock ordered an investigation. White was arrested late Saturday night and spirited to Charleston, because it was feared the mob would free him. Citizens swore to kill every officer in Bluefield unless White was brought back. Ugly threats were made today. Five hundred excited citizens followed White into the office of Justice of the Peace Dillard when he was arraigned. All of them were clamoring for his release. The negroes are making the situation worse. Secure in the belief that the state is behind them, they are openly condemning the lynching of Johnson. The special grand jury impaneled by Criminal Judge J. Frank Maynard has begun its investigation of the lynching.

Making it worse, openly condemning Johnson's lynching? You read that right. And, apparently, the arresting officers cut his telephone line when they took him into custody, and Mary was none too pleased. From the *Bluefield Daily Telegraph*, September 21, 1912:

WAS TOLD BY SHERIFF TO DISCONNECT 'PHONE
Special Officer Kahle Appears Before Board to Answer Charges Made by Mrs. White.

The Board of Affairs met yesterday afternoon with all of the members present except Commissioner Kahle, who is absent from the city. Special Officer C. F. Kahle appeared in answer to the charge made against him by Mrs. Gordon White of disconnecting the telephone at her home on the day of her husband's arrest by Kahle and others. Mr. Kahle stated, in his defense, that he, with others, was deputized by the sheriff of the county to make the arrest and that plans were laid in the office of Mr. Maynard before going out to arrest the man. He said it was deemed advisable by the sheriff to disconnect the telephone and that it was suggested that he do it.

But, Gordon, nor anyone else, paid for the crime. *The Advocate* was an African-American interest newspaper in Charleston, published from 1901 – 1913. It foresaw the conclusion of events, on Sept. 26. 1912:

The End of the Chapter.

The Advocate derives no pleasure from the fulfillment of its prophecy that Mercer County's effort to punish the lynchers of Walter Johnson would prove a fiasco. Press reports of the sympathy of the public with the act made it a foregone conclusion that the actors would never be brought to justice. It was upon this sympathy our prophecy was based.

The hope is held out that the regular grand jury is yet to consider the inexcusable murder of the man, generally believed now to be innocent, and that many true bills will be found, but none except the most optimistic indulge in such a hope. To do so would be to disregard all traditions and precedents and to place Mercer citizens upon a higher plane than the average.

The latter position is not tenable as any one knows who is acquainted with Mercer's people — white people- mostly recent inhabitants of Virginia, deep-dyed with all of Virginia's prejudice against color. They are Republicans of recent conversion, and, consequently, of the lily-white persuasion which would deny to the black man common justice.

With such a constituency and against such public sympathy for the mob, the officers of the law, conscientious as they may be, will make no headway. An innocent man has been murdered, his murderers and the man guilty of the crime for which he suffered are free, and West Virginia hangs her head in shame. Thus readeth the chapter and thus it ends.

The same year that Walter Johnson was brutally murdered, Black delegate John Coleman introduced an anti-lynching bill in the West Virginia legislature. Three lynchings, including Johnson's, took place in southern West Virginia while the bill was being considered, but it was voted down. It was not until 1921 that one was passed.

As difficult as the subject matter is to research and read about, we have to acknowledge the impact of lynching on West Virginia. Throughout this book, we talk about Black families who migrated here from Virginia and North Carolina and Alabama and Louisiana during the 1890 – 1930 period, because of the insatiable need for coal laborers. Jobs, yes, but there was another, darker reason: Lynching was so common in the south that many felt a move "north" to West Virginia would allow them to live a safer life. After *Plessy v. Ferguson* upheld "separate but equal" without defining "equal," states, especially in the former Confederacy, felt they were again unconstrained by those pesky Constitutional rights for the Black population, and, for the next fifty years, they were basically correct. Throughout the region, Blacks had practically no vote, no protection, no rights, no voice. They came for coal jobs by the thousands (there were 32,000 Blacks in West Virginia in 1890, and 43,000 only ten years later; the number continued to swell until the Great Depression) but the state was pitifully unprepared for the population influx. It's government controlled by the mine and timber interests, there was only token taxation on industry, so professional policing was just an afterthought. Coal companies hired Baldwin Felts and Pinkerton "detectives" to act with the full authority that should have been held by government, and with impunity for wrongdoing.

Almost 60 African-American West Virginians were lynched in our state between 1882 and the year Walter Johnson was brutally murdered, and he was not the last. As late as November 1931, a mob broke Tom Jackson and George Banks out of the Greenbrier County jail in Lewisburg and hung them from an unusually short telephone pole, with their feet just inches from the ground. They were still struggling, not yet asphyxiated, when the mob began shooting them repeatedly. Investigators later retrieved a half-gallon of empty shell casings from the scene.

Men were arrested for murdering Jackson and Banks, but the Grand Jury returned no indictments. Surprised?

The Whites were native to Wythe County, Virginia. The 1910 census shows Gordon and Mary with a large family: Robert, Oliver, Neta, Mary E., George, Iola, Dorothy, and Preston, with Robert age 25, Preston a baby, and all the rest scattered between. Unlike Walter Johnson, the Whites went on with their lives, Gordon and Mary eventually returning to their native Wythe County, Virginia. Gordon Preston White (1865 – 1955) and Mary Arrena Sutherland (1867 – 1946) married in 1883, and today rest side by side in the Davis Cemetery, Cripple Creek. Neta (sometimes spelled Neata) married an

Owen, and died at her home on Lyndale Avenue in Bluefield on January 23, 1962 of pneumonia.

I have spent a lot of time in Princeton and Bluefield. In fact, my wife is from Princeton. When I worked for the federal court, I spent a couple of days a month in the Bluefield federal courthouse, and always looked forward to it. It was usually pretty quiet, and I walked down the street to browse an antique store at lunch. In fact, I spent my last day on the job in that office, locking my laptop, Glock, and other tools of my trade in the vault and walking out a retiree ready to begin a new life, having just turned 51 years old. In a way, I am glad I didn't know this story back then.

But, maybe I shouldn't be. Maybe we should all know it, and remember it, every day.   Walter Johnson. Say his name.

Heyward Shepherd (1813 – 1859), John Brown's victim.   *Though he was a family man simply doing his job, his legacy still stirs controversy after more than a century and a half.*

The story of Heyward Shepherd, who lived in Winchester, Virginia but worked, and died, in Harpers Ferry should be interesting to us today because it gives a look into the relatively little-documented lives of "Free Blacks" in our area before the Civil War. But, his would most likely be a tale completely forgotten were it not for the tragically ironic manner of his death.

It has to begin with someone else. John Brown was born in Connecticut, the son of abolitionist Owen Brown, a successful cattleman and tanner whose own father was a soldier in the American Revolution. The family descended from New England Puritans. Brown's mother, Ruth Mills Brown, died when he was only eight years old, by which time the family had "gone west" to Ohio. Among the employees at the Brown tannery was Jesse R. Grant, whose son Ulysses would someday successfully command our Union troops.

He was active in abolitionist circles, and participated in the Underground Railroad, helping runaway slaves escape to free soil. Living in Springfield, Massachusetts, he tried to organize regional wool farmers in order to improve quality and bypass the stranglehold wool merchants had on the trade. His plan didn't work out very well, because European buyers were also more interested in price than quality. During this time, he met abolitionists Frederick Douglass and Sojourner Truth. My second novel, *Thoreau's Wound*, also describes his meeting Ralph Waldo Emerson and Henry David Thoreau in Concord.

John's move from activist to violence came in 1856, in "Bloody Kansas," which was essentially a mini-Civil War leading up to the much bigger one. It was based on control of Congress, which had tip-toed a tenuous balance between Free states and Slave states for years. As new territories in the west prepared for statehood, the balance was inevitably going to be tilted toward freedom. Kansas was allowed to decide the issue for itself via popular referendum, and it was fairly clear, in those days before public opinion polls, that it would vote to become free soil, and the pro-slavery forces were willing to prevent that at any cost. Armed militias from bordering Missouri, a slave state, invaded, and anti-slavery militias responded. Immigrants on both sides flowed into the state, specifically to establish residence and vote, armed by their supporters back east. It became open warfare, even involving artillery stolen from the army. On May 24, 1856, John Brown and his sons and their band invaded a small pro-slavery settlement at Pottawatomie Creek, hacking five men to death with swords.

Pottawatomie Creek was Brown's Rubicon. One of his sons was eventually killed in the Kansas violence, and John Brown was now on a Mission from God. A Holy War. Jihad.

Successful Jihad requires soldiers and weapons. Brown's soldiers were to be not only fellow Abolitionists, but those held in bondage themselves, fighting for their own freedom when given guns. Thousands of guns. Where to find that many guns? John took advantage of a lull in the Kansas conflict to return to New England and, over the next three years, plan the great emancipation's first step:

Harpers Ferry. He was to attack the arsenal there with a force of 4,500 well-armed men. On October 16, 1859, he and his force did just that.

All twenty-one of them. When you are convinced God is on your side, little else seems to matter, I suppose. Harpers Ferry, at the confluence of the Potomac and Shenandoah Rivers, had been founded by Robert Harper in the mid-1700s, and had been visited by both Thomas Jefferson and George Washington, whose brothers settled nearby. Seeing the need for protection of a westward-moving population, the federal government bought land from Harper's heirs in 1796 to build its second armory and arsenal. Along with the older one in Springfield, Massachusetts, the arsenals manufactured most of the small arms for the Army, Navy, and Marine Corps. It was up and running by 1801 and operated until it was destroyed in 1861 in order to prevent its falling into Confederate hands. During that time, it produced more than six-hundred-thousand muskets, rifles, and pistols, and became an early adapter of interchangeable parts in firearms manufacture.

If you are interested, by the way, many Harpers Ferry firearms still exist, and come onto the market for gun collectors. A quick search finds a nice one available right now, in excellent overall condition, for $12,950.00. To avoid sticker shock, lower quality ones can be found for considerably less, especially muskets that were later "converted" with percussion mechanisms.

Very little went to plan for Brown in Harpers Ferry. Shepherd, 46, lived with his family on North Kent Street in Winchester, and worked as baggage handler for the B & O Railroad. He was in charge of the Harpers Ferry depot overnight. His shift began on Sunday, October 16, 1859, like any other. After midnight, the history of the United States changed forever.

Part of Brown's quest has a strange, almost *Raiders of the Lost Ark* feel. He knew that George Washington's great-great-nephew, Colonel Lewis Washington, lived nearby on his Beall-Air plantation. Washington, like his famous uncle, was a slave holder, and also the inheritor of a couple of George's prized possessions: a sword presented to Washington by Frederick the Great, and a pair of pistols given by the Marquis de Lafayette. For some reason, Brown saw these objects as talismans that would ensure success, and he sent a party to capture Lewis Washington and the objects while he stayed out of sight in Harpers Ferry, cutting the telegraph line so a call for help could not be sent when the shooting started. While doing this, Brown and his men were encountered by a night watchman, whom they took hostage. The watchman managed to escape, though, and flagged down the express train coming eastbound from Wheeling, around 1:15 AM. When Heyward Shepherd and four other men went to investigate, Brown's men yelled for them to stop, but instead they turned around to return to the safety of the depot.

And that's when the abolitionists shot a free Black man in the back.

The town doctor, John Starry, lived across from the bridge and, hearing the commotion, came out to investigate. He found the abolitionists and the wounded Shepherd, with whom he was acquainted. He tended to Shepherd, but it was clear the victim could not survive. Starry was allowed to leave on the condition he go back into his house and not raise an alarm. Instead, he ran to the Lutheran church and began ringing the bell, and sent others to summon help from Charles Town and other nearby settlements. It was on, as the saying goes. But, throughout the beginning of the siege and into the next morning, Heyward lingered, finally dying twelve agonizing hours after being wounded.

Looking at the record, I do not find Heyward in the 1850 Winchester census. Is it possible he was still enslaved at that time, and only won his freedom later, sometime prior to 1859? Perhaps. But it is likely the family of Sarah A. Shepherd, 36, listed as a Mulatto Housekeeper found living in the 1860 census is Heyward's widow and children. Besides Sarah, the home included Martha, 16; Mary, 12; Lucy, 9; Fanny, 7; and John H., 4. Who knows what Sarah had to go through over the next four years to keep her family safe?

We know how the Brown raid ended after the arrival of Colonel Robert E. Lee and Lieutenant J.E.B. Stuart, and to what it led. Brown would also have the distinction of being a non-native West Virginian (or, what became West Virginia in 1863) who died in the state, when he was hung in nearby Charles Town on December 2, 1859. For security, during the execution, a professor at Virginia Military Institute in Lexington, who was a native of Clarksburg, marched a contingent of young soldiers to the event. The nation's most famous poet, himself an abolitionist, was also there. So was an actor from a prominent thespian family in Maryland. If the primitive photography of the day were as advanced as it is now, it may be possible to pick out Thomas J. "Stonewall" Jackson, Walt Whitman, and John Wilkes Booth all in the same shot on that cold day.

Before the War even ended, its narrative began to be crafted to fit the views of those telling it. Today, we call that "spin." I have heard historians say that the Union won the shooting war, but the Confederacy won the narrative war, and those battles continue even today. Sadly, Heyward's story became a pawn in that conflict. In the 1930s, the United Daughters of the Confederacy and the Sons of Confederate Veterans (no offense to any of my readers who may be members) erected a monument to Hayward in Harpers Ferry, inscribed, "On the night of October 16, 1859, Heyward Shepherd, an industrious and respected colored freeman, was mortally wounded by John Brown's raiders. In pursuance of his duties as an employee of the Baltimore and Ohio Railroad Company, he became the first victim of this attempted insurrection. This boulder is erected by the United Daughters of the Confederacy and the Sons of Confederate Veterans as a memorial to Heyward Shepherd, exemplifying the character and faithfulness of thousands of negros who, under many temptations throughout subsequent years of war, so conducted themselves that no stain was left upon a record which is the peculiar heritage of the American people, and an everlasting tribute to the best in both races."

Heyward certainly deserves to be remembered, as a guy doing his job and wrongly killed. He left a wife and several children over in Winchester. But, plainly, the monument was placed to advance the "Happy, faithful servant" element of the patient, persistent, and largely successful "Lost Cause" revisionist campaign which began the day after Lee's surrender and continues unabated. It started a "plaque war" of sorts at Harpers Ferry, with subsequent plaques placed by the NAACP and National Park Service to contextualize the Heyward monument, and there are several. The newest, placed by the NPS in 1994, states, in part, "In 1905, the United Daughters of the

Confederacy stated that erecting the monument (to Shepherd) would influence for good the present and coming generations, and prove that *the people of the South who owned slaves valued and respected their good qualities as no one else ever did or will do."* (emphasis added)

Valued and respected? Go home, Karen.

I am not against monuments. But, whenever I see one, I ask: When was it erected, and for what purpose? Is it objective, or making a political statement? Who erected it, and was it done with community input? Does it stand as a positive example for young people today?

Rest in Peace, Heyward.

ACKNOWLEDGEMENTS AND SOURCES

First, thanks to Janice Davis Young, recently retired from her service at the Drain-Jordan Library at West Virginia State University. Over the years, she has done a tremendous job with the Archives, met a "Who's Who" in the world of Black History, and been referenced in many publications, including *Goldenseal.* Godspeed for a long, well-deserved, and productive retirement! Also thanks to former West Virginia State Senator Marie Redd, author Dr. Adam Starks (*Broken Child Mended Man*), Pastor Charles Shaw, and musician Doris Fields, all of whom graciously responded to my inquiries and made suggestions.

And, thanks to my wife Sandy, who puts up with the obsessive behavior writing requires; Dave Lewis (to whom this book is dedicated) for his mentorship, encouragement, and friendship during my career with the court; and to Dr. Henry Lewis Gates Jr., whom, though we have never met, inspires in me and so many others a love of history and pride in our West Virginia heritage. Skip, I am still available for that beer with you and Barack. Call me.

These articles incorporate much public domain material from government and out-of-copyright historical source materials. Genealogical information in this book comes primarily from United States Census records, vital research records from the West Virginia State Archives, and Ancestry.com. That work, of course, is posted by individual researchers interested in the subject family, and there is no guarantee of its correctness, so please take that into consideration. The *West Virginia Encyclopedia* online, a project of the West Virginia Humanities Council, has also been used as a great overall resource. A few articles, including the ones on Raleigh County natives/residents Doris Payne, Bill Withers, and Cornelius Carlton, appeared in some form (either shortened or lengthened) in *Fresh History, Brewed Daily: Raleigh County (WV) People, Places, Happenings 1750 – Present (Favoritetrainers.com Books, 2015),* and are not further referenced. Along with some of my other books, that one is available at Tamarack in Beckley, and online.

Period newspaper and other references made within the body of the book are not repeated here:

Mather, Frank Lincoln (27 June 2019). "Who's who of the Colored Race: A General Biographical Dictionary of Men and Women of African Descent." Ethel Caffie-Austin, West Virginia Music Hall of Fame archive, Dr. Ethel Caffie-Austin: West Virginia's First Lady of Gospel Music, Joe Fitzwater, WOWK 2020, "A Different World: Symposium on Diversity, Change, and Appalachian Youth". www.marshall.edu. Haran. "A Different World: Symposium on Diversity, Change, and Appalachian Youth" We Are Marshall exciting, emotional for Bluefield family, Archer, Bill. Bluefield Daily Telegraph, December 13, 2006, Dennis Blevins College States, www. Sports-reference.com. RV senior Michael Blevins honors fallen great uncle on Friday nights, AZ Central.com, 2017, Robert Burnette Obituary, Death Notice, and Service, www.legacy.com, "CAIN, Richard Harvey". Biographical Directory of the United States Congress. United States Congress. Retrieved December 5, 2016. Edgar, Walter. South Carolina Encyclopedia (2006) pp. 119-120, University of South Carolina Press, Columbia, South Carolina, Bailey, N. Louise, Morgan, Mary L., and Taylor, Carolyn R. Biographical Directory of the South Carolina Senate: 1776-1985, v. I, pp. 246-248, 1986, University of South Carolina Press, Columbia, South Carolina, Butler, Dee. The Emergence of Women in West Virginia History: A Title IX Project for Social Studies. West Virginia Department of Education, Capitol Complex, Building 6, Room 252, Charleston, WV 25302., 1987. Peeks, Edward (June 5, 1977). "Remembering Miss Fannie". West Virginia Archives and History. Charleston Sunday Gazette-Mail. Retrieved February 13, 2016. Matz, Barbara and Janet Craig (Project Director and Project Coordinator). Missing Chapters: West Virginia Women In History. Charleston: Women's Commission, 1983, pp. 3-5, 21-23 and 41- 43. March 29, 1973: Educator Fannie Cobb Carter Dies in Charleston". WV Public Radio. Retrieved 22 November2016. Rice, Connie Park (2007). ""Don't Flinch nor Yield an Inch": J. R. Clifford and the Struggle for Equal Rights in West Virginia". West Virginia History: A Journal of Regional Studies. 1 (2): 45–68. Rice, Connie Park (2007 Simmons, William J.; Turner, Henry McNeal (1887). Men of Mark: Eminent, Progressive and Rising. G. M. Rewell & Company. p. 273. Men of Mark: Eminent, Progressive and Rising. Gilbert, David T.

(August 11, 2006). "The Niagara Movement at Harpers Ferry" State v. Dean, 134 W. Va. 257, 58 S.E.2d 860 (1950), Butler, G. (2007, March 13). Martin Robison Delany (1812 – 1885) BlackPast.org., Victor Ullman, Martin R. Delany: The Beginnings of Black Nationalism (Boston, Beacon Press, 1971), Jim Haskins, Black Stars: African-American Military Heroes (John Wiley and Sons, Inc. New York), Blowers, Diana (February 22, 1995). "Delany made his mark as a doctor, writer, black nationalist, officer". Dayton Daily News (Dayton, Ohio). p. 25 MARTIN ROBISON DELANY MONUMENT Archived 2016-01-06 at the Wayback Machine, lwfaam.net. Retrieved January 27, 2019.Ann Kathryn Flagg, UNCAP: Guide to the Ann Kathryn Flagg Papers, University of Chicago, Actress and Playwright Ann Kathryn Flagg Died: WV Public Radio, October 27, 2016, Maya Jaggi (July 6, 2002). "Henry the first". The Guardian. O'Hagan, Sean (July 20, 2003). "The biggest brother: interview with Henry Louis Gates, black America's foremost intellectual". The Observer. London. Bruce Cole (2002). "Henry Louis Gates Jr. Interview". National Endowment for the Humanities. Charge Dropped against Harvard scholar, The Washington Times, July 22, 2009, Contemporary Black Biography. Vol. 67. Gale, 2008. Reproduced in Biography Resource Center, Farmington Hills, Mich.: Gale, 2009. "Mrs. Gilmore's Defining Black History". Democratic Underground.com. Feb 12, 2012. "Elizabeth Harden Gilmore House". National Park Service. Hal Greer, Basketball Reference.com "Marshall basketball legend Hal Greer dies at 81 | Marshall University". wvgazettemail.com. "June 26, 1936: NBA Hall of Famer Hal Greer Born in Huntington | West Virginia Public Broadcasting". "Basketball legend returns home | Marshall Sports". herald-dispatch.com. February 9, 2012 West Virginia's First African-American Female Delegate, WV Public Radio, May 15, 2020, Talbott, I. D. "Duke"; Charles M. Murphy (November 30, 2012). "Minnie Buckingham Harper". e-WV: The West Virginia Encyclopedia. Dr. Patrice Harris, AMA-ORG/About, AMA Past President Dr. Patrice Harris advocates for Equity, Healthcareitnews.com, Feb. 10, 2021, "Patrice Harris, WVU grad and Bluefield native, becomes first African-American woman to lead American Medical Association Board of Trustees | Eberly College of Arts and Sciences | West Virginia University". Eberly.wvu.edu. Retrieved 2018-08-14. "Black Woman Named President of American Medical Association, Makes History - EBONY". EBONY. 2018-07-02. Rozen, Leah (October 3, 2014). "Steve Harvey on Success and His Hard-Won Life Lessons: "I'm Living Proof You Can Reinvent Yourself"". Parade. Athlon Media Group. Strohm, Emily; Kimble, Lindsay (May 25, 2016). "Living Out of His Car and Surviving on Bologna Sandwiches: Inside Steve Harvey's Struggle with Homelessness as He Tried to Make It as a Comedian". People.com. Finn, Natalie (May 11, 2017). "The Determined Rise of Steve Harvey: From Homeless Stand-Up Comic to $100 Million TV Machine Who Doesn't Have Time for an

Ambush". *E! News Online.* State v. Hickman, West Virginia Supreme Court of Appeals, December 12, 1985, Suspect surrenders after pleas from family, UPI Archives, June 27, 1981, Websites, The Potter's Church and TD Jakes, Shayne Lee, T.D. Jakes: America's New Preacher, NYU Press, USA, 2007, p. 22 *Cusic, Don, ed. (12 November 2009).* Encyclopedia of Contemporary Christian Music. *p. 221.* "Meet the SuperSoul100: The World's Biggest Trailblazers in One Room". *O Magazine. August 1, 2016.* James Jett, AllTime-Athletics.com, James Jett, Sports-Reference.com, Pro-Football Reference.com/players/J/Jett, *Stewart, Shirley L. (July 8, 2020).* "Johnnie Johnson". *e-WV: The West Virginia Encyclopedia.* Ratliff, Ben (April 14, 2005). "Johnnie Johnson, 80, Dies; Inspired 'Johnny B. Goode'". The New York Times. *Fricke, David (May 5, 2005). "Johnnie Johnson". Rolling Stone. p. 26. Lawson Family Genealogy, WVCulture.Org, African-Americans in West Virginia,* "Lou Myers Dead – Mr. Vernon Gaines From 'A Different World' Dies at 77". *TMZ.com. February 20, 2013* Lou Myers profile, filmreference.com; http://www.wvstateu.edu/About/History-and-Traditions/Lou-Myers.aspx NCBI: In Memorium, John C. Norman, 2014, Charleston native a pioneer in transplant procedures, Charleston Daily Mail, May 9, 2019, Dr. John C. Norman Collection, West Virginia State Department of Culture, Simmons, William J., and Henry McNeal Turner. Men of Mark: Eminent, Progressive and Rising. GM Rewell & Company, 1887. Spanish–American War: 2nd Regiment West Virginia Infantry". Wvculture.org. Archer, William R. "Bill". Bluefield, Arcadia Publishing (2000), page 101, Jasen, David A. A Century of American Popular Music, Routledge (2002), page 121, Lawrence, A. H. Duke Ellington and His World: A Biography Routledge (2001), Analysis of Redd's Campaign, Marshall University, George "Spanky" Roberts, CAFRISEABOVE.org, George "Spank" Roberts, West Virginia Department of Transportation, Spanky Roberts, WV's First African-American Aviation Hero, 130 AW, February 3, 2018, Siggers: Reviews, RateYourMusic.Com, Reuben Siggers and his Fabulous Kool Kats, Rocky-52, Siggers, Doo-Wop.blogg.org, Mr. Arthur Simmons, The Raleigh Register, Val Wilmer, Art Simmons. The New Grove online, Curtis, Nancy C. (1996). Black Heritage Sites: An African-American Odyssey and Finder's Guide. Chicago, Illinois: American Library Association. Progressive Americans of the twentieth century : containing biographical sketches of distinguished Americans. Chicago, Illinois: Progressive Publishing Company. 1910. *Powell, Bob.* "April 3, 1908: Samuel Starks State Librarian Dies". *WV Public Broadcasting.* Retrieved 2 April 2019, Strauder v. West Virginia, 1879, Encyclopedia.com, Strauder v. West Virginia, West Virginia Supreme Court of Appeals, October 1879, Sullivan, Leon H. (1998). Moving Mountains: The Principles and Purposes of Leon Sullivan. Judson Press. Columbus Salley (1998). The Black 100: A Ranking of the Most Influential African-Americans, Past and Present. Citadel Press.

PlanPhilly | Nation's first black-owned shopping center celebrates 50.Fairmont's Last Living Slave:" Aunt Hat," West Virginia Department of Culture, Little Hat Jones Wilson Whitely, West Virginia History On View, Byron W. Woodson, Sr., A President in The Family, (Westport CT, Praeger, 2001, Carter G. Woodson, Charles Harris Wesley, The Negro in Our History, Associated Publishers, 1922, p. 140 (digitized from original at University of Michigan Library), "Thomas Jefferson and Sally Hemings: A Brief Account", Plantation & Slavery, Monticello, Ed Austin, The Raleigh Register (as cited), C. C. Barnett, American Negro Index, Barnette Family History, WikiTree, Barnett Hospital and Nursing School, National Register Information System, Nomination Form, John Warren Davis, West Virginia Department of Arts, Culture, and History Archives, John Warren Davis, adviser to five presidents, The Record. Hackensack, NJ, July 13, 1980, *Trotter, Joe (1993)*. Black Women in America. *Brooklyn, NY: Carlson Publishing, Casto, James E. (2013)*. Legendary Locals of Huntington. *Arcadia Publishing,* Peeks, E. (February 10, 2004). "Memphis Garrison helped open doors for blacks". ProQuest Miller Elected Criminal Judge, Welch Daily News, November 13, 1968, Leon P. Miller, Political Graveyard, Leon P. Miller, Find-a-Grave, "Mildred Mitchell-Bateman, M.D." National Institutes of Health. National Institutes of Health. Bickley, Ancella. "Mildred Mitchell-Bateman". The West Virginia Encyclopedia, Mildred Mitchell-Bateman Papers, 1941-2006, Accession No. 2017/10.0839, Special Collections Department, Marshall University, Huntington, WV, West Virginia State University ROTC Alumni". West Virginia State University ROTC Official Website. "U.S. Army Ordnance Corps Official Webpage Former Chiefs of Ordnance". *U.S. Army Ordnance Corps Official Webpage.* Jeff Wiltse, Contested Waters: A Social History of Swimming Pools in America, Univ of North Carolina Press, 2009, Nutter, Isaac Henry", Who's Who of the Colored Race: A General Biographical Dictionary of Men and Women of African Descent, ed. Franklin Lincoln Mather, Chicago: 1915, Byrd Prillerman, The HistoryMakers.com, Byrd Prillerman School, U. S. National Park Service, Byrd Prillerman Obituary, Legacy.com., "Ira De Augustine Reid papers". New York Public Library. Ira De A. Reid House Rededicated". Haverford College. 13 February 2013. Shetterly, Margot Lee; Loff, Sarah (2016-11-22). "Dorothy Vaughan Biography". NASA. "Hidden Figure: Dorothy Vaughan". *Spelman College.* Shetterly, Margot Lee (2016a). "The Hidden Black Women Who Helped Win the Space Race". New York. Daryl Michael Scott, "The History of Black History Month" Archived July 23, 2011, at the Wayback Machine, "Carter G. Woodson: Winona, WV - New River Gorge National Park anPreserve (U.S. National Park Service)". *www.nps.gov.* Winston, Michael R. (1975). "Carter Godwin Woodson: Prophet of a Black Tradition". The Journal of Negro History. University of Chicago Press. John Hardy: BobDylanRoots.com, *Stephen Wade*

(2 September 2002). "John Henry, Present at the Creation". *NPR. Grimes, William (2006-10-18)*. "Taking Swings at a Myth, With John Henry the Man (Published 2006)". *The New York Times. Janney, Caroline E. (2006)*. "Written in Stone: Gender, Race, and the Heyward Shepherd Memorial". *Civil War History*. Johnson, Mary (1997). "An 'Ever Present Bone of Contention': the Heyward Shepherd Memorial". West Virginia History. "Robert Page Sims". *West Virginia Department of Arts, Culture and History Caldwell, Arthur Bunyan, ed. (1923). "Hamilton Hatter"*. History of the American Negro. "Vietnam War Medal of Honor recipients (M-Z)". Medal of Honor citations. United States Army Center of Military History. "Richard Nixon: Remarks on Awarding the Congressional Medal of Honor to Twelve Members of the Armed Services". The American Presidency Project. University of California, Santa Barbara. Joe Turner: The Decorated West Virginia Military Pilot You've Never Heard Of, West Virginia Public Broadcasting, August 22, 2019, Inductees, West Virginia Aviation Wall of Valor/WVAMA.org, ."Katherine Johnson Biography;" Gutman, David. "WV native, NASA mathematician to receive Presidential Medal of Freedom," WV Gazette Mail, November 16, 2015; Bartels, Meghan. "The unbelievable life of the forgotten genius who turned Americans' space dreams into reality," Business Insider, August 22, 2016; (1984). No Sacrifice Too Great: The Life of Lewis L. Strauss. Charlottesville, Virginia: University Press of Virginia; "Leon Howard Sullivan: American clergyman and civil rights leader," Biography, Encyclopedia Britannica; Goodloe, Trevor "Leon Howard Sullivan Jr.," BlackPast, April 21, 2008; Sullivan, Leon (estate). Official Website; Sullivan, Leon H. (1998). Moving Mountains: The Principles and Purposes of Leon Sullivan. Judson Press; Wilson, Kendall (2001-04-27). "Leon Sullivan's Living Legacy". The Philadelphia Tribune; Find-a-Grave, West Virginia.)," "Booker T. Washington," Encyclopedia of Southern Culture, University of North Carolina Press, 1989; Tuskegee University, Official Website. "Dr. Booker Taliaferro Washington – Founder and First President of Tuskegee Normal and Industrial Institute;" West, Michael Rudolph (2006). The Education of Booker T. Washington: American Democracy and the Idea of Race Relations. New York: Columbia University Press; Harlan, Louis R (Oct 1970), "Booker T. Washington in Biographical Perspective," American Historical Review.

AUTHOR AND DESIGNER

AUTHOR: Danny R. Kuhn, M.A., was born in what was, at the time, called the Miners Memorial Hospital (now Appalachian Regional Hospital) in Beckley, West Virginia. The descendant of three generations of coal miners, he grew up on a small farm in Raleigh County, and holds degrees from Marshall and West Virginia Universities, with additional post-graduate work at West Virginia Wesleyan College. He began his career as a social worker in Williamson, West Virginia and later taught science at Marsh Fork and Shady Spring High Schools. In 1990, he became a United States Probation Officer for the federal court, and was appointed Deputy Chief U. S. Probation Officer for the Southern District of West Virginia in 2001, retiring from that position in 2010. He relocated to Myrtle Beach, South Carolina with his wife Sandra (though he retains an off-grid cabin in the eastern section of the Mountain State), and is a corporate trainer in writing, communication, and team building with Favoritetrainers.com.

Danny's books include novels *Fezziwig: A Life* (2015) and *Thoreau's Wound* (2017), both published by Knox Robinson Publishing of London and Atlanta, and nonfiction works *Fresh History, Brewed Daily: Raleigh County (WV) People, Places, Happenings 1750 – Present* (2015), *Daily Inspiration for Progressive America* (2016), and *Probation and Parole: Writing for Clarity* (2018), and *O, Mountaineers! Noted (or Notorious) West Virginians Born-Lived-Died Volume I,* all published by Favoritetrainers.com Books. He is an Editor of and a Contributor to three collections, including *Mountain Mysts: Myths and Fantasies of the Appalachians* (Headline Books, 2015), *Not Taking a Fence – Verses, Stories, and Memories from the Heart of Appalachia: Volume 1* (Favoritetrainers.com Books, 2016), and *Tales Irish* (Favoritetrainers.com Books, 2017). His articles have appeared in national publications, most recently *Commonweal* and *The Sun*.

DESIGNER: Seth Ellison, M.F.A, is a graduate of the Savannah College of Art and Design (B.F.A., Fine and Studio Arts) and The University of the Arts, Philadelphia (M.F.A., Fine and Studio Arts). He is a web content editor for Educational Testing Service, Princeton, New Jersey. His other cover designs include *Daily Inspiration for Progressive America, Probation and Parole: Writing for Clarity,* and *O, Mountaineers! Noted (or Notorious) West Virginians Born-Lived-Died,* as mentioned above.

YOU MAY ALSO BE INTERESTED IN THESE OTHER WORKS BY DANNY KUHN (Available online or selected titles at TAMARACK, Beckley WV)

O, Mountaineers! Noted (or Notorious) West Virginians (Favoritetrainers.com Books) West Virginians, whether by birth, residence, or death, have reached the pinnacle of success in almost every field, including entertainment, business, science, the military, politics, and sports. They include a shoe salesman who "brought down" the father of the atomic bomb, two of Hollywood's biggest stars who came to play ball, a legendary stripper, one of Washington's spies, and a couple of the most famous criminals of the twentieth century. You will find historical figures such as "Stonewall" Jackson and John W. Davis, but also contemporary notables Jennifer Garner and Brad Paisley. There is even an apple...and a horse. Many are household names; others, though influential, you will meet here for the first time. Some stories are inspirational, some disturbing, but all fascinating. Join the party, Mountaineers!

Mountain Mysts: Myths and Fantasies of the Appalachians (Headline Books, LONDON BOOK FESTIVAL HONORABLE MENTION) The ancient Appalachian Mountains offer panoramic views on a clear day. Their rugged beauty highlights simple, heartwarming stories of hearth and home. But then, the Mysts roll in…

These sixteen stories, all set in West Virginia, cover the breadth of central Appalachian fantasy and mythology, from modern day fables to ancient creatures, laugh-out-loud teenage hijinks to 19th-century mysteries that refuse to remain unsolved. There are Ghent-le Giants and coal mining dwarves, confused cemetery flower deliveries and slick-haired evangelists, all adding to the lore of the region. *Foreword by Joyce DeWitt, actress (Three's Company)*

Not Taking A Fence – Verses, Stories, and Memories from the Heart of Appalachia: From Contemporary Poems to Grave Robbing and Home Wakes *(Favoritetrainer.com Books)* To be really great in little things...is a virtue so great as to be worthy of canonization." - Harriet Beecher Stowe. What constitutes 'little things' is relative in the soaring Appalachian Mountains. Amid nature's grandeur, the people have, for centuries, struggled to bring civilization to the rugged landscape. Or, is it really the other way around? The answer is in the little things. This eclectic collection of poems, songs, and short prose, both fiction and poignant actual experiences, has been collected from more than thirty Appalachian authors, most of whom are never-before-published. It will immerse the reader in the Appalachian experience, both ancient and modern, and guide you from the angst of small town pizza delivery to the tender oral history memories of saying goodbye to loved ones by "sitting up with the dead." "...an Appalachian literary smorgasbord, with both tears and laughter for everyone, from every region.

Fresh History, Brewed Daily: Raleigh County (WV) People, Places, Happenings 1750 – Present (Favoritetrainers.com Books) The history of Raleigh County, West Virginia began long before it achieved official status in 1850. The earliest settlers carved a harsh living from the wilderness, but their stories show them to be people just like us, with similar dreams and foibles. Written with the traditions of the late Rev. C. Shirley Donnelly and journalist Jim Wood as models, this collection of articles on Raleigh County is like a series of conversations, history stories told among friends and family to pass along to subsequent generations. Using nearly a hundred sources from genealogical studies to old newspaper articles, Fresh History Brewed Daily: Raleigh County (WV) People, Places, Happenings 1750 - Present covers over 250 years of local heritage, from the earliest frontier families and the still-present divisions caused by the Civil War to immigrant coal miners and airplane crashes. You will find coalfield baseball, talented singers and writers, unsolved murders, and hometown heroes like Basil Plumley and Bill Withers. There is a special salute to Raleigh County men and women who sacrificed for our country, from the Revolution to Vietnam. If you are from the area, you are sure to find something still recognizable today. These stories are told with enough documentation and analysis to satisfy history lovers, but also plenty of humor and connection to the present to keep everyone else interested as well. You may even learn something about your own family, because it is Fresh History, Brewed Daily!

Fezziwig: A Life (Favoritetrainers.com Books) In the midst of Britain's Industrial Revolution, one of Charles Dickens' most beloved characters is living a full life, adventurous and lusty, but touched by scandal. Born in rural Lincolnshire in 1721, as a boy, William Fezziwig is displaced from his impoverished home through treachery and left alone in the world. Against the odds, Fezziwig rises to a prominent position in 18th century London when opportunities are presented by a respectable gentleman smuggler who sees promise in the waif. Prominence brings peril and Fezziwig must brave the War of Jenkins' Ear in order to pursue trade in Barbados and colonial Charleston, South Carolina. In the Americas there are threats on many fronts, from Spanish warships to his conflicted feelings toward the beguiling Eliza Lucas, heiress to one of the largest plantations in the Carolinas. Quixotic American Benjamin Franklin and a bevy of eccentric characters destined to become some of history's most influential figures upend Fezziwig's desire for a quieter life. Fezziwig finds himself in the position of mentor to his famous friend, as well as a certain ambitious young apprentice in need of lessons on life…and love. Social, political, intellectual, and economic revolution is in the air, and an old mystery resurfaces that could change the course of Fezziwig's and Franklin's careers.

Thoreau's Wound (Knox Robinson Publishing) Young Finbar Laverty, displaced by Ireland's Tithe Wars and family treachery, attempts a new start by moving with his volatile wife Maggie, a follower of the Old Religion, from the Cork countryside to bustling Dublin. He is recruited by his friend Dr. James Wilde to help disinter the body of Dean Jonathan Swift during the renovation of St. Patrick's Cathedral, but commits an act of vengeance and is forced to flee Ireland.

Seeking fortune in London, Finbar's inadvertent participation in a Royal conspiracy involving a young court reporter puts him on the run again, this time to America.

The Lavertys begin to think they have found peace in New Hampshire, but suspicion surrounding a female body revealed by the melting ice on Bodge's Pond and the anti-Irish Catholic frenzy ignited by the Know-Nothings sends Finbar to Concord, Massachusetts. His new bosses' son, Henry David Thoreau, introduces him to new ideas, Abolitionist activism, and the most influential circle of literary figures in America's history.

While Finbar's adopted country is about to be torn apart by civil war, his family is also threatened when the consequences of old sins return to haunt him.

Praise for Thoreau's Wound:

"The Irish have been coming to America forever, or so it seems, and yet the story keeps on reviewing itself each time the torch, in John F. Kennedy's words, is passed to a new generation. Stories of sibling rivalry, lost mothers, complicated fathers and mysterious young passions, are as old as the hills, yet they continue to renew themselves and never cease to captivate us. In Thoreau's Wound, in the adventures and misadventures of Finbar Laverty, every reader will recognize something of him or her self. I was taken by the story. You will be too." -**Alphie McCourt, author and brother of Angela's Ashes' Frank McCourt**

"Ah, the Irish! Treat yourself to this wonderful journey as Danny Kuhn studs Finbar's adventure with lore from the Auld Sod and figures out of history!" -**Mike Farrell, author and actor (M*A*S*H*)**

Tales Irish (Favoritetrainers.com Books) These twenty-three new tales of Eire, gathered from authors in four countries, capture the spirit of the Irish at home and abroad. From the ancient past on the wild west coast and devout 6th-century monks braving uncharted seas to explore the mysterious land across the Atlantic to the gritty streets of modern Dublin, they will engulf the reader with the sights and sounds, the loves, losses, humour, and myths of the Emerald Isle, no matter where that reader calls home.

Made in the USA
Middletown, DE
25 June 2021